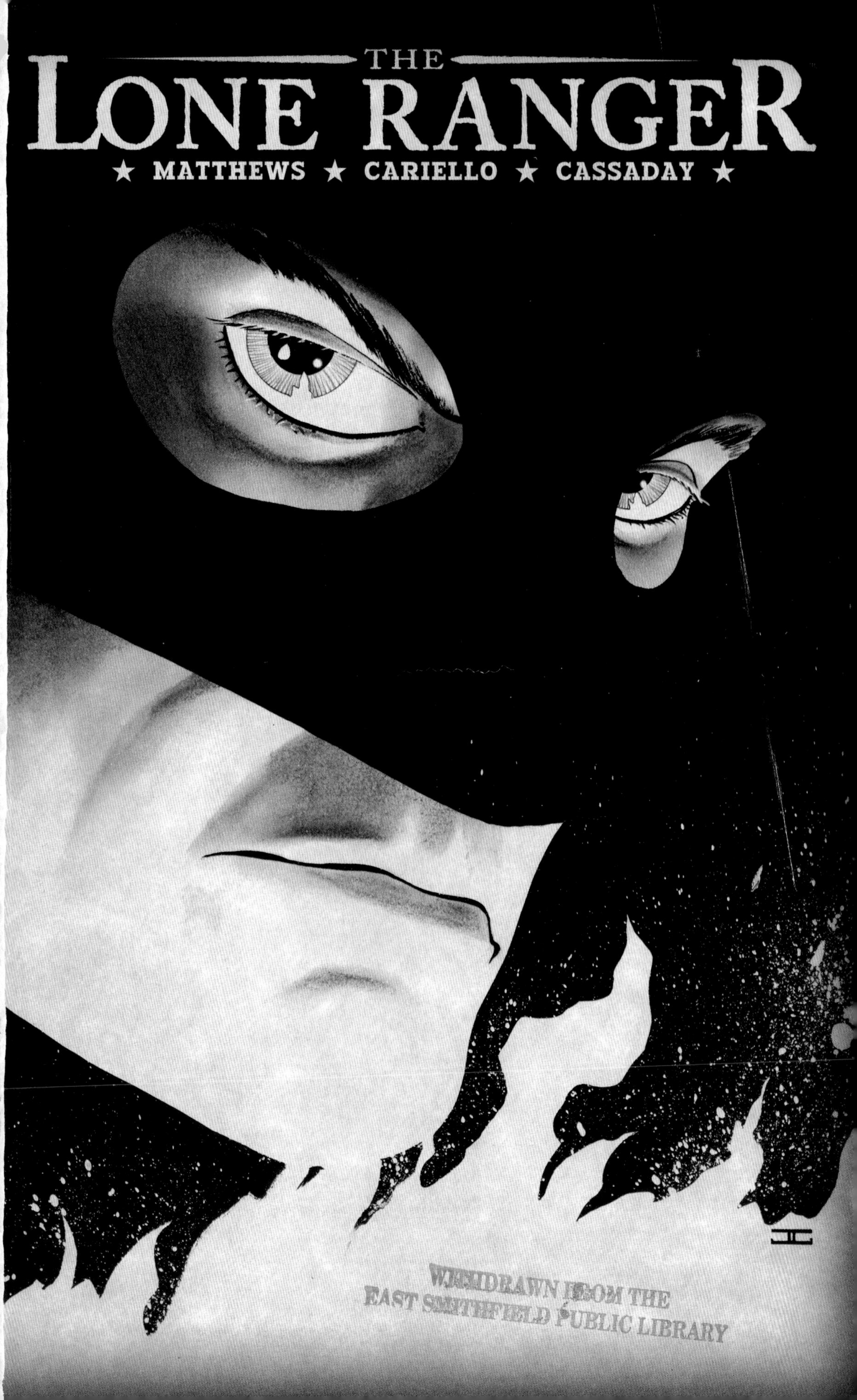
THE
LONE RANGER
★ MATTHEWS ★ CARIELLO ★ CASSADAY ★

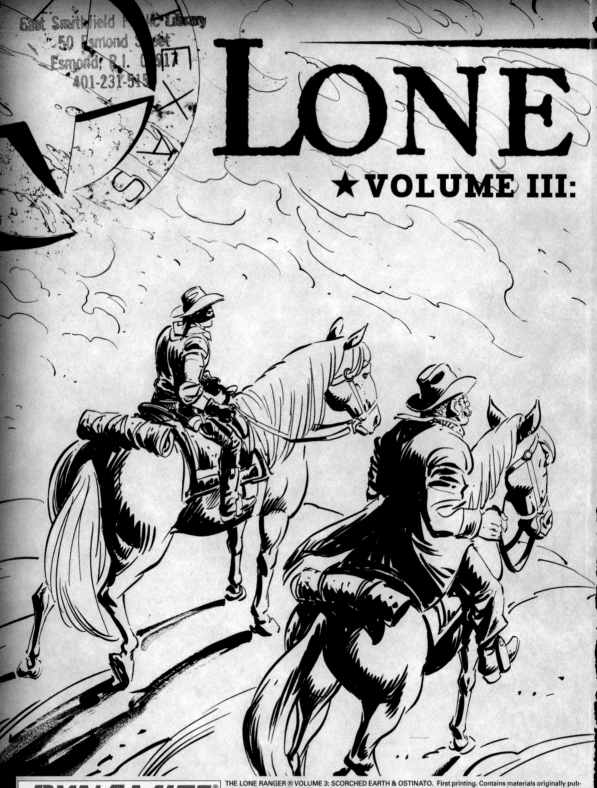

LONE

★VOLUME III:

THE LONE RANGER ® VOLUME 3: SCORCHED EARTH & OSTINATO. First printing. Contains materials originally published in THE LONE RANGER #12-16. Published by Dynamite Entertainment. 155 Ninth Ave. Suite B, Runnemede, NJ 08078. Lone Ranger: © 2009 Classic Media, Inc. THE LONE RANGER and associated character names, images and other indicia are trademarks of and copyrighted by Classic Media, Inc., an Entertainment Rights group company. All rights reserved. "DYNAMITE," "DYNAMITE ENTERTAINMENT" and its logo ® & © 2009 DFI. All names, characters, events, and locales in this publication are entirely fictional. Any resemblance to actual persons (living or dead), events or places, without satiric intent, is coincidental. No portion of this book may be reproduced by any means (digital or print) without the written permission of Dynamite Entertainment except for review purposes. The scanning, uploading and distribution of this book via the Internet or via any other means without the permission of the publisher is illegal and punishable by law. Please purchase only authorized electronic editions, and do not participate in or encourage electronic piracy of copyrighted materials.

For information regarding media rights, foreign rights, promotions, licensing, and advertising:
marketing@dynamiteentertainment.com

Printed in China

WWW.DYNAMITEENTERTAINMENT.COM

NICK BARRUCCI	•	PRESIDENT
JUAN COLLADO	•	CHIEF OPERATING OFFICER
JOSEPH RYBANDT	•	ASSOCIATE EDITOR
JOSH JOHNSON	•	CREATIVE DIRECTOR
JASON ULLMEYER	•	GRAPHIC DESIGNER

To find a comic shop in your area,
call the comic shop locator service
toll-free **1-888-266-4226** or visit
comicshoplocator.com

First Printing
HARDCOVER ISBN-10: 1-60690-031-5   ISBN-13: 978-1-60690-031-4
SOFTCOVER ISBN-10: 1-60690-041-2   ISBN-13: 978-1-60690-041-3
10 9 8 7 6 5 4 3 2 1

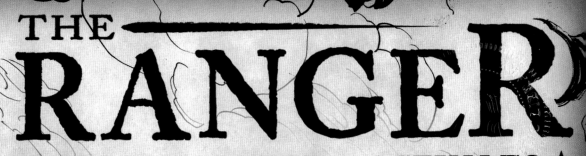

THE RANGER

SCORCHED EARTH & OSTINATO★

Writer: Brett Matthews

Artist: Sergio Cariello

Cover Artist: John Cassaday

Letterer: Simon Bowland

Colorist: Marcelo Pinto of Impacto Studio

Collection Design: Jason Ullmeyer

Special Thanks To:
Lynn Kim, Kim Anthony Jones, Tony Knight, Mike Weiss & John Fraser

This volume collects issues 12-16 of the Dynamite Entertainment series.

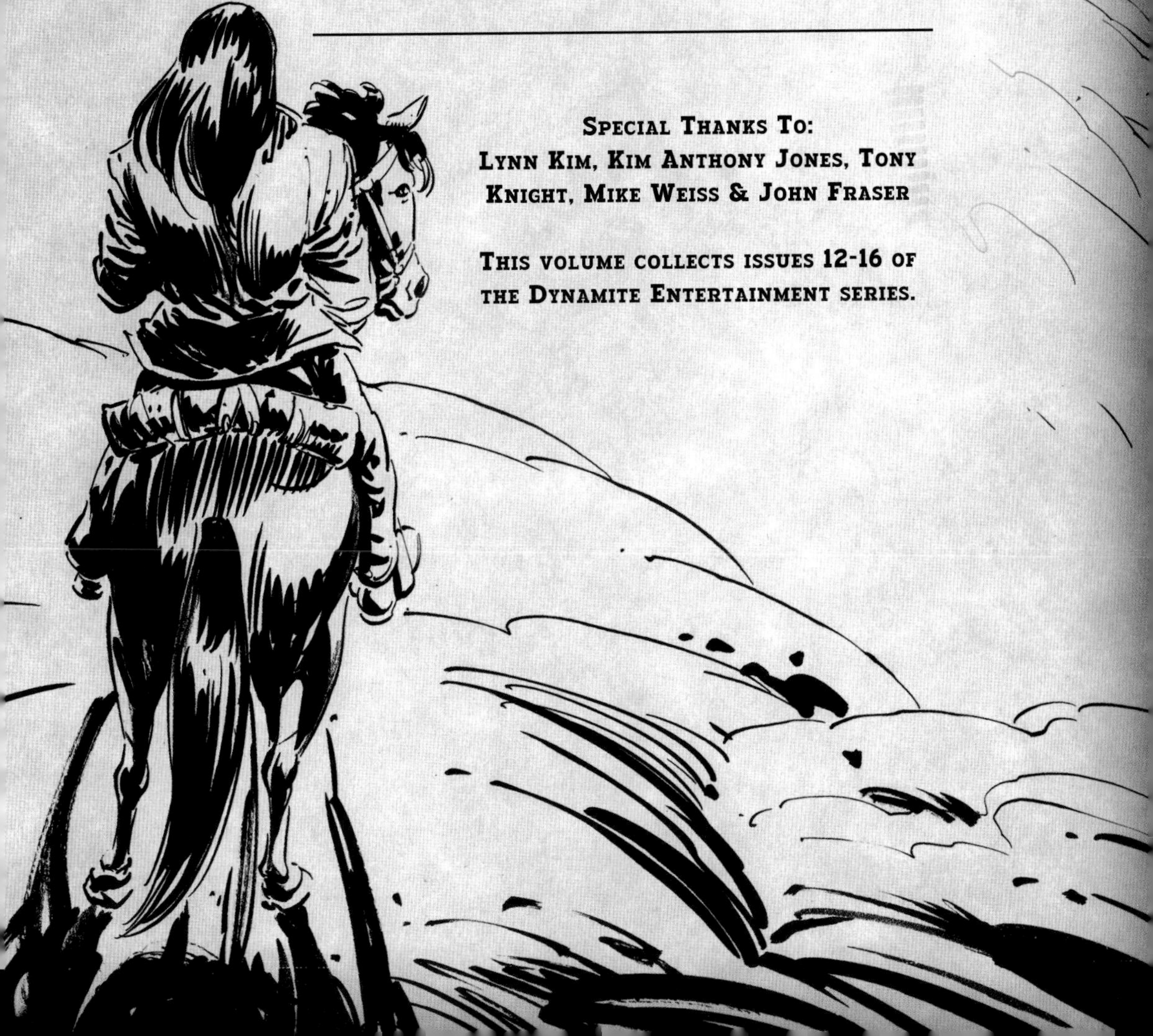

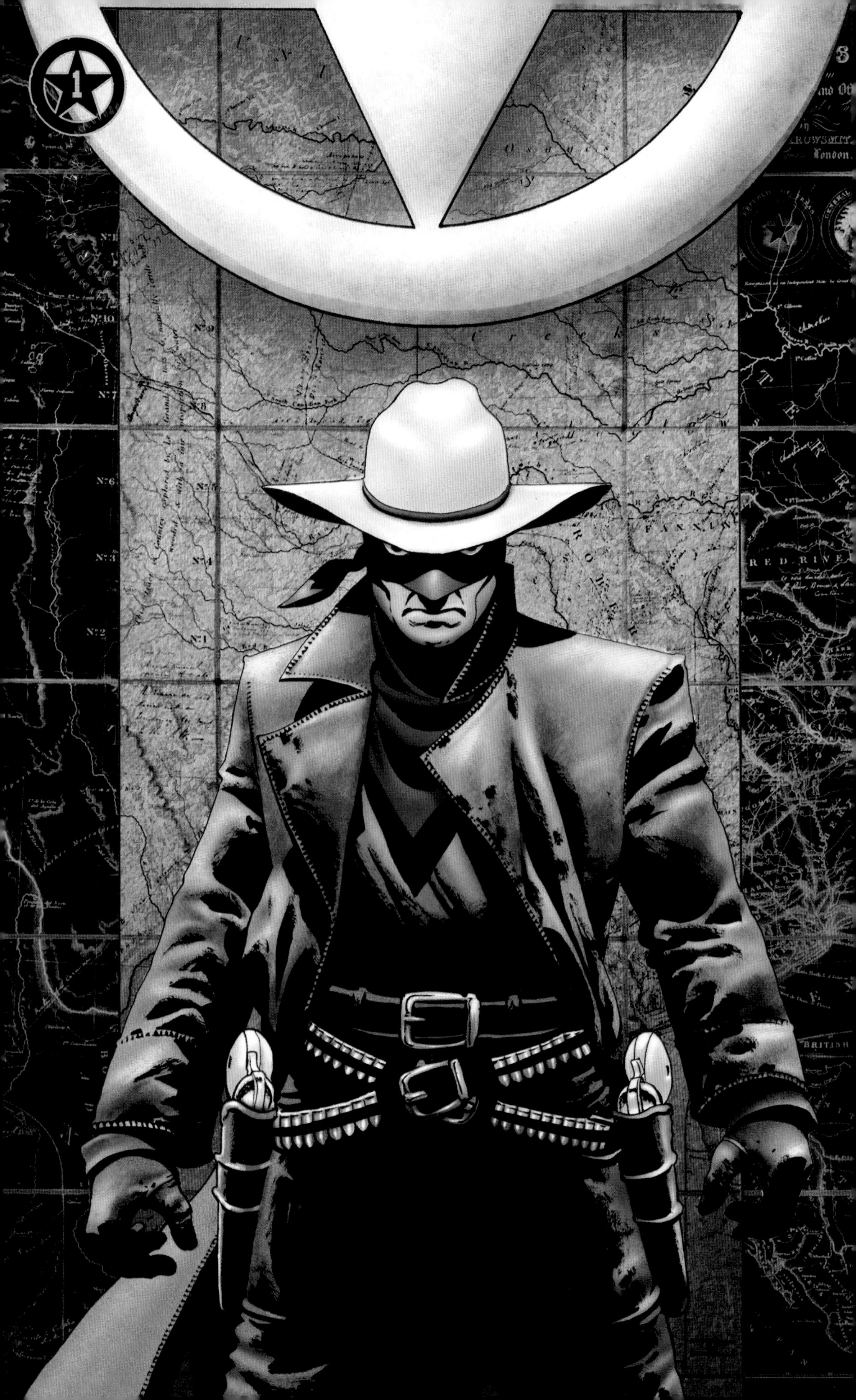

1
London.
BRITISH

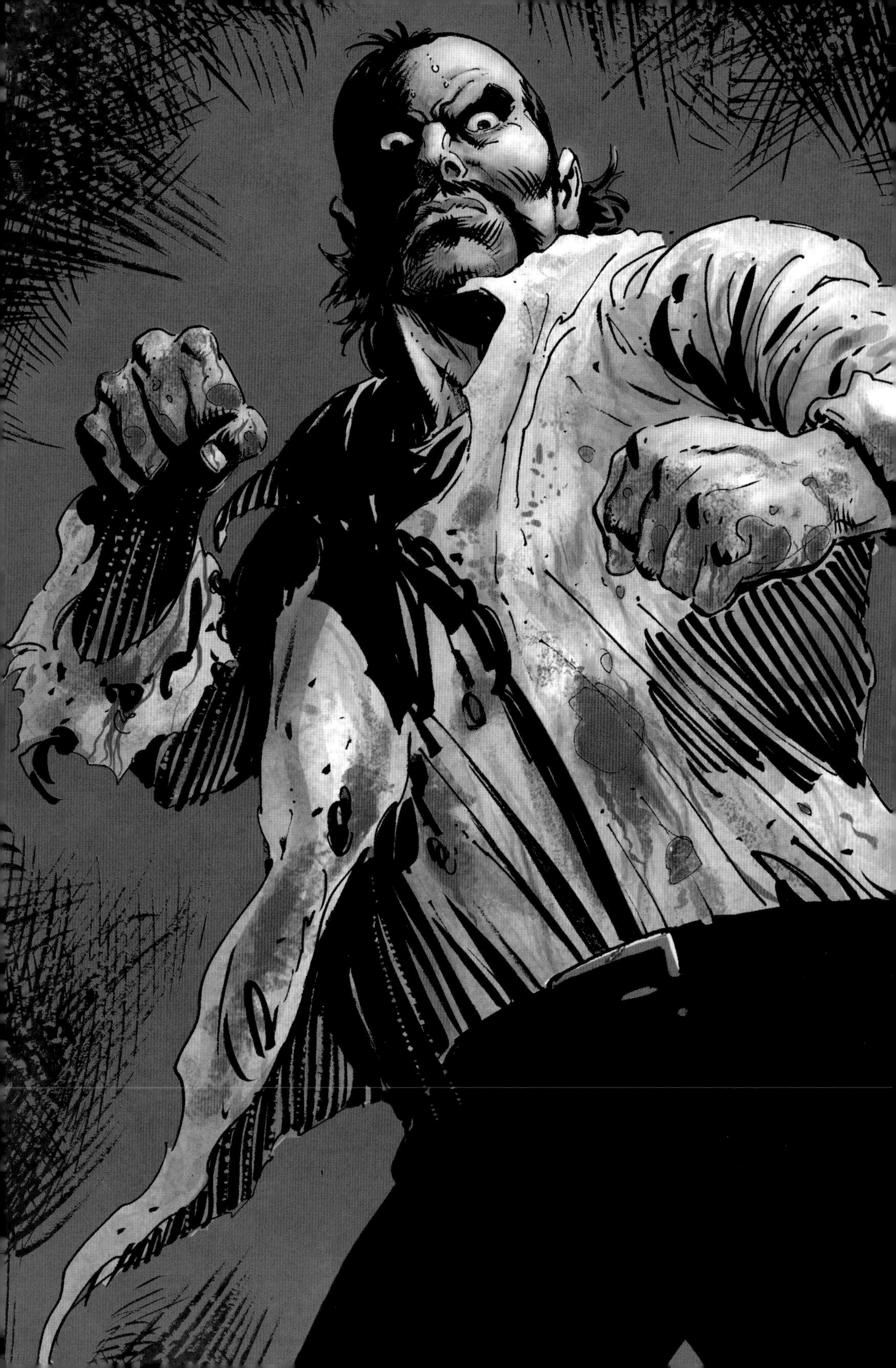

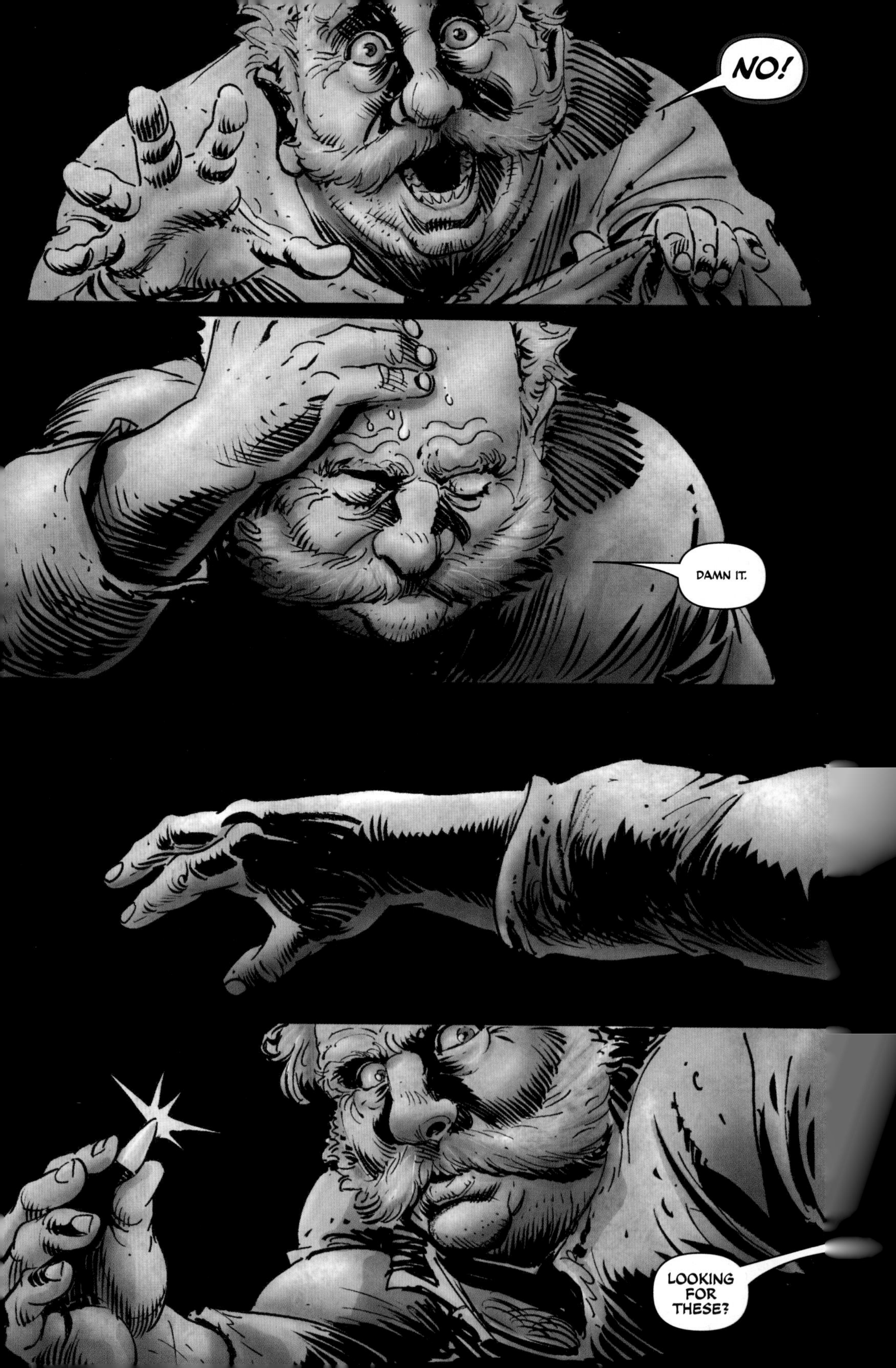
NO!
DAMN IT.
LOOKING FOR THESE?

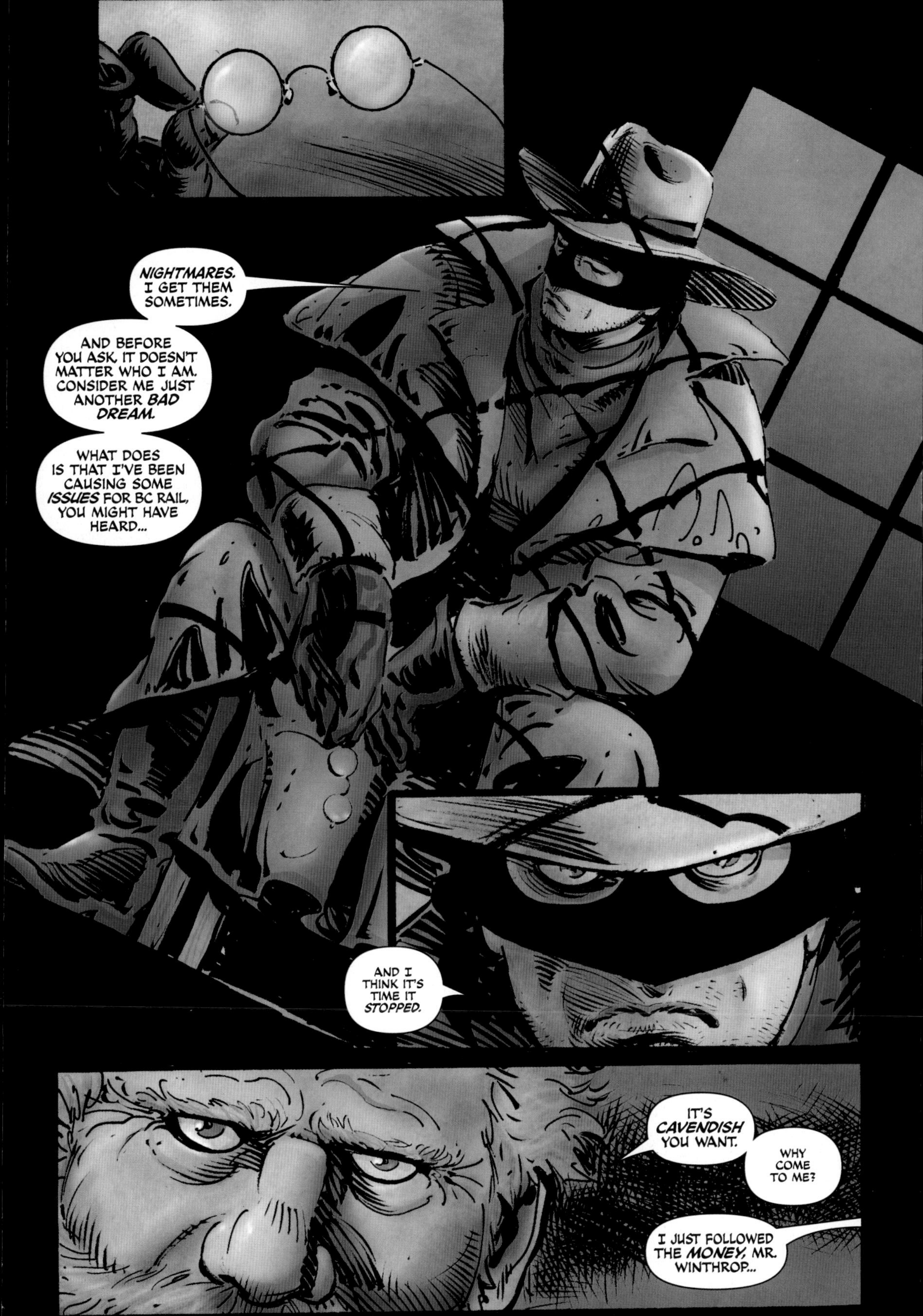
NIGHTMARES. I GET THEM SOMETIMES.
AND BEFORE YOU ASK, IT DOESN'T MATTER WHO I AM. CONSIDER ME JUST ANOTHER BAD DREAM.
WHAT DOES IS THAT I'VE BEEN CAUSING SOME ISSUES FOR BC RAIL, YOU MIGHT HAVE HEARD...
AND I THINK IT'S TIME IT STOPPED.
IT'S CAVENDISH YOU WANT.
WHY COME TO ME?
I JUST FOLLOWED THE MONEY, MR. WINTHROP...

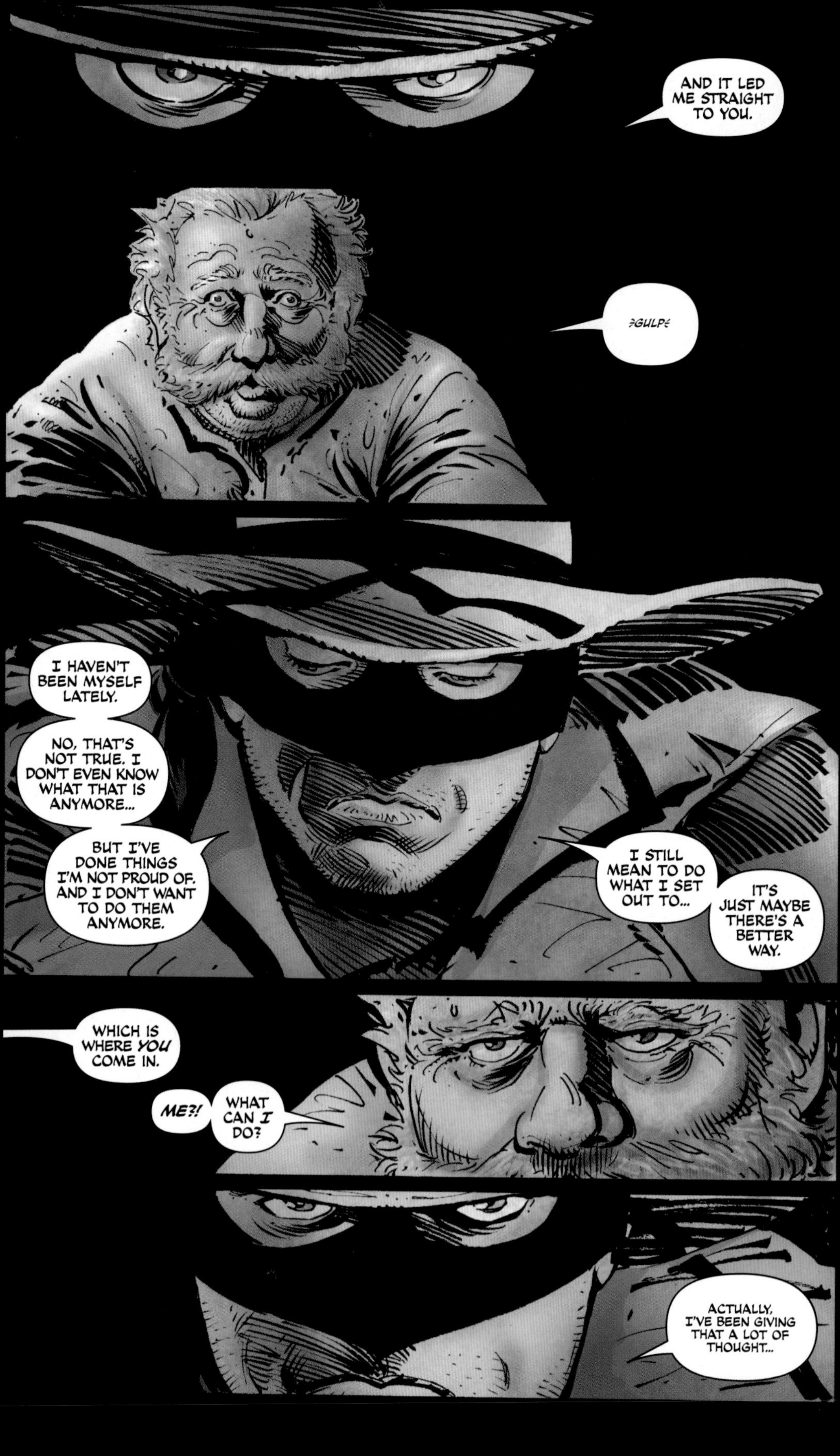
AND IT LED ME STRAIGHT TO YOU.
≥GULP≤
I HAVEN'T BEEN MYSELF LATELY.
NO, THAT'S NOT TRUE. I DON'T EVEN KNOW WHAT THAT IS ANYMORE...
BUT I'VE DONE THINGS I'M NOT PROUD OF. AND I DON'T WANT TO DO THEM ANYMORE.
I STILL MEAN TO DO WHAT I SET OUT TO...
IT'S JUST MAYBE THERE'S A BETTER WAY.
WHICH IS WHERE YOU COME IN.
ME?!
WHAT CAN I DO?
ACTUALLY, I'VE BEEN GIVING THAT A LOT OF THOUGHT...

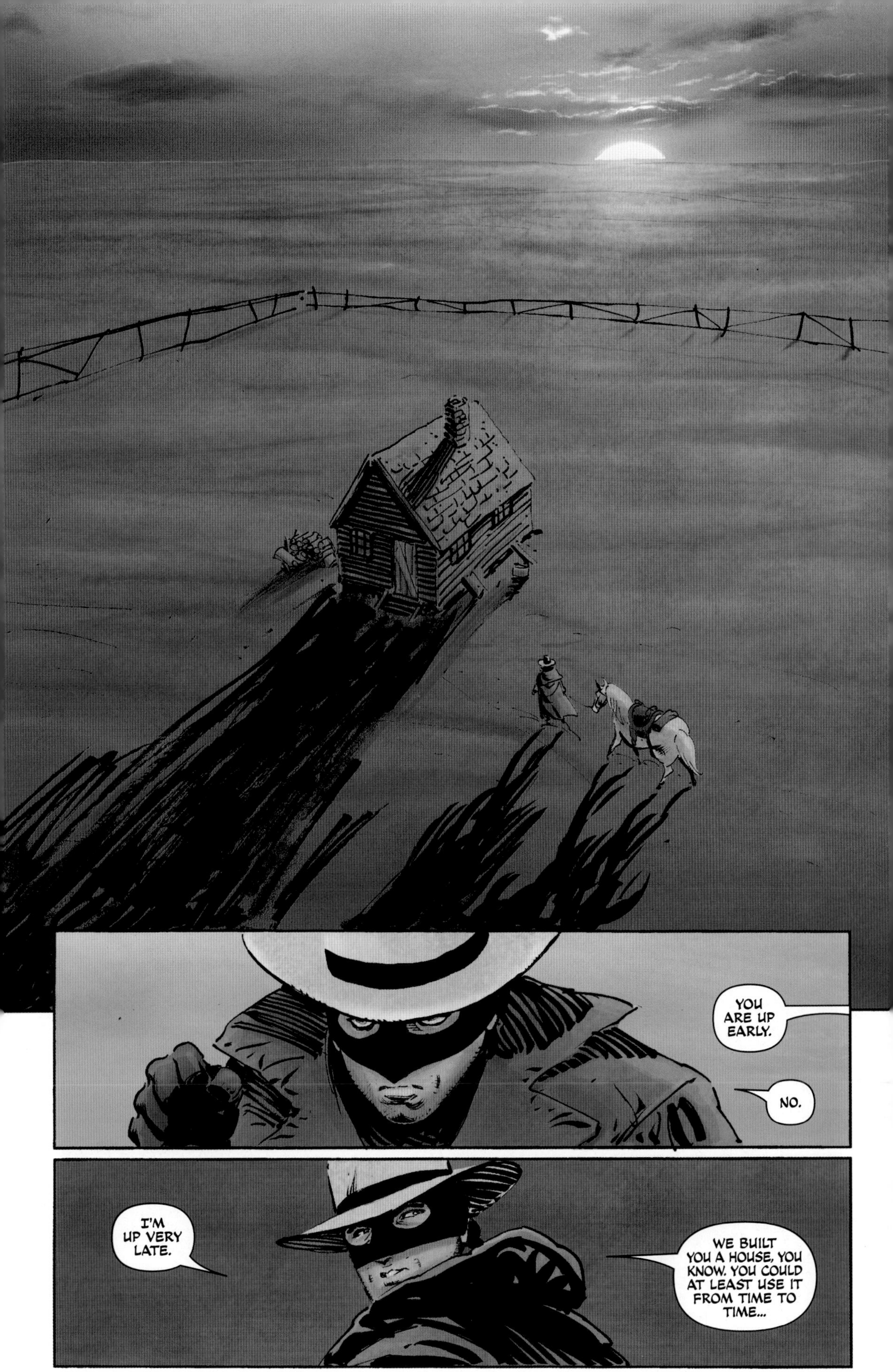
YOU ARE UP EARLY.
NO.
I'M UP VERY LATE.
WE BUILT YOU A HOUSE, YOU KNOW. YOU COULD AT LEAST USE IT FROM TIME TO TIME...

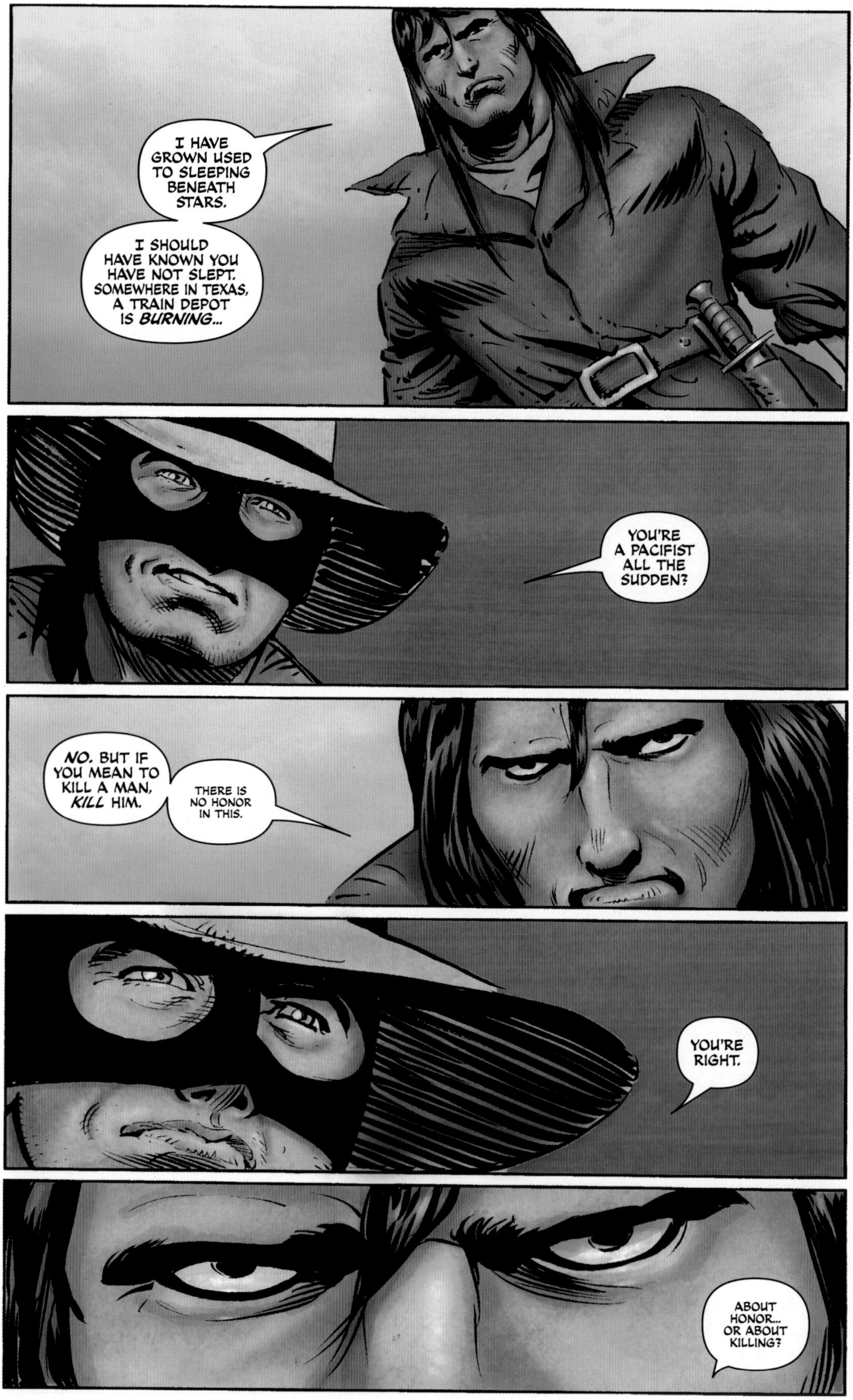
I HAVE GROWN USED TO SLEEPING BENEATH STARS.
I SHOULD HAVE KNOWN YOU HAVE NOT SLEPT. SOMEWHERE IN TEXAS, A TRAIN DEPOT IS *BURNING*...
YOU'RE A PACIFIST ALL THE SUDDEN?
NO. BUT IF YOU MEAN TO KILL A MAN, *KILL* HIM.
THERE IS NO HONOR IN THIS.
YOU'RE RIGHT.
ABOUT HONOR... OR ABOUT KILLING?

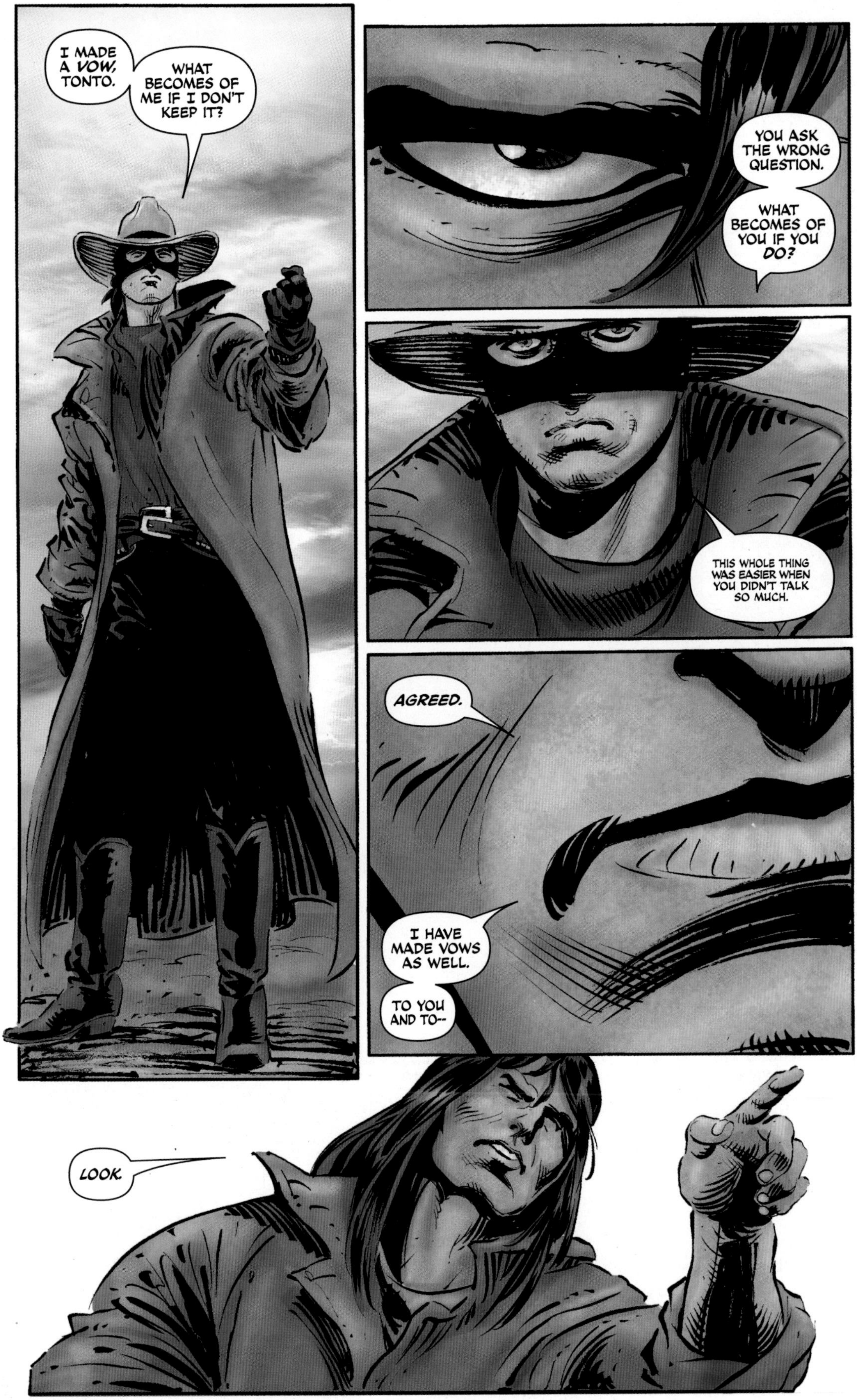
I MADE A *VOW,* TONTO.
WHAT BECOMES OF ME IF I DON'T KEEP IT?
YOU ASK THE WRONG QUESTION.
WHAT BECOMES OF YOU IF YOU *DO?*
THIS WHOLE THING WAS EASIER WHEN YOU DIDN'T TALK SO MUCH.
AGREED.
I HAVE MADE VOWS AS WELL.
TO YOU AND TO--
LOOK.

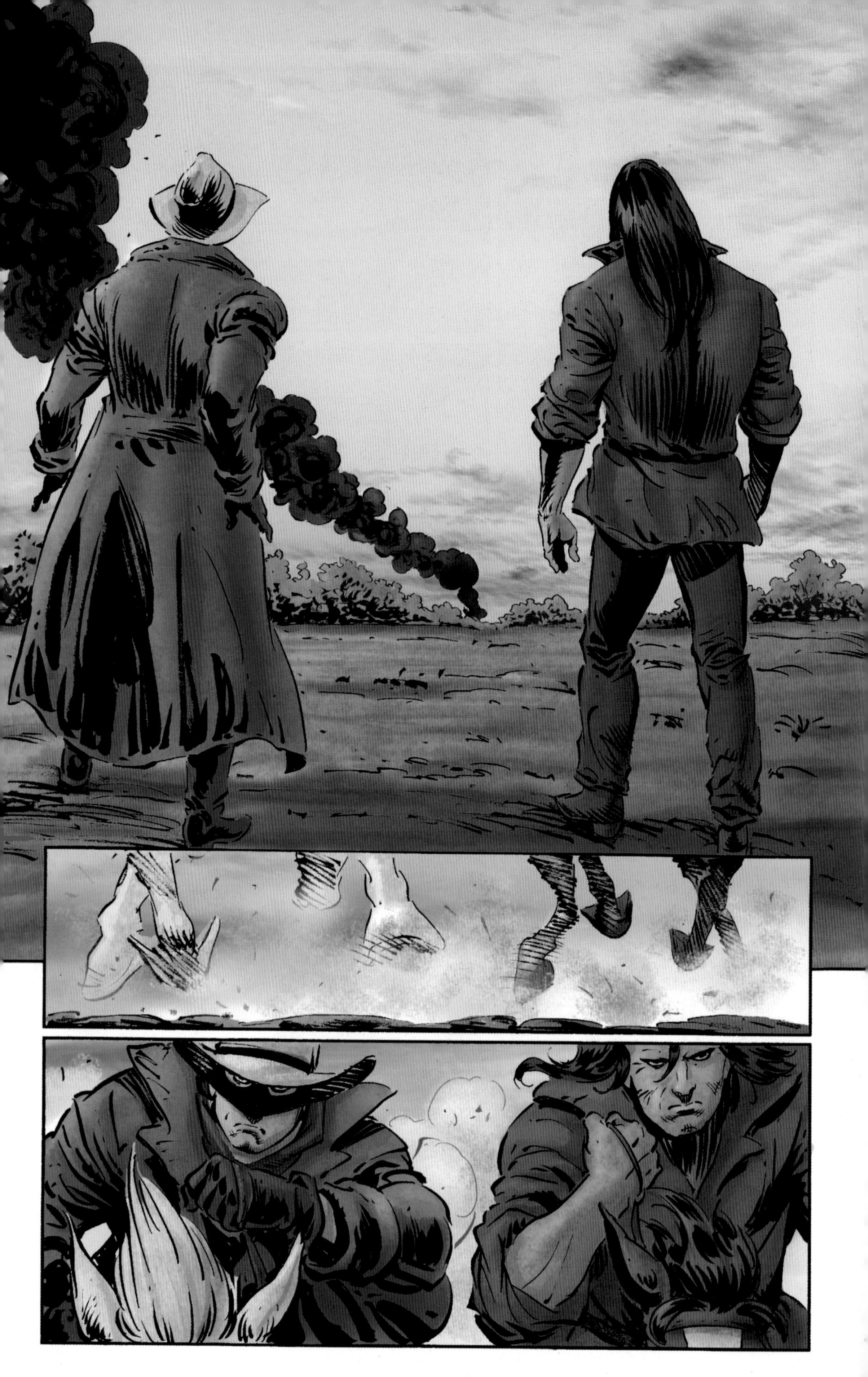

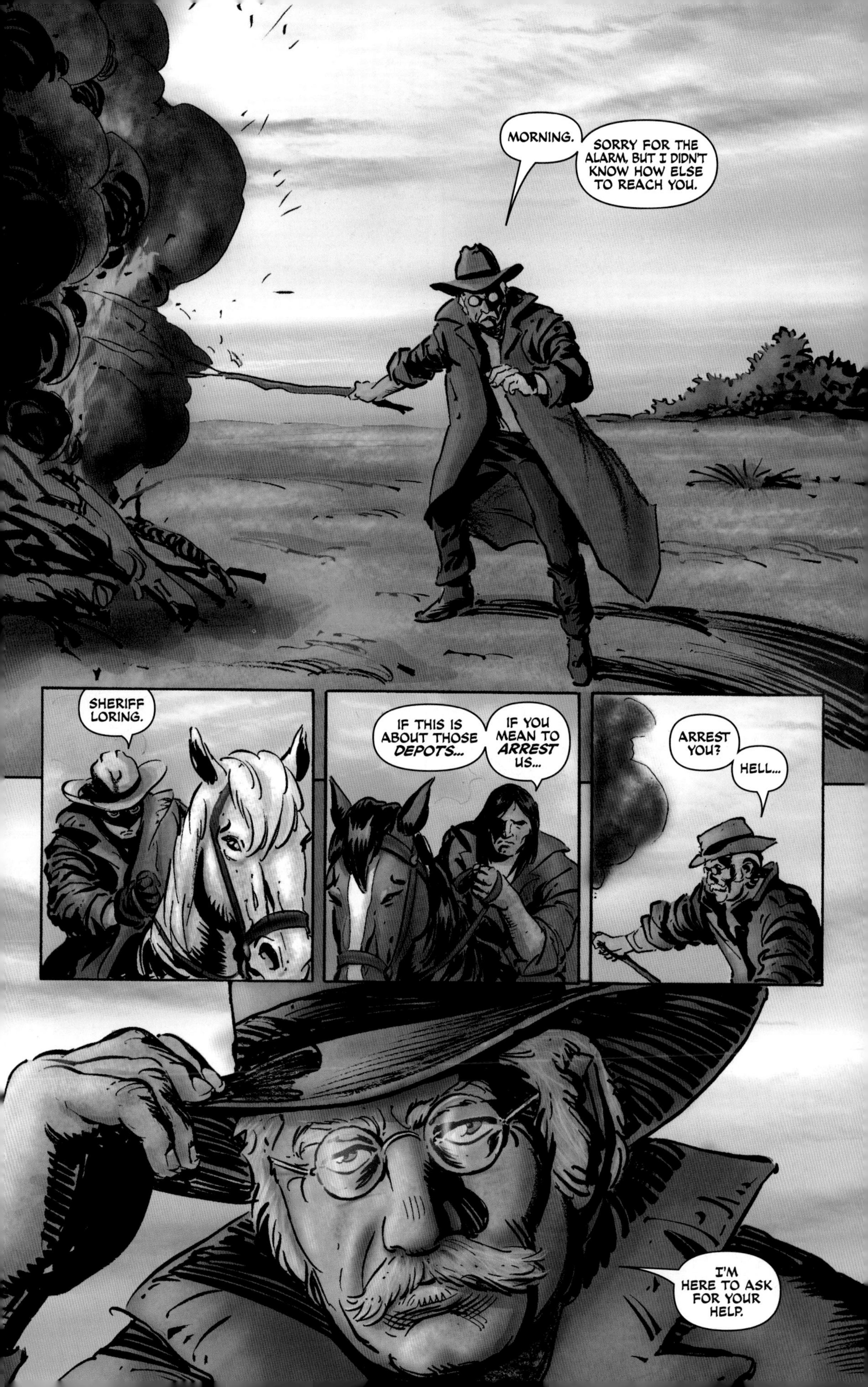
MORNING.
SORRY FOR THE ALARM, BUT I DIDN'T KNOW HOW ELSE TO REACH YOU.
SHERIFF LORING.
IF THIS IS ABOUT THOSE *DEPOTS...*
IF YOU MEAN TO *ARREST* US...
ARREST YOU?
HELL...
I'M HERE TO ASK FOR YOUR HELP.

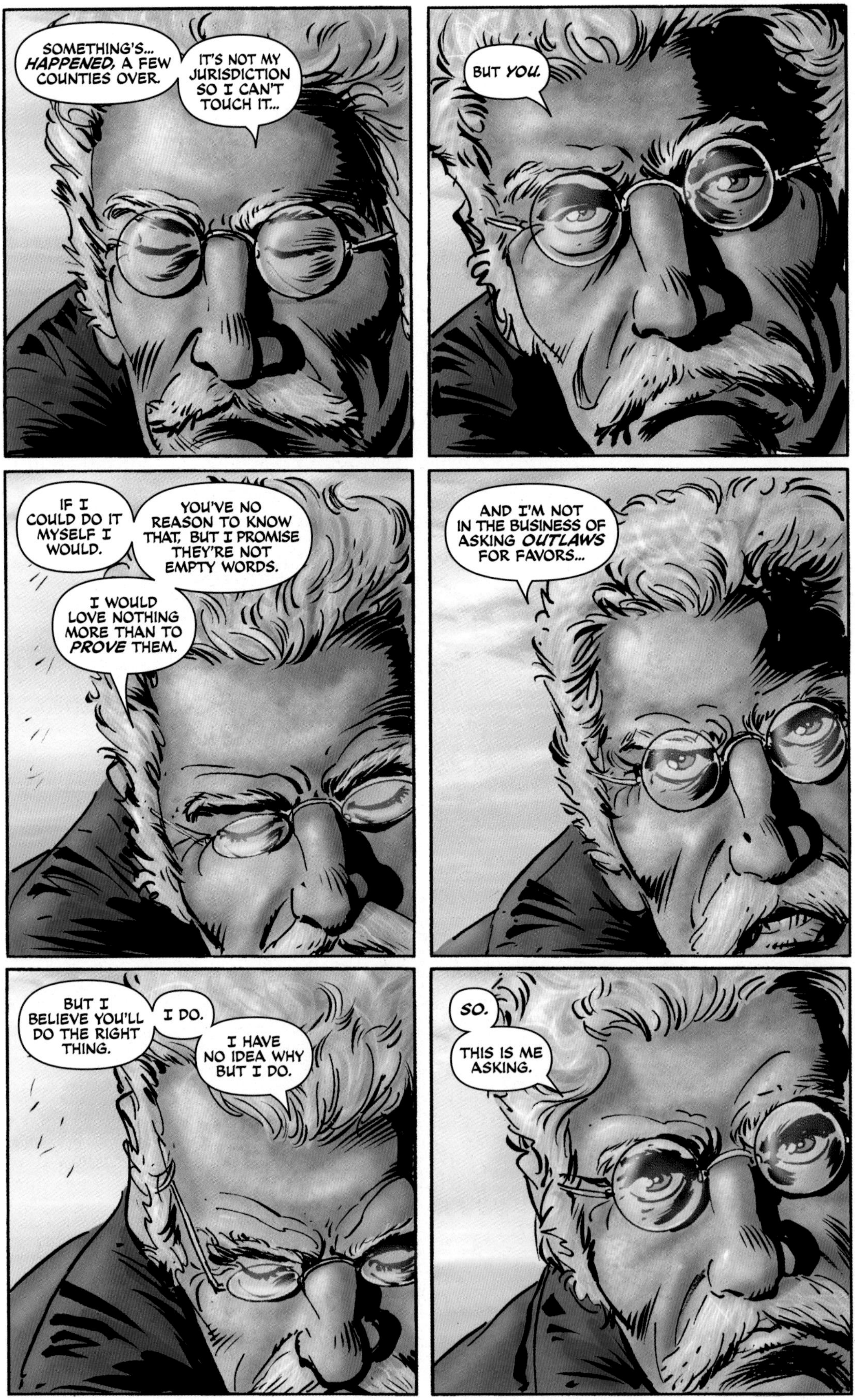
SOMETHING'S... HAPPENED, A FEW COUNTIES OVER.
IT'S NOT MY JURISDICTION SO I CAN'T TOUCH IT...
BUT YOU.
IF I COULD DO IT MYSELF I WOULD.
YOU'VE NO REASON TO KNOW THAT, BUT I PROMISE THEY'RE NOT EMPTY WORDS.
I WOULD LOVE NOTHING MORE THAN TO PROVE THEM.
AND I'M NOT IN THE BUSINESS OF ASKING OUTLAWS FOR FAVORS...
BUT I BELIEVE YOU'LL DO THE RIGHT THING.
I DO.
I HAVE NO IDEA WHY BUT I DO.
SO.
THIS IS ME ASKING.

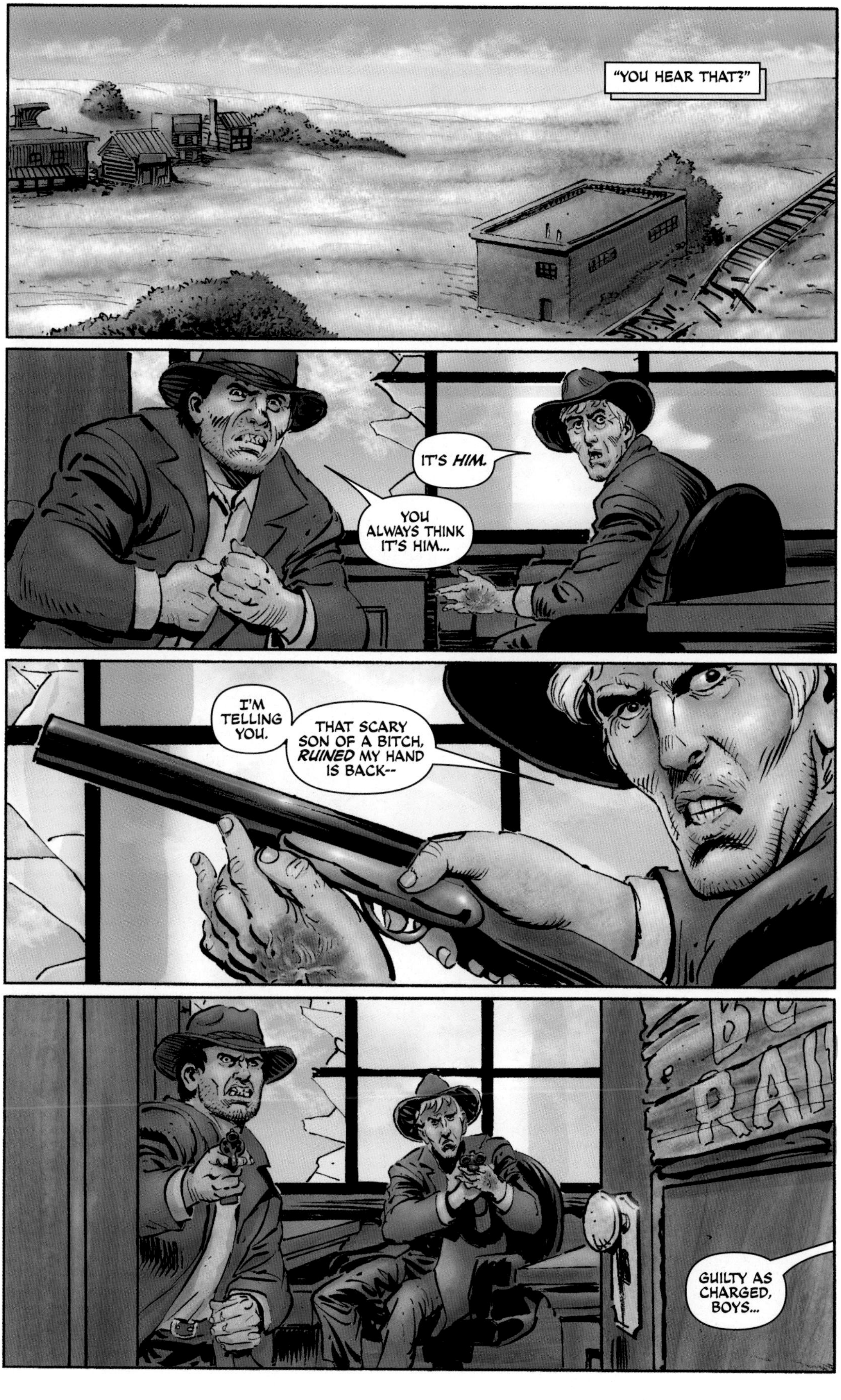
"YOU HEAR THAT?"
IT'S *HIM.*
YOU ALWAYS THINK IT'S HIM...
I'M TELLING YOU.
THAT SCARY SON OF A BITCH, *RUINED* MY HAND IS BACK--
GUILTY AS CHARGED, BOYS...

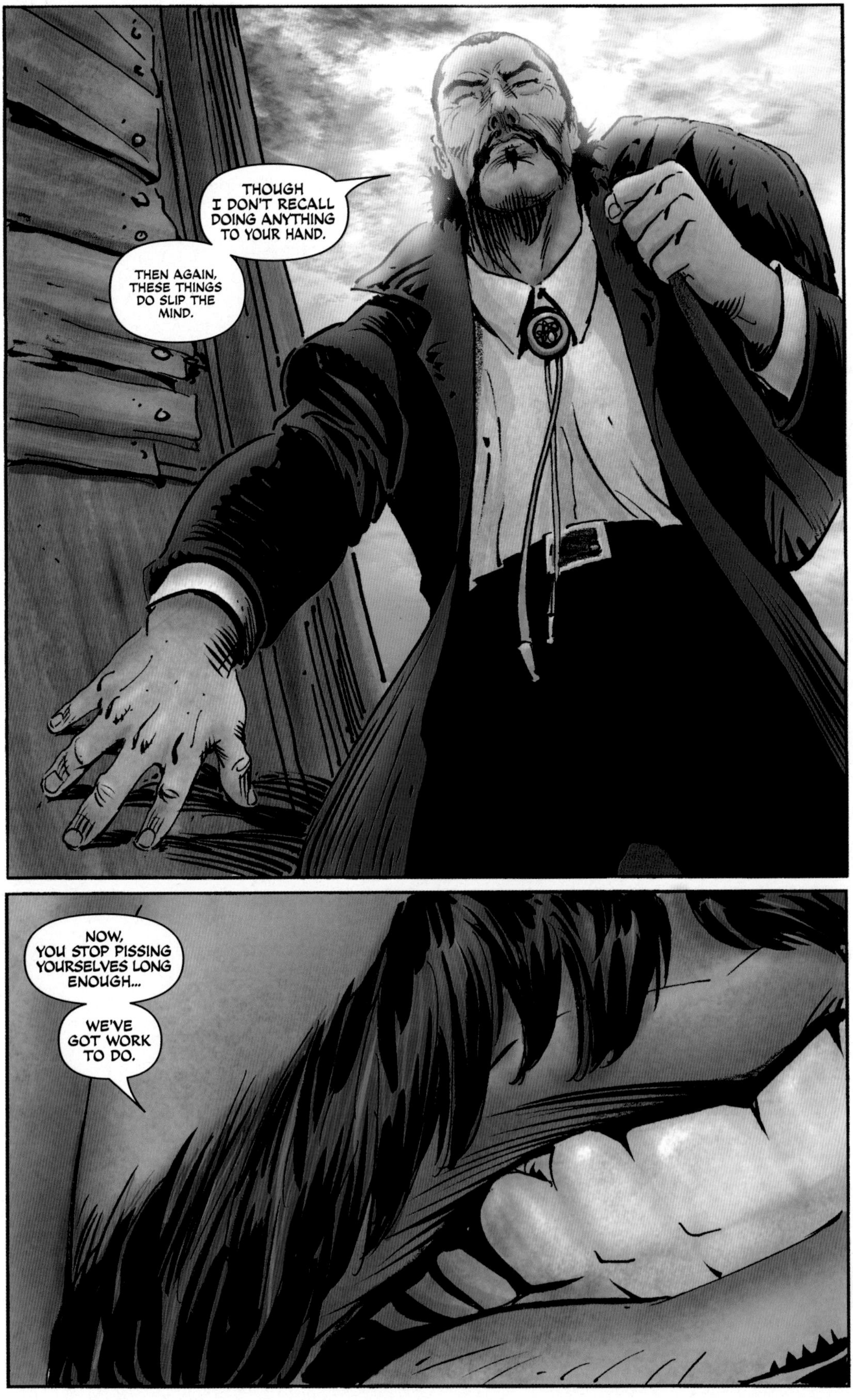
THOUGH I DON'T RECALL DOING ANYTHING TO YOUR HAND.
THEN AGAIN, THESE THINGS DO SLIP THE MIND.
NOW, YOU STOP PISSING YOURSELVES LONG ENOUGH...
WE'VE GOT WORK TO DO.

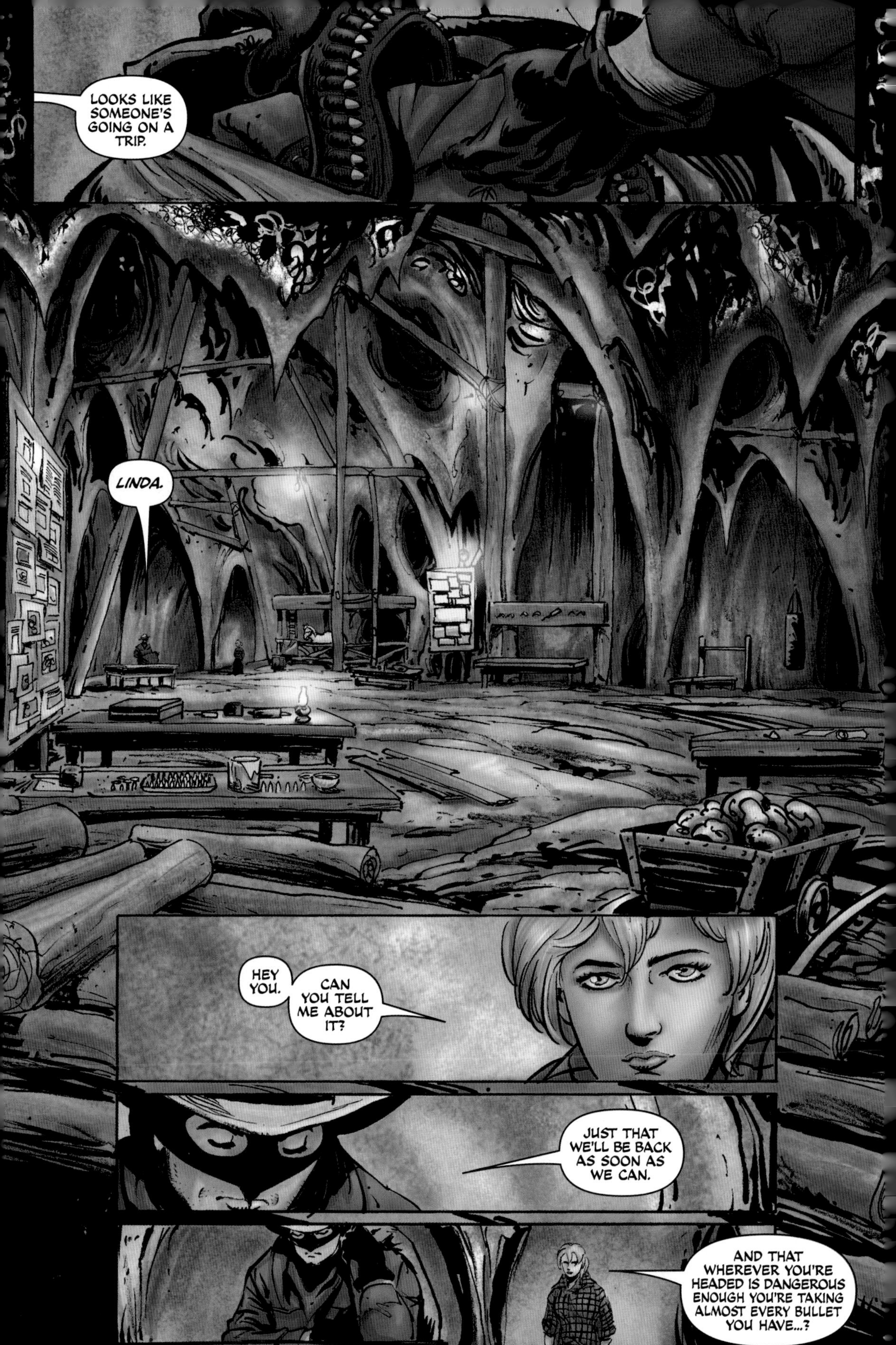
LOOKS LIKE SOMEONE'S GOING ON A TRIP.
LINDA.
HEY YOU.
CAN YOU TELL ME ABOUT IT?
JUST THAT WE'LL BE BACK AS SOON AS WE CAN.
AND THAT WHEREVER YOU'RE HEADED IS DANGEROUS ENOUGH YOU'RE TAKING ALMOST EVERY BULLET YOU HAVE...?

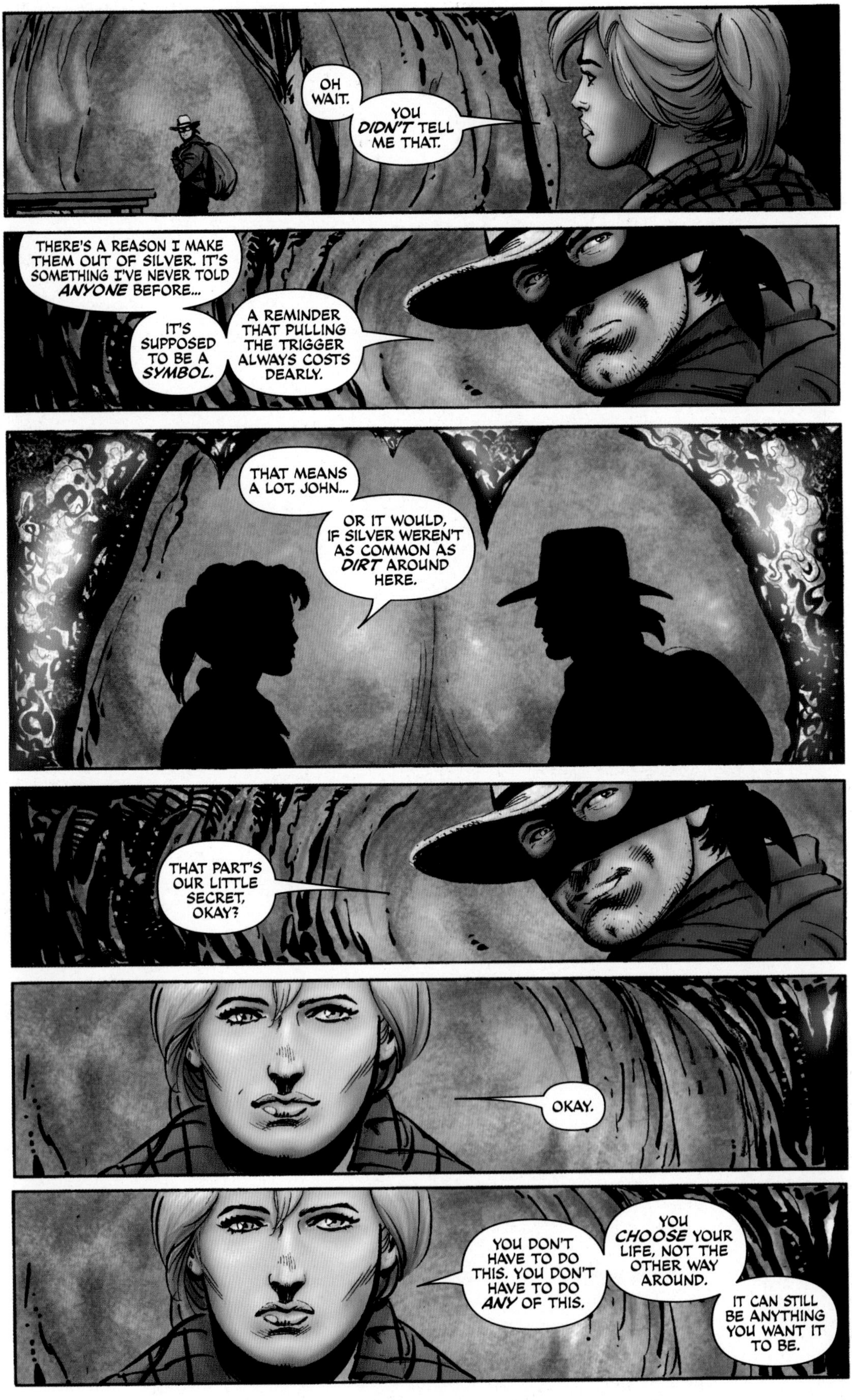
OH WAIT.
YOU DIDN'T TELL ME THAT.
THERE'S A REASON I MAKE THEM OUT OF SILVER. IT'S SOMETHING I'VE NEVER TOLD ANYONE BEFORE...
IT'S SUPPOSED TO BE A SYMBOL.
A REMINDER THAT PULLING THE TRIGGER ALWAYS COSTS DEARLY.
THAT MEANS A LOT, JOHN...
OR IT WOULD, IF SILVER WEREN'T AS COMMON AS DIRT AROUND HERE.
THAT PART'S OUR LITTLE SECRET, OKAY?
OKAY.
YOU DON'T HAVE TO DO THIS. YOU DON'T HAVE TO DO ANY OF THIS.
YOU CHOOSE YOUR LIFE, NOT THE OTHER WAY AROUND.
IT CAN STILL BE ANYTHING YOU WANT IT TO BE.

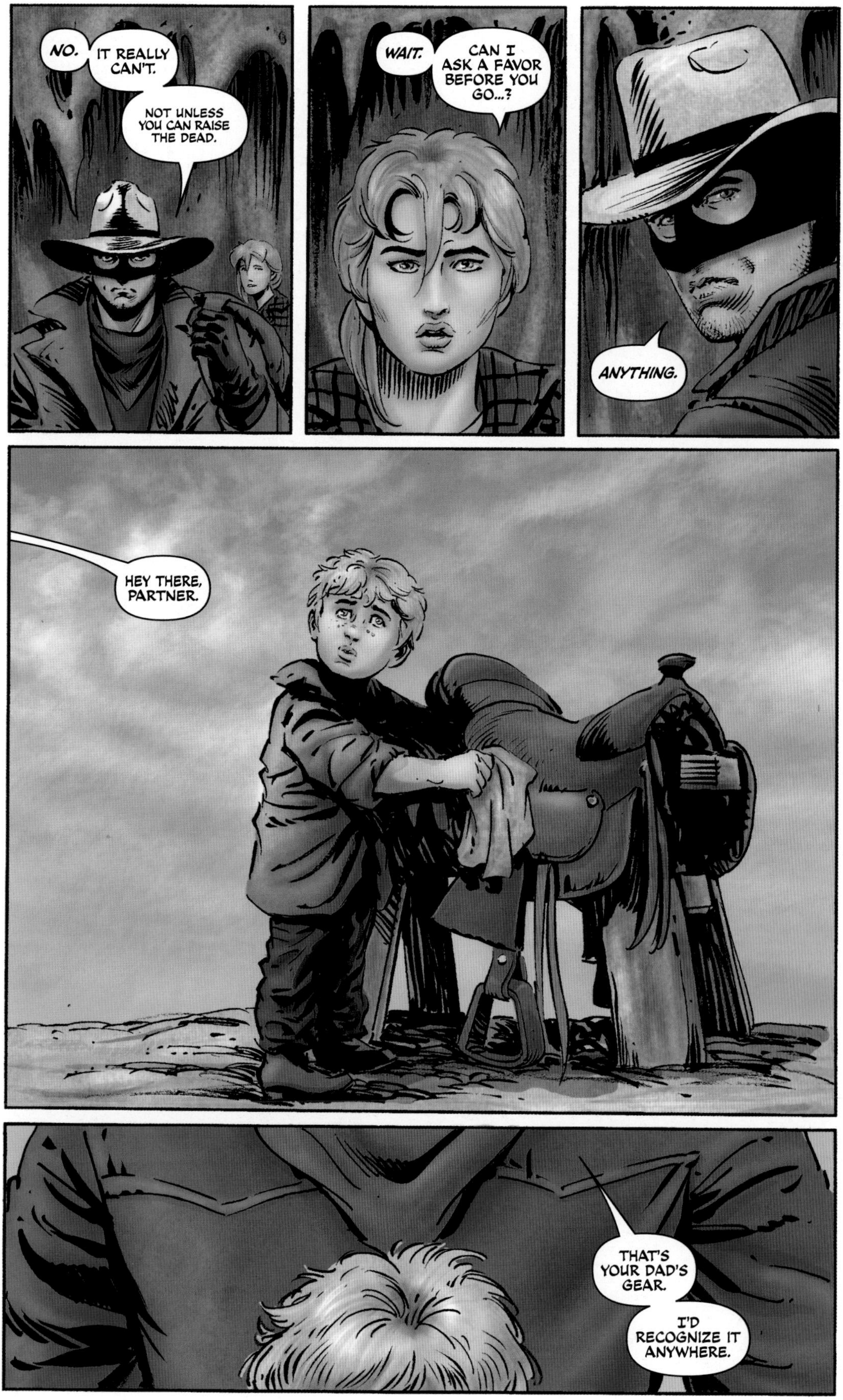
NO.
IT REALLY CAN'T.
NOT UNLESS YOU CAN RAISE THE DEAD.
WAIT.
CAN I ASK A FAVOR BEFORE YOU GO...?
ANYTHING.
HEY THERE, PARTNER.
THAT'S YOUR DAD'S GEAR.
I'D RECOGNIZE IT ANYWHERE.

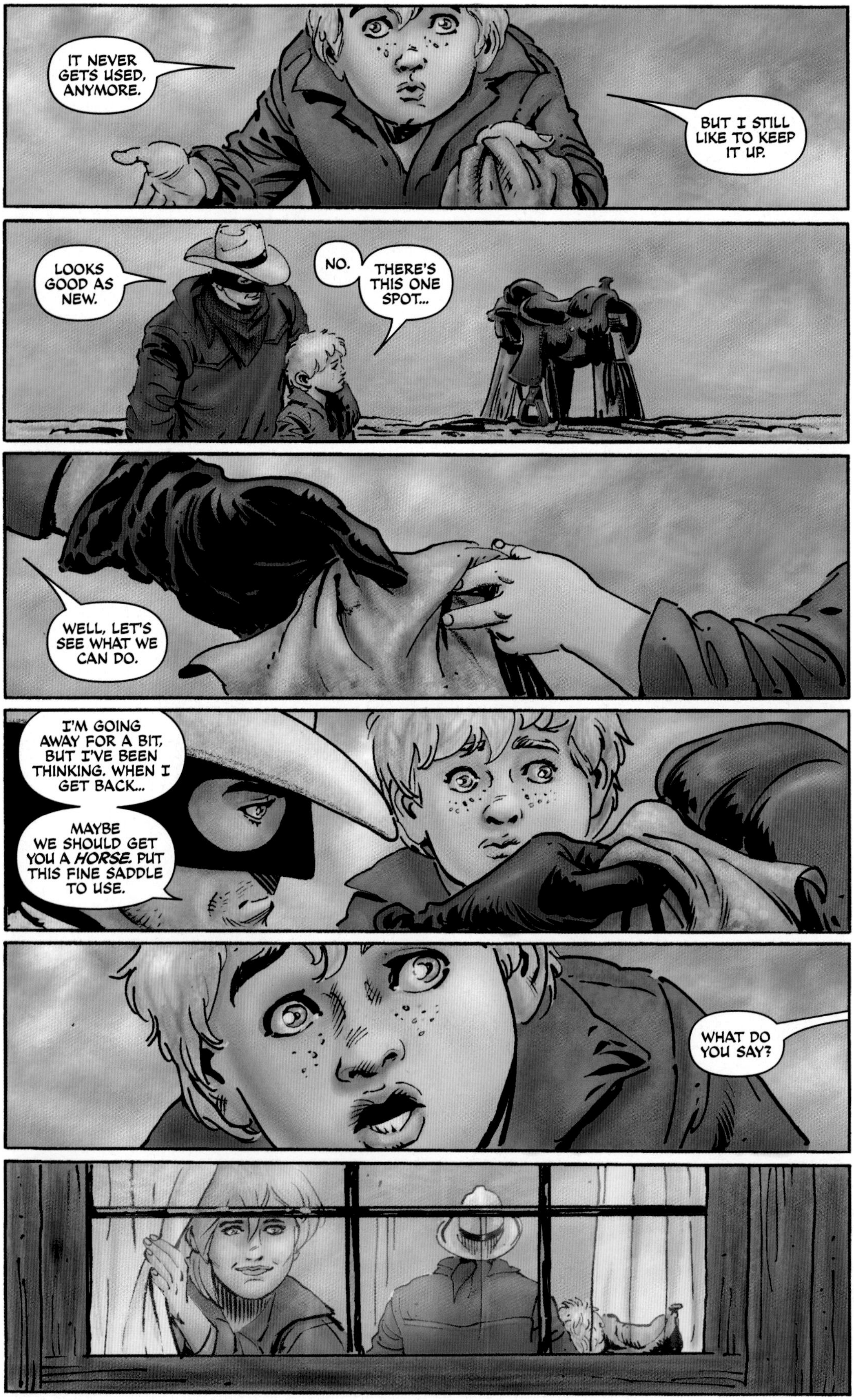
IT NEVER GETS USED, ANYMORE.
BUT I STILL LIKE TO KEEP IT UP.
LOOKS GOOD AS NEW.
NO.
THERE'S THIS ONE SPOT...
WELL, LET'S SEE WHAT WE CAN DO.
I'M GOING AWAY FOR A BIT, BUT I'VE BEEN THINKING. WHEN I GET BACK...
MAYBE WE SHOULD GET YOU A *HORSE.* PUT THIS FINE SADDLE TO USE.
WHAT DO YOU SAY?

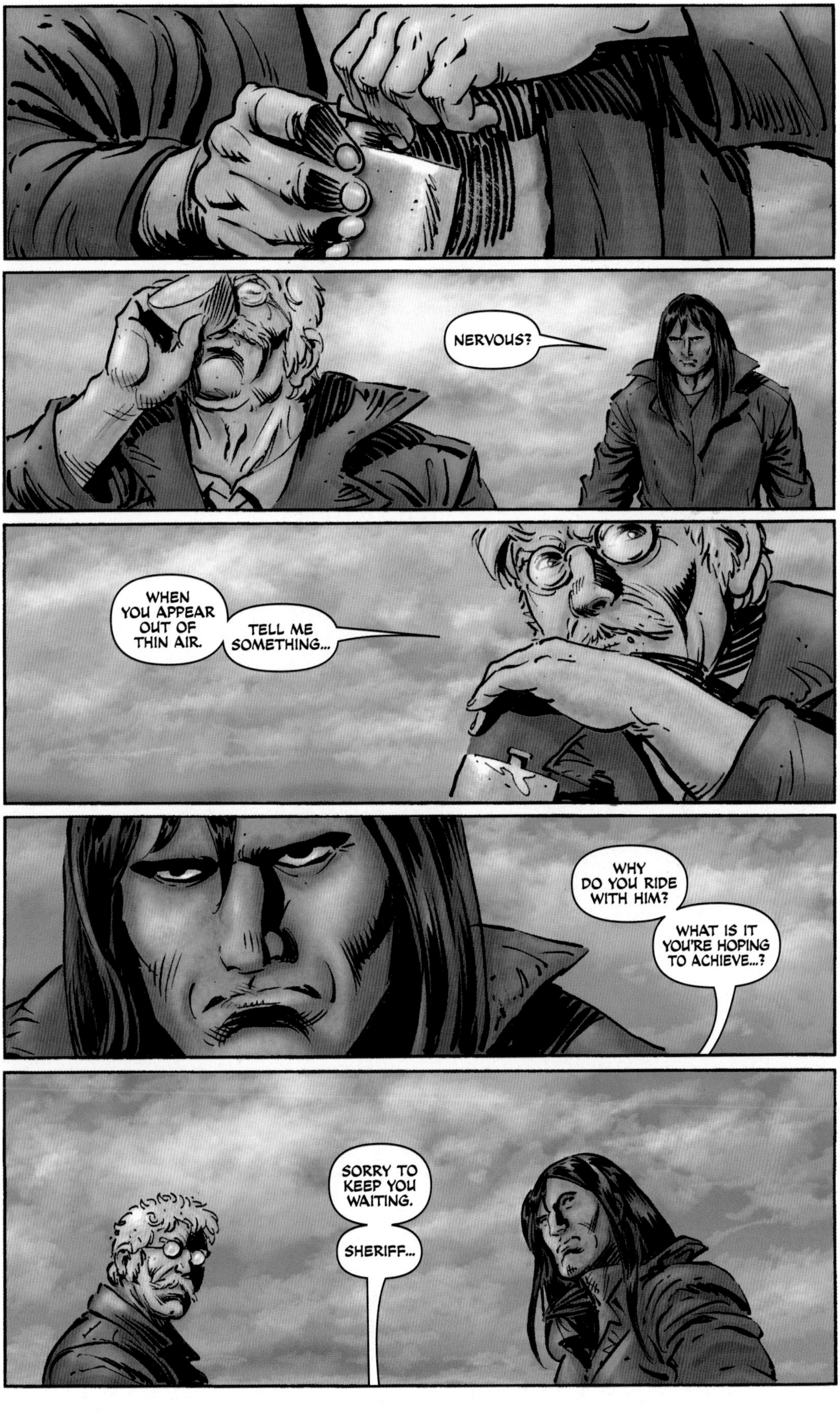
NERVOUS?
WHEN YOU APPEAR OUT OF THIN AIR.
TELL ME SOMETHING...
WHY DO YOU RIDE WITH HIM?
WHAT IS IT YOU'RE HOPING TO ACHIEVE...?
SORRY TO KEEP YOU WAITING.
SHERIFF...

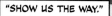

"SHOW US THE WAY."

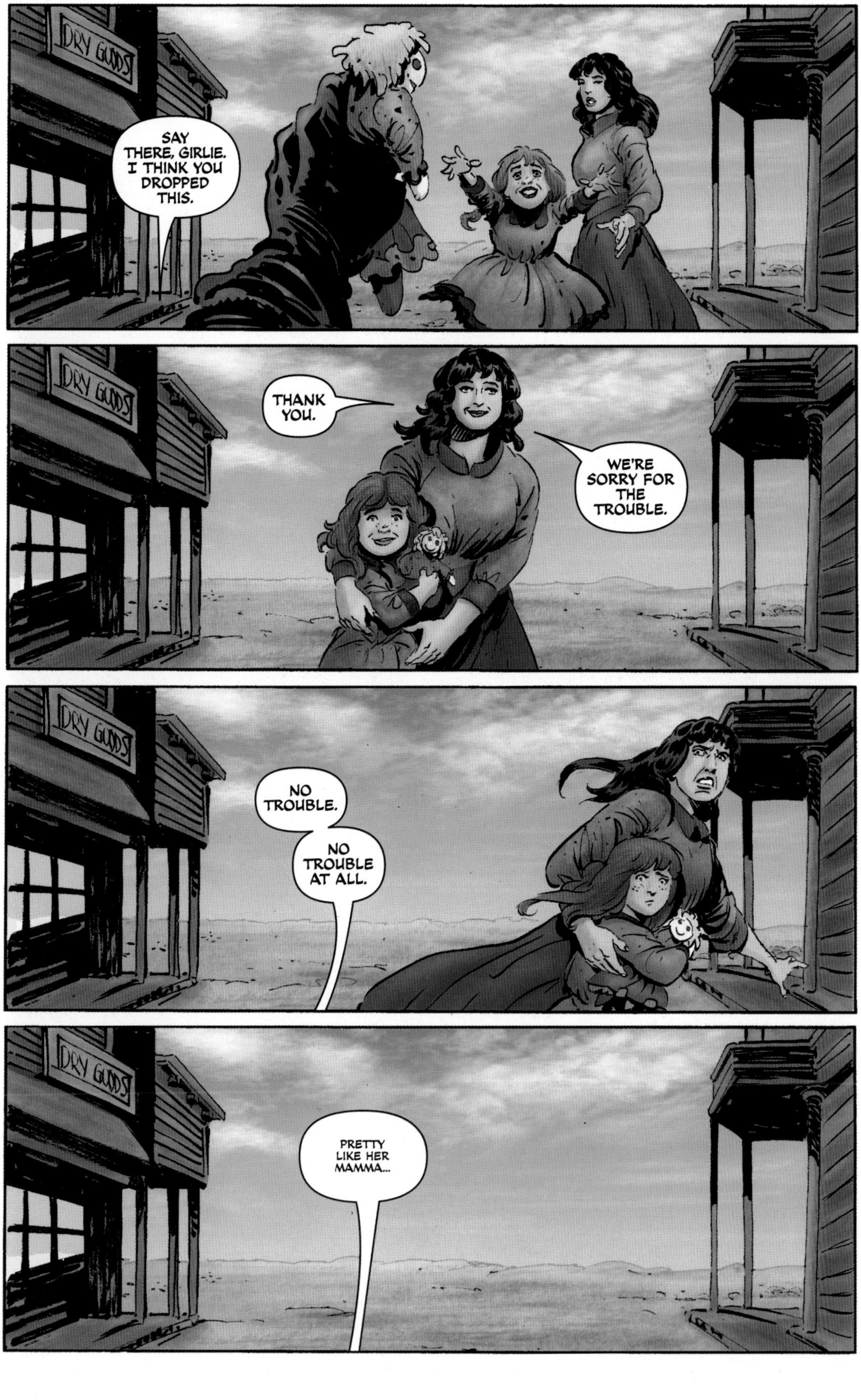
SAY THERE, GIRLIE. I THINK YOU DROPPED THIS.
THANK YOU.
WE'RE SORRY FOR THE TROUBLE.
NO TROUBLE.
NO TROUBLE AT ALL.
PRETTY LIKE HER MAMMA...
DRY GOODS

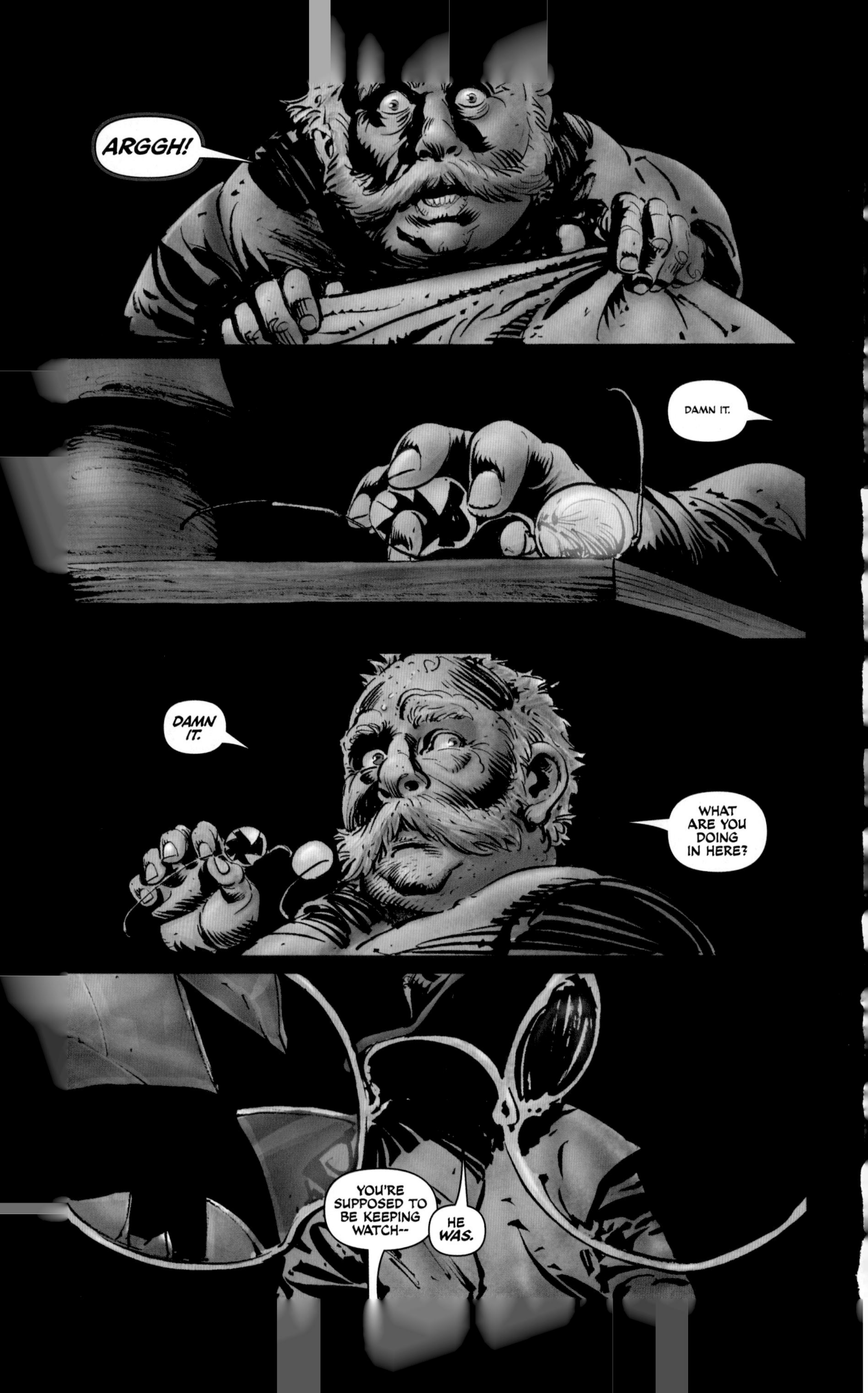
ARGGH!
DAMN IT.
DAMN IT.
WHAT ARE YOU DOING IN HERE?
YOU'RE SUPPOSED TO BE KEEPING WATCH--
HE WAS.

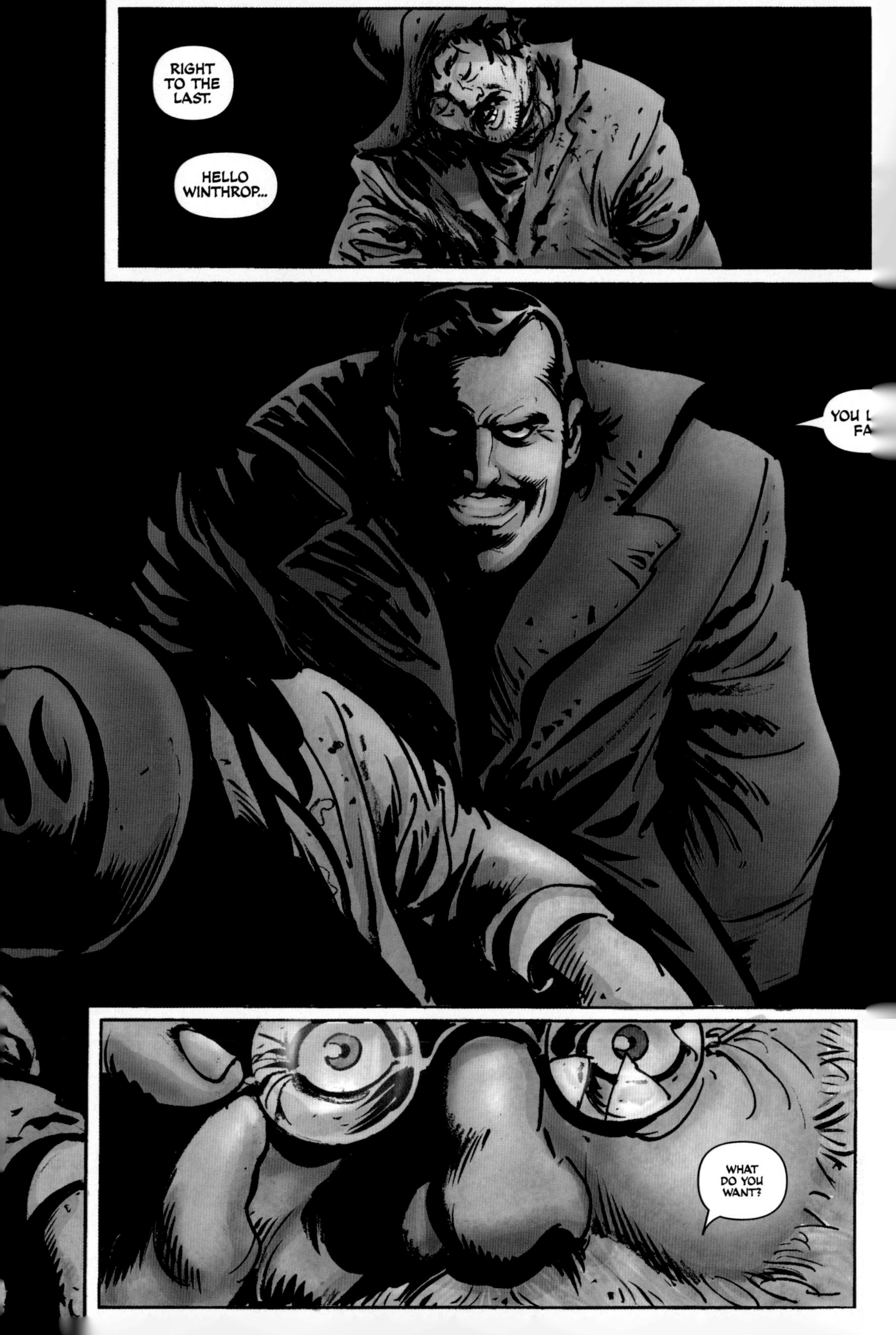
RIGHT TO THE LAST.
HELLO WINTHROP...
WHAT DO YOU WANT?

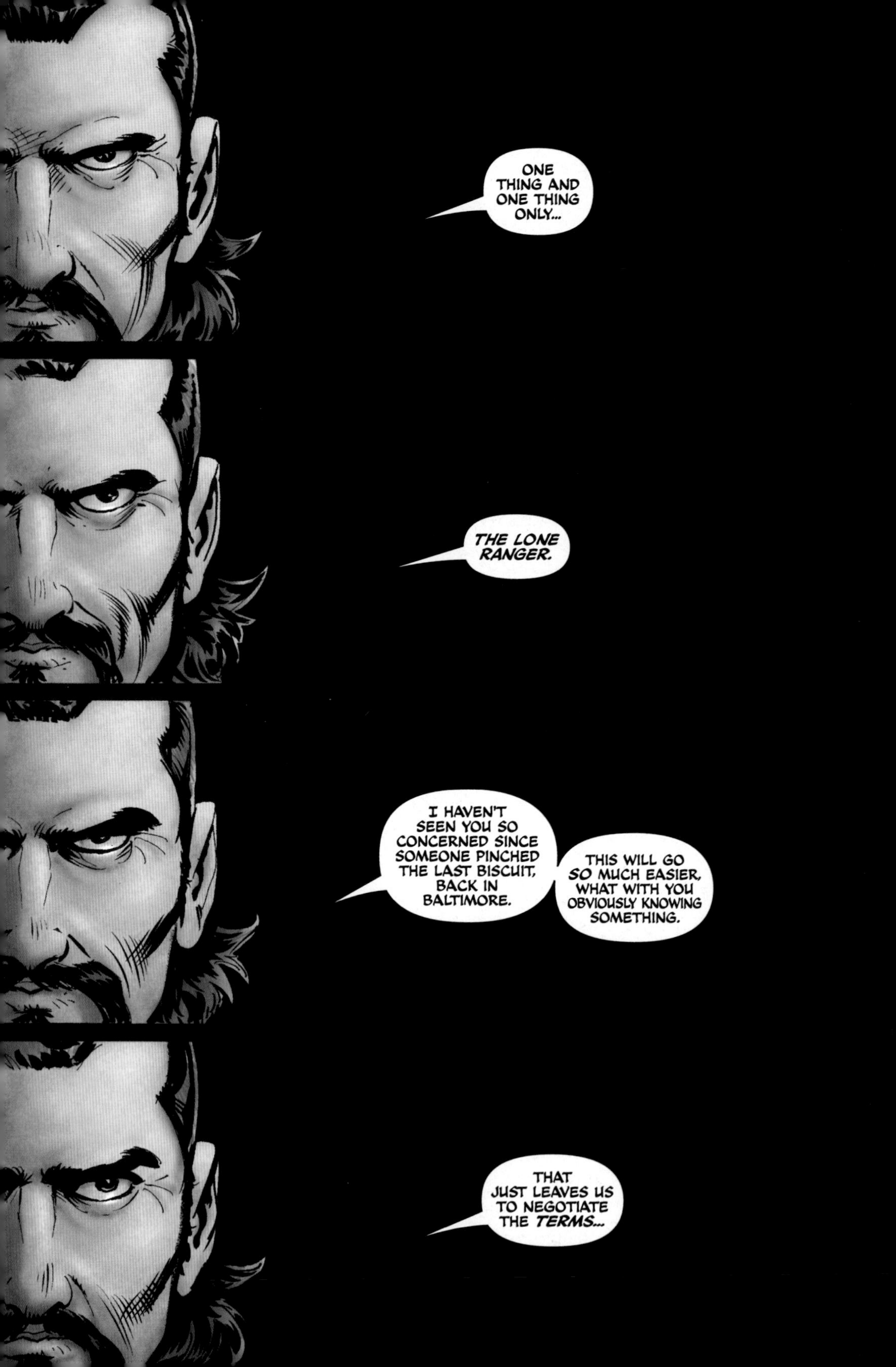
ONE THING AND ONE THING ONLY...
THE LONE RANGER.
I HAVEN'T SEEN YOU SO CONCERNED SINCE SOMEONE PINCHED THE LAST BISCUIT, BACK IN BALTIMORE.
THIS WILL GO *SO* MUCH EASIER, WHAT WITH YOU OBVIOUSLY KNOWING SOMETHING.
THAT JUST LEAVES US TO NEGOTIATE THE *TERMS*...

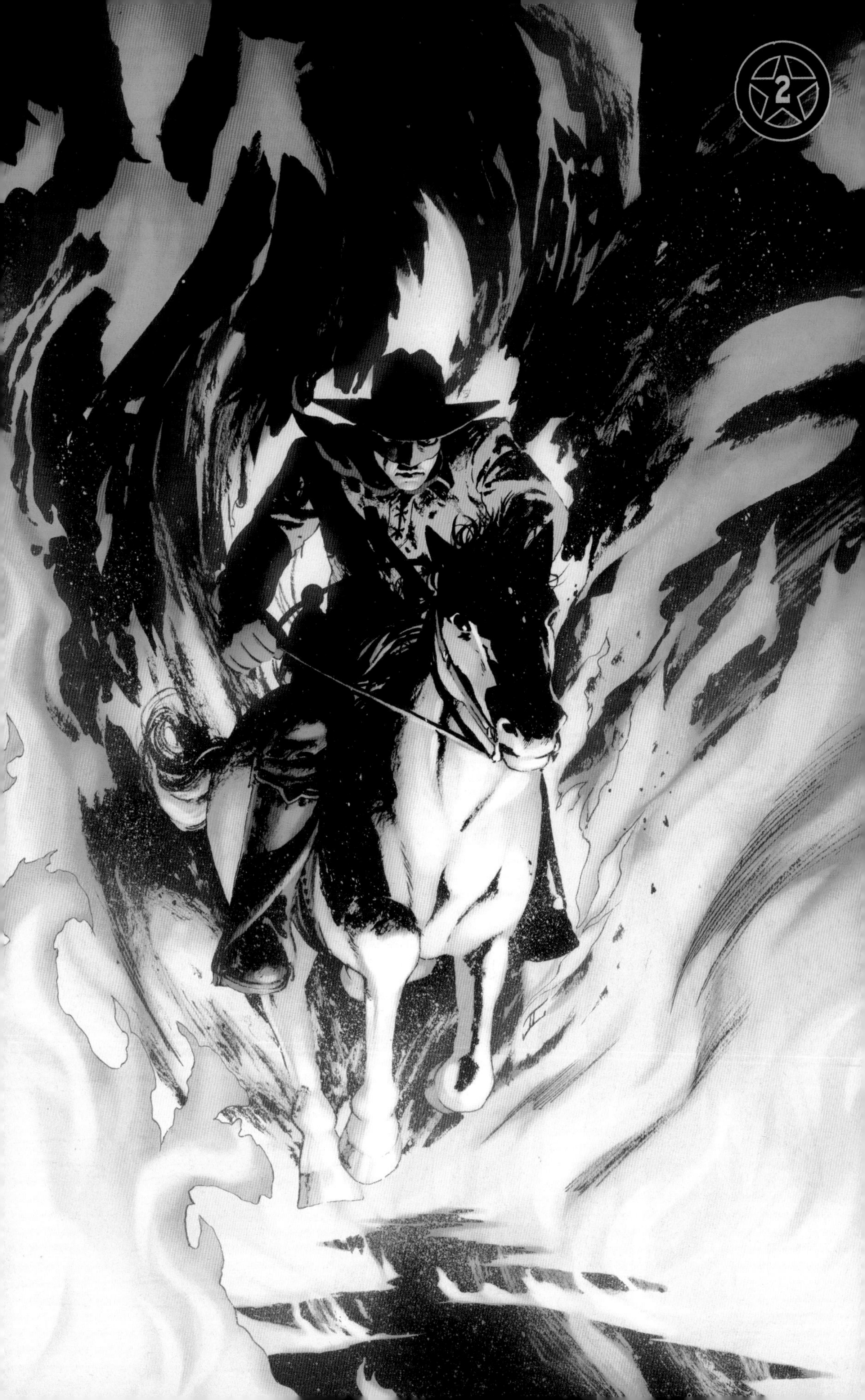
2

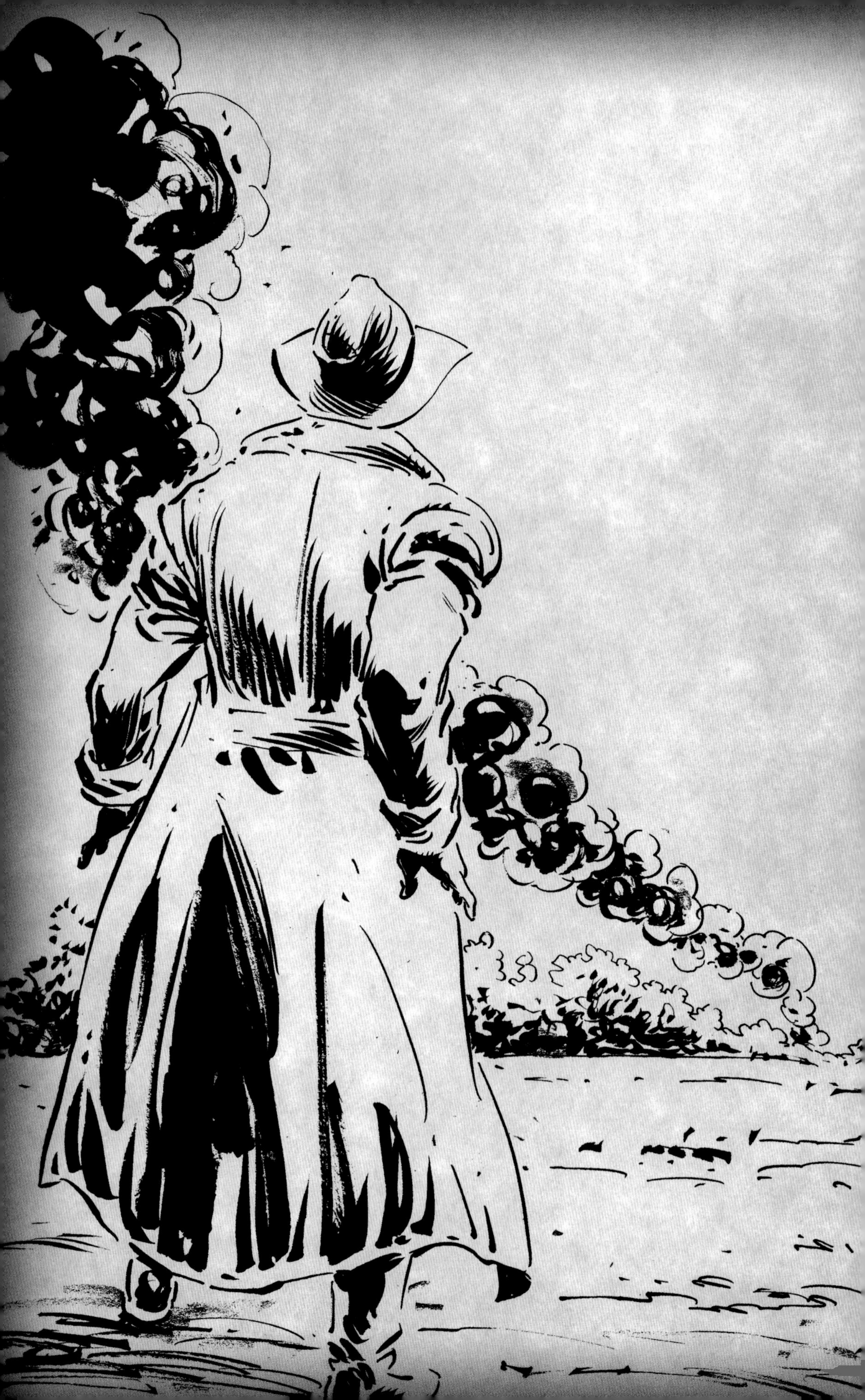

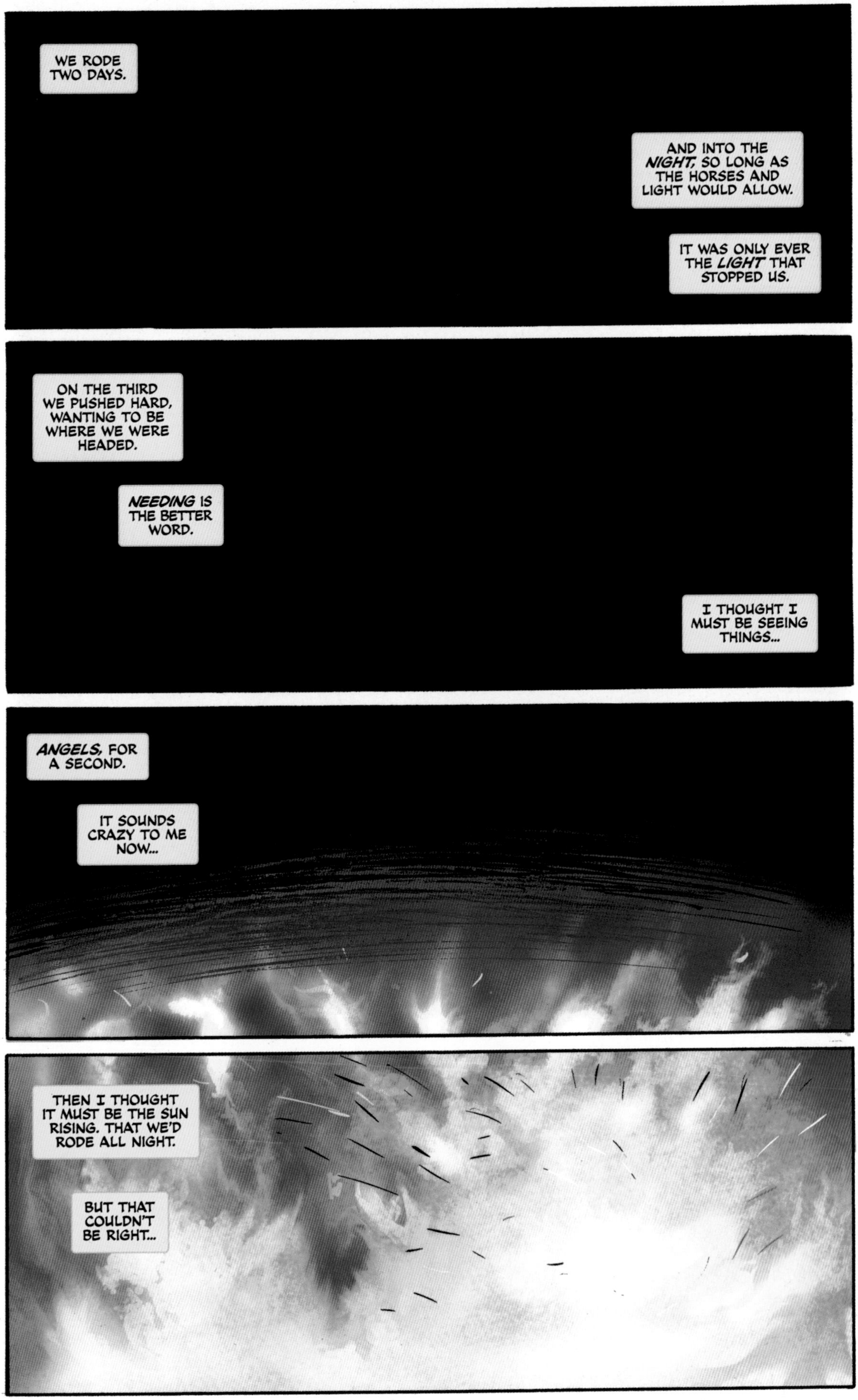
WE RODE TWO DAYS.
AND INTO THE *NIGHT,* SO LONG AS THE HORSES AND LIGHT WOULD ALLOW.
IT WAS ONLY EVER THE *LIGHT* THAT STOPPED US.
ON THE THIRD WE PUSHED HARD, WANTING TO BE WHERE WE WERE HEADED.
NEEDING IS THE BETTER WORD.
I THOUGHT I MUST BE SEEING THINGS...
ANGELS, FOR A SECOND.
IT SOUNDS CRAZY TO ME NOW...
THEN I THOUGHT IT MUST BE THE SUN RISING. THAT WE'D RODE ALL NIGHT.
BUT THAT COULDN'T BE RIGHT...

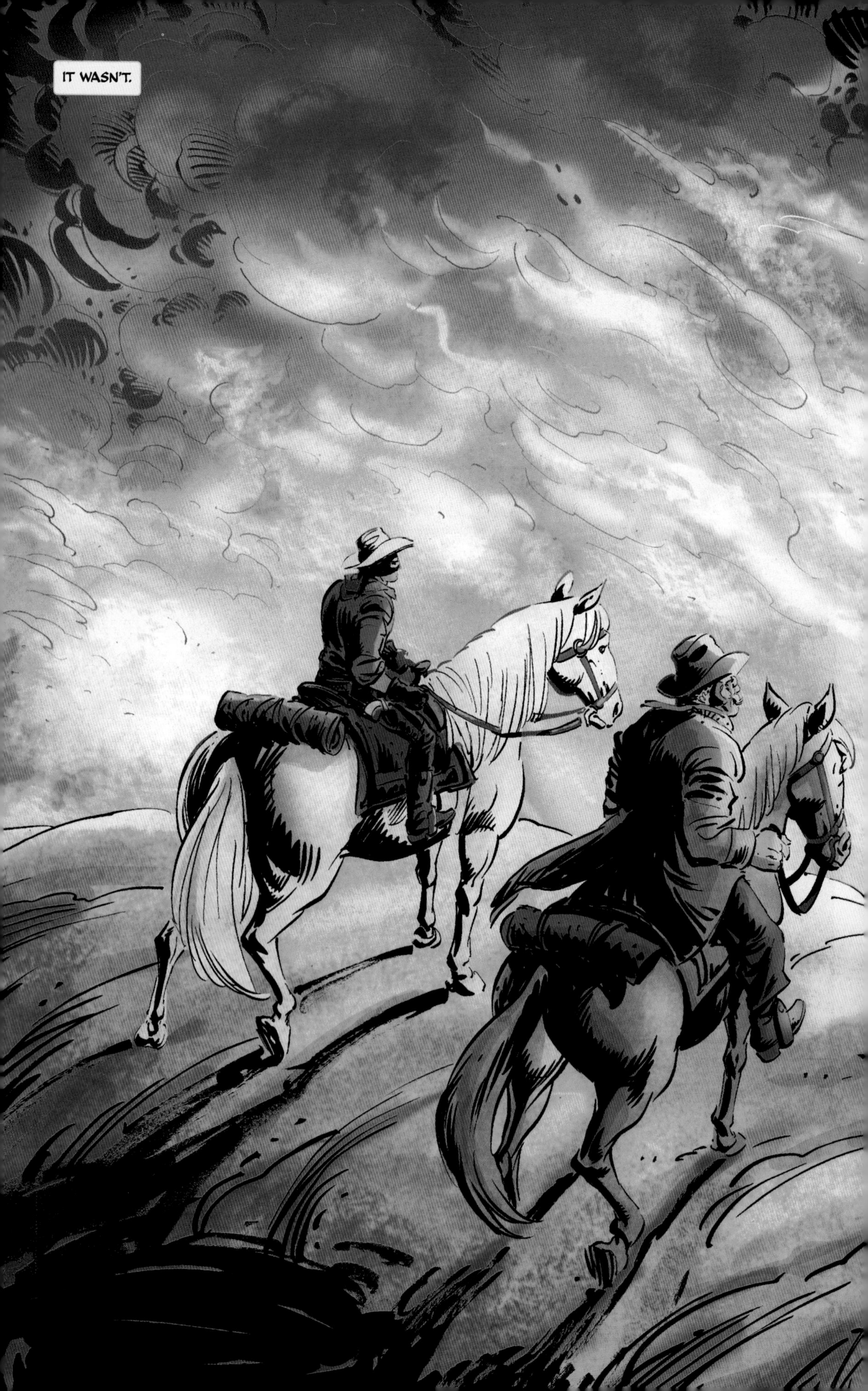
IT WASN'T.

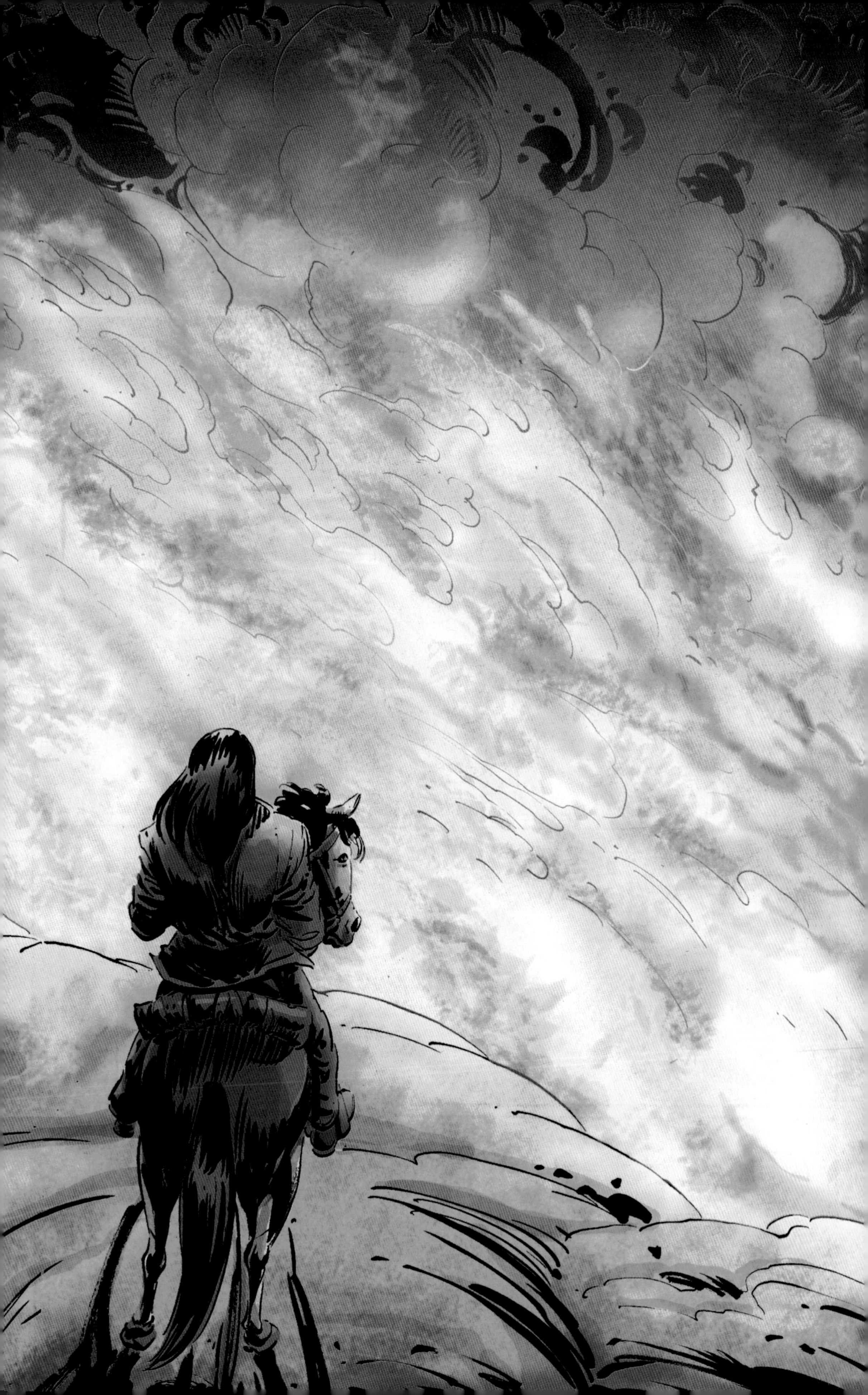

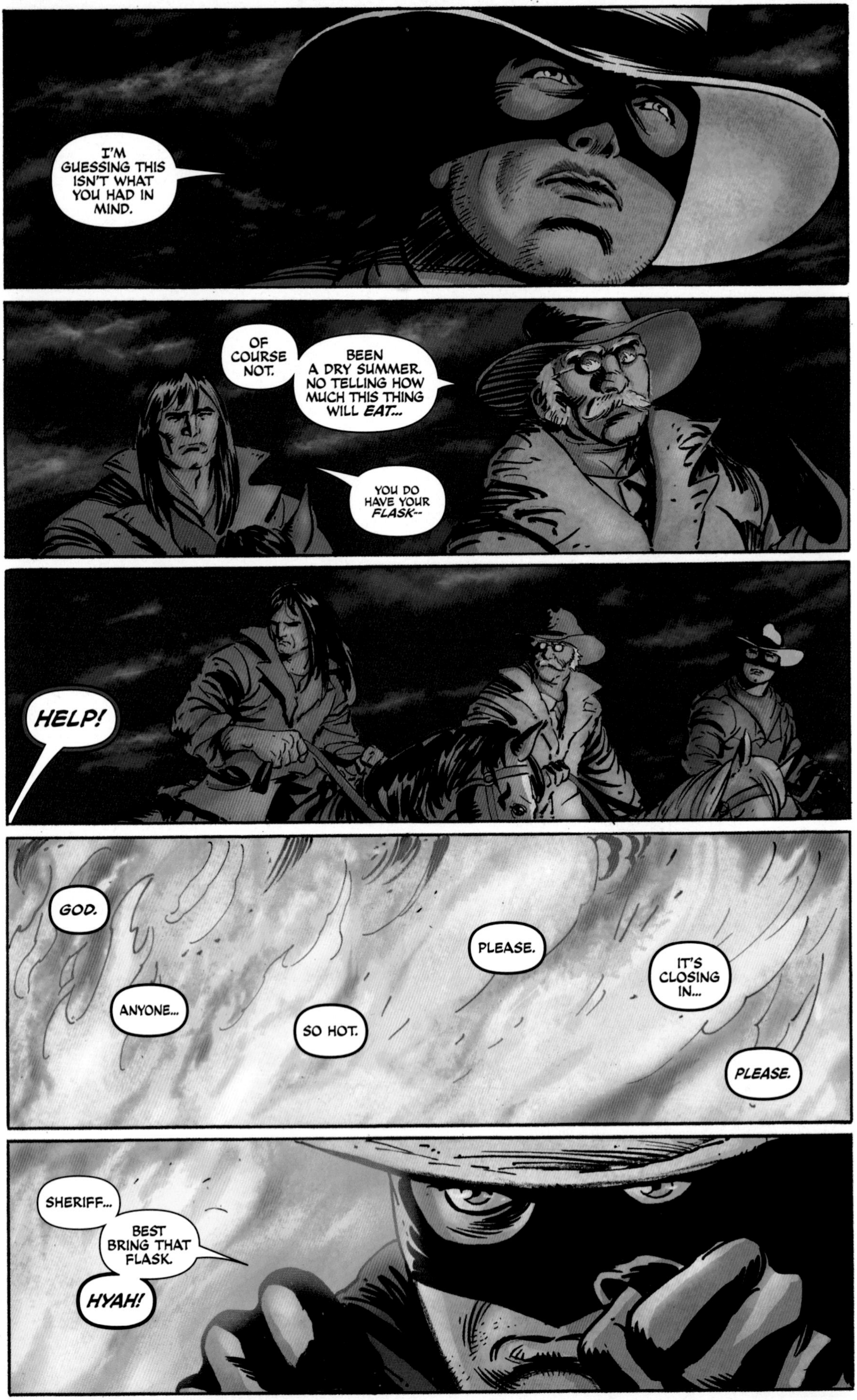
I'M GUESSING THIS ISN'T WHAT YOU HAD IN MIND.
OF COURSE NOT.
BEEN A DRY SUMMER. NO TELLING HOW MUCH THIS THING WILL *EAT*...
YOU DO HAVE YOUR *FLASK*--
HELP!
GOD.
ANYONE...
SO HOT.
PLEASE.
IT'S CLOSING IN...
PLEASE.
SHERIFF...
BEST BRING THAT FLASK.
HYAH!

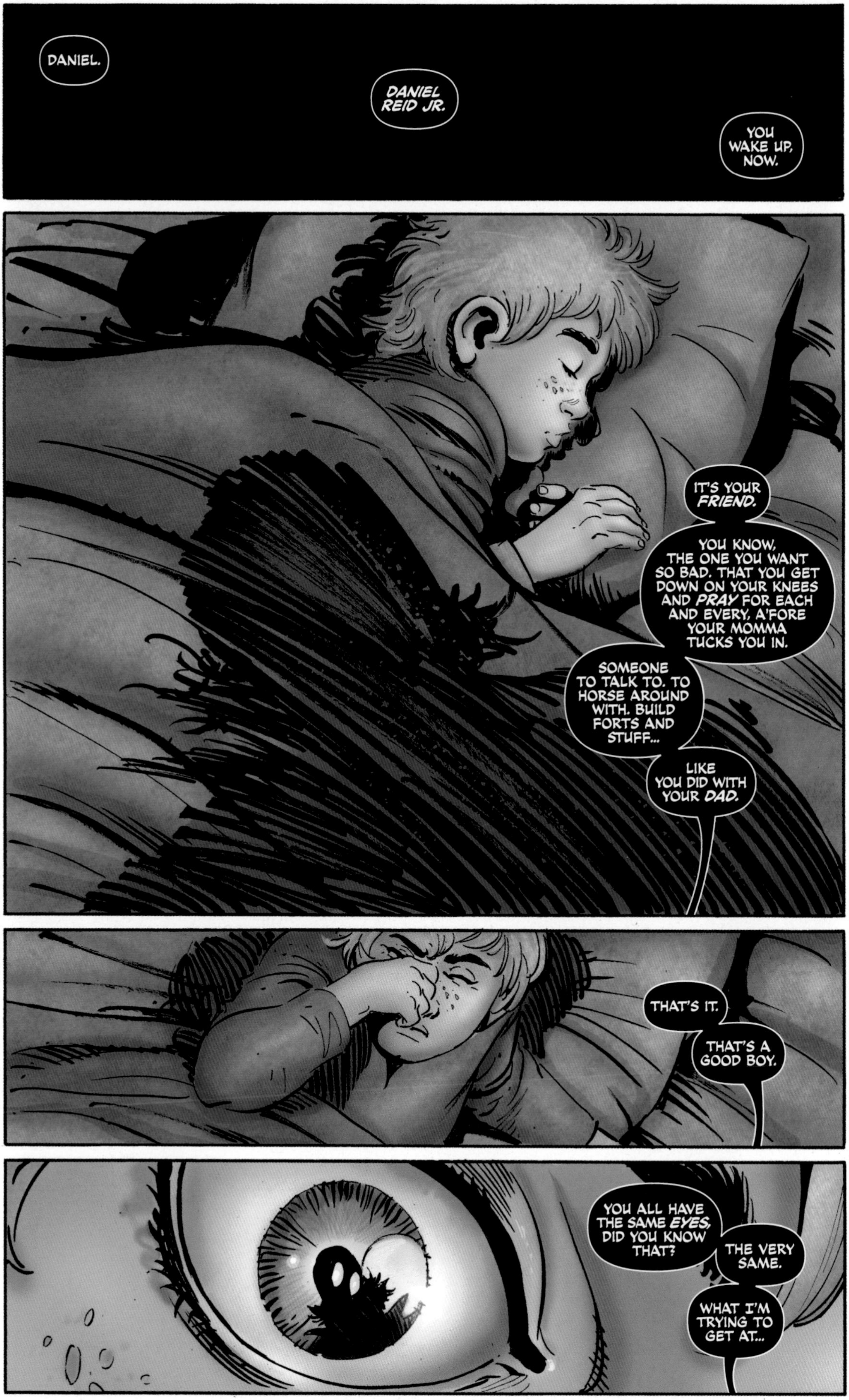
DANIEL.
DANIEL REID JR.
YOU WAKE UP, NOW.
IT'S YOUR FRIEND.
YOU KNOW, THE ONE YOU WANT SO BAD. THAT YOU GET DOWN ON YOUR KNEES AND PRAY FOR EACH AND EVERY, A'FORE YOUR MOMMA TUCKS YOU IN.
SOMEONE TO TALK TO. TO HORSE AROUND WITH. BUILD FORTS AND STUFF...
LIKE YOU DID WITH YOUR DAD.
THAT'S IT.
THAT'S A GOOD BOY.
YOU ALL HAVE THE SAME EYES, DID YOU KNOW THAT?
THE VERY SAME.
WHAT I'M TRYING TO GET AT...

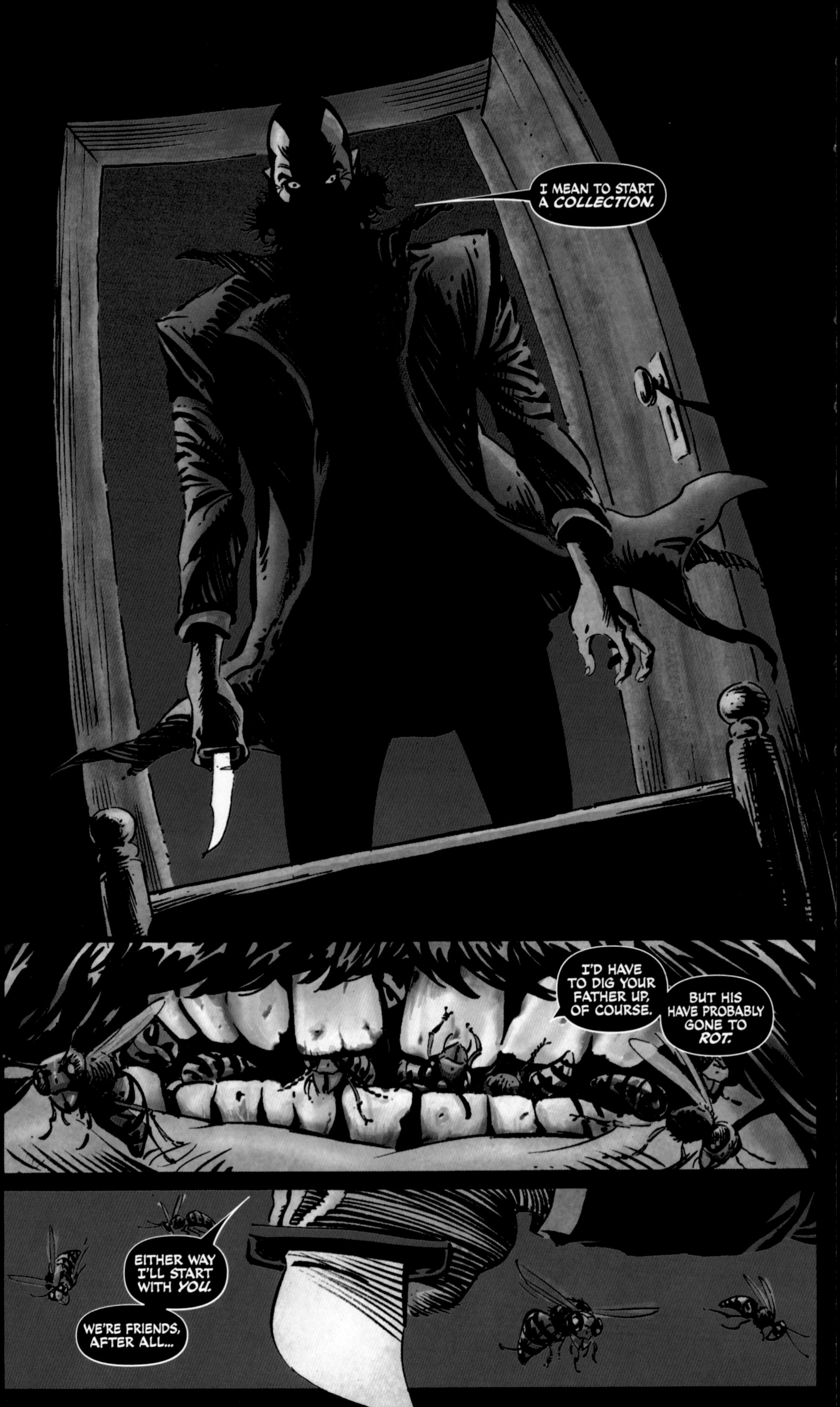
I MEAN TO START
A COLLECTION.
I'D HAVE
TO DIG YOUR
FATHER UP,
OF COURSE.
BUT HIS
HAVE PROBABLY
GONE TO
ROT.
EITHER WAY
I'LL START
WITH YOU.
WE'RE FRIENDS,
AFTER ALL...

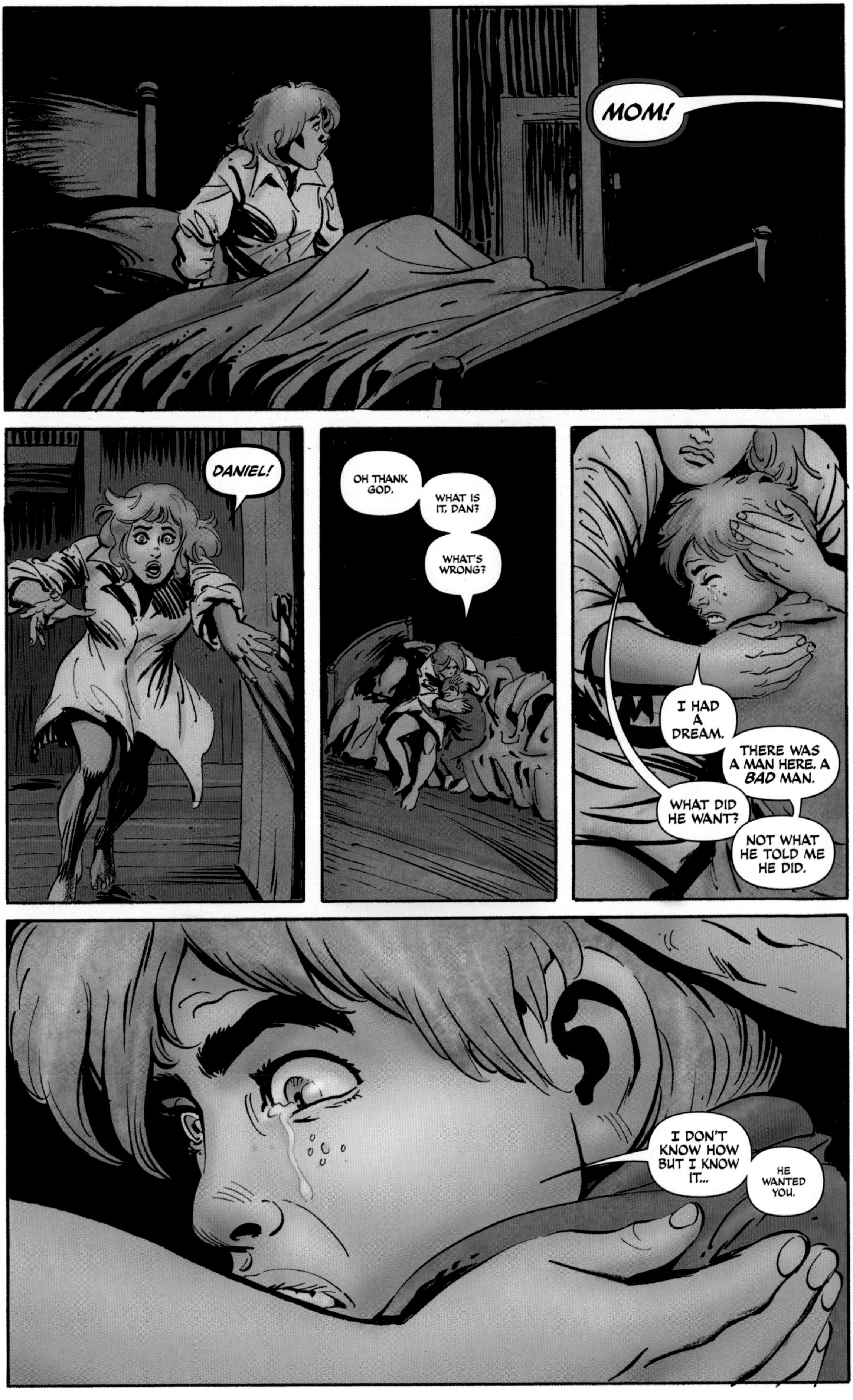
MOM!
DANIEL!
OH THANK GOD.
WHAT IS IT, DAN?
WHAT'S WRONG?
I HAD A DREAM.
THERE WAS A MAN HERE. A *BAD* MAN.
WHAT DID HE WANT?
NOT WHAT HE TOLD ME HE DID.
I DON'T KNOW HOW BUT I KNOW IT...
HE WANTED YOU.

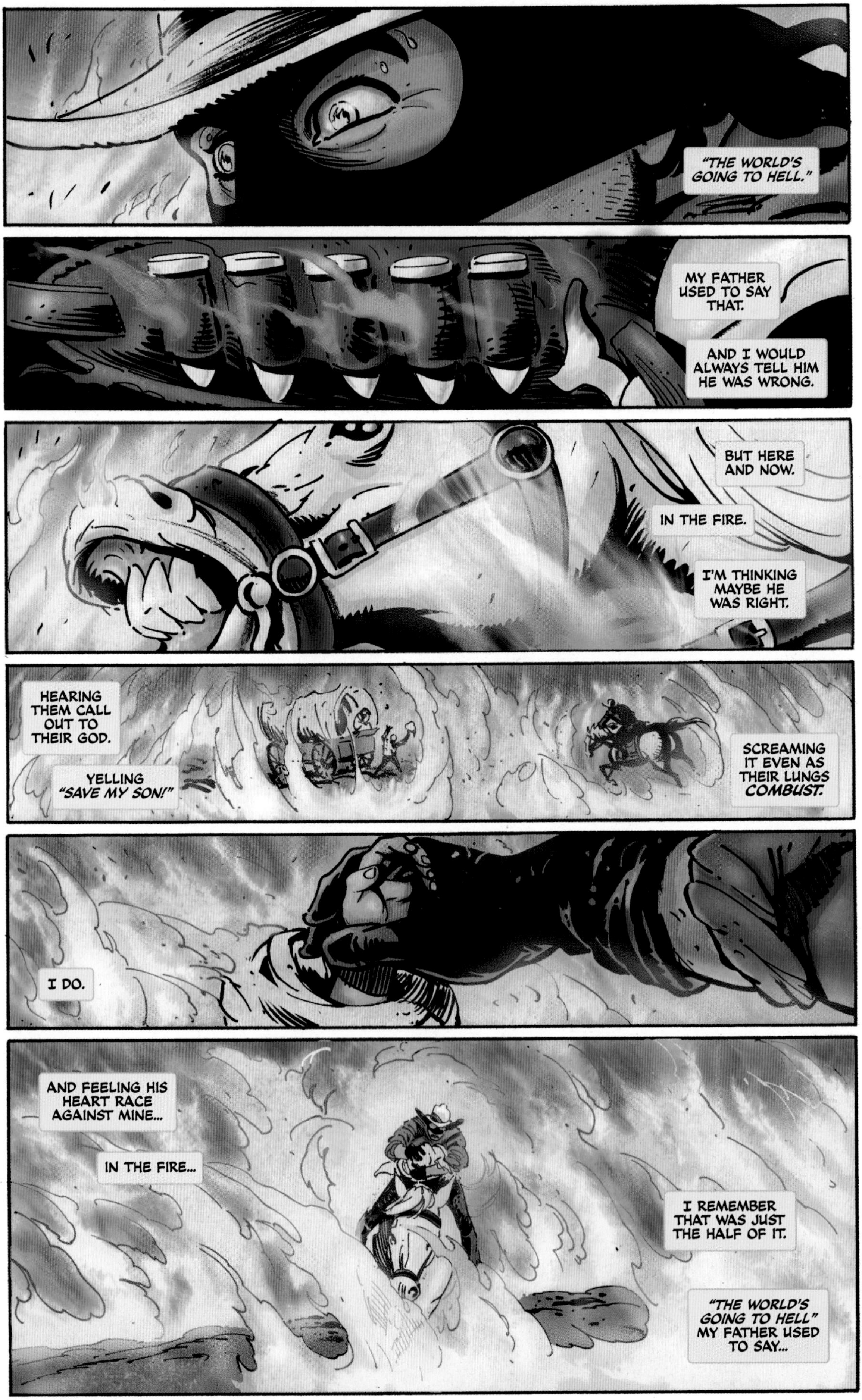
"THE WORLD'S GOING TO HELL."
MY FATHER USED TO SAY THAT.
AND I WOULD ALWAYS TELL HIM HE WAS WRONG.
BUT HERE AND NOW.
IN THE FIRE.
I'M THINKING MAYBE HE WAS RIGHT.
HEARING THEM CALL OUT TO THEIR GOD.
YELLING "SAVE MY SON!"
SCREAMING IT EVEN AS THEIR LUNGS COMBUST.
I DO.
AND FEELING HIS HEART RACE AGAINST MINE...
IN THE FIRE...
I REMEMBER THAT WAS JUST THE HALF OF IT.
"THE WORLD'S GOING TO HELL" MY FATHER USED TO SAY...

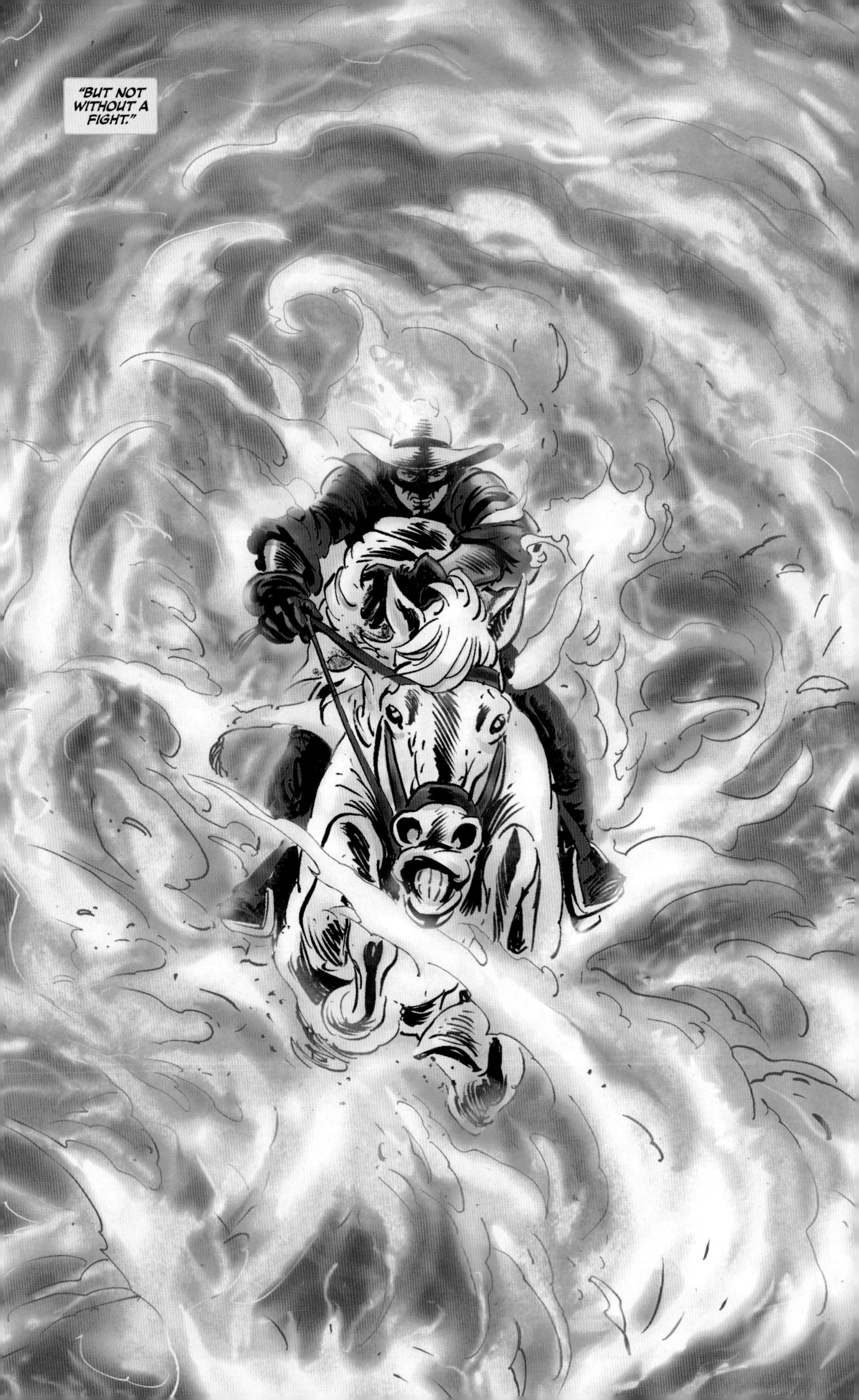
"BUT NOT WITHOUT A FIGHT."

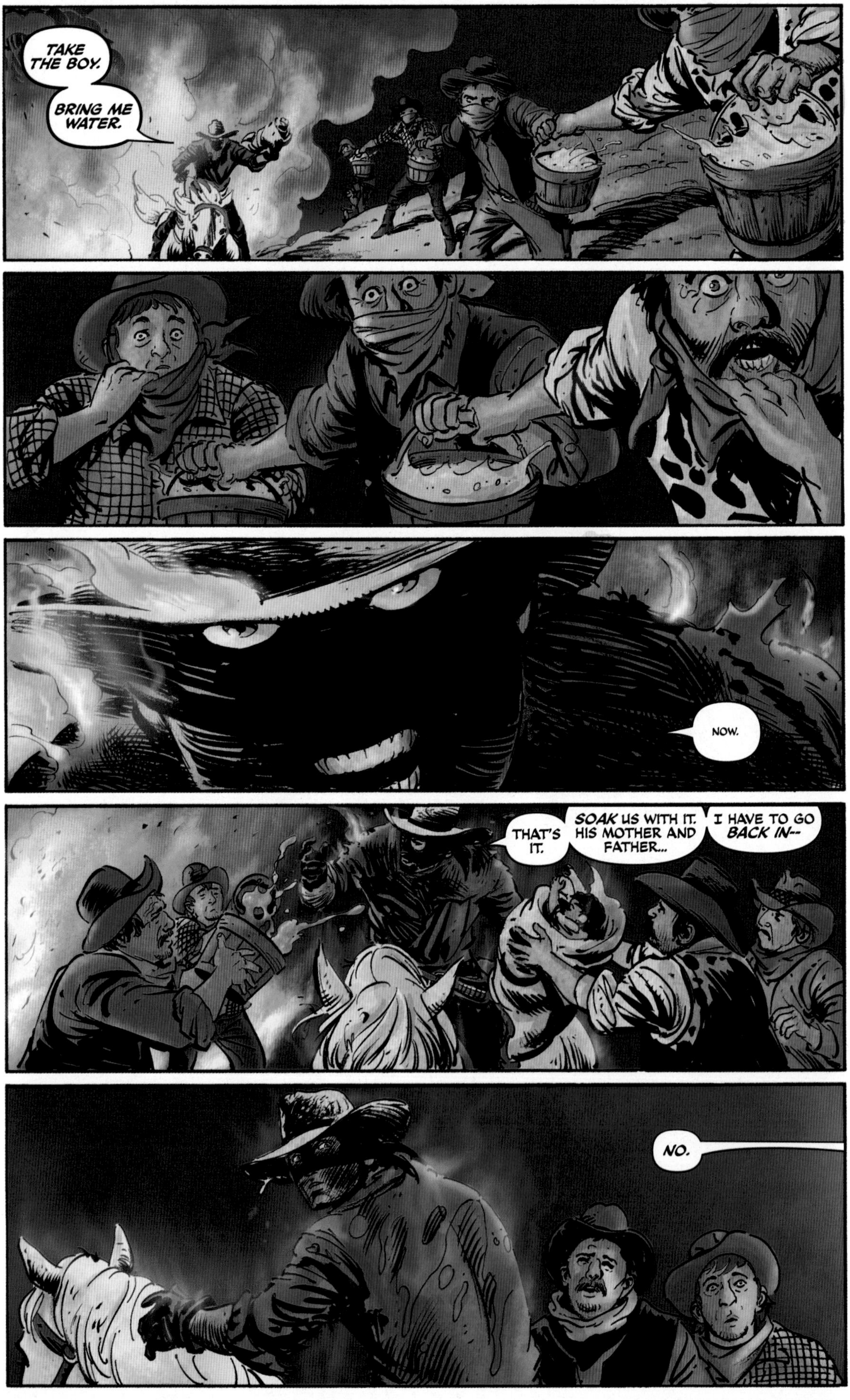
TAKE THE BOY.
BRING ME WATER.
NOW.
THAT'S IT.
SOAK US WITH IT. HIS MOTHER AND FATHER...
I HAVE TO GO BACK IN--
NO.

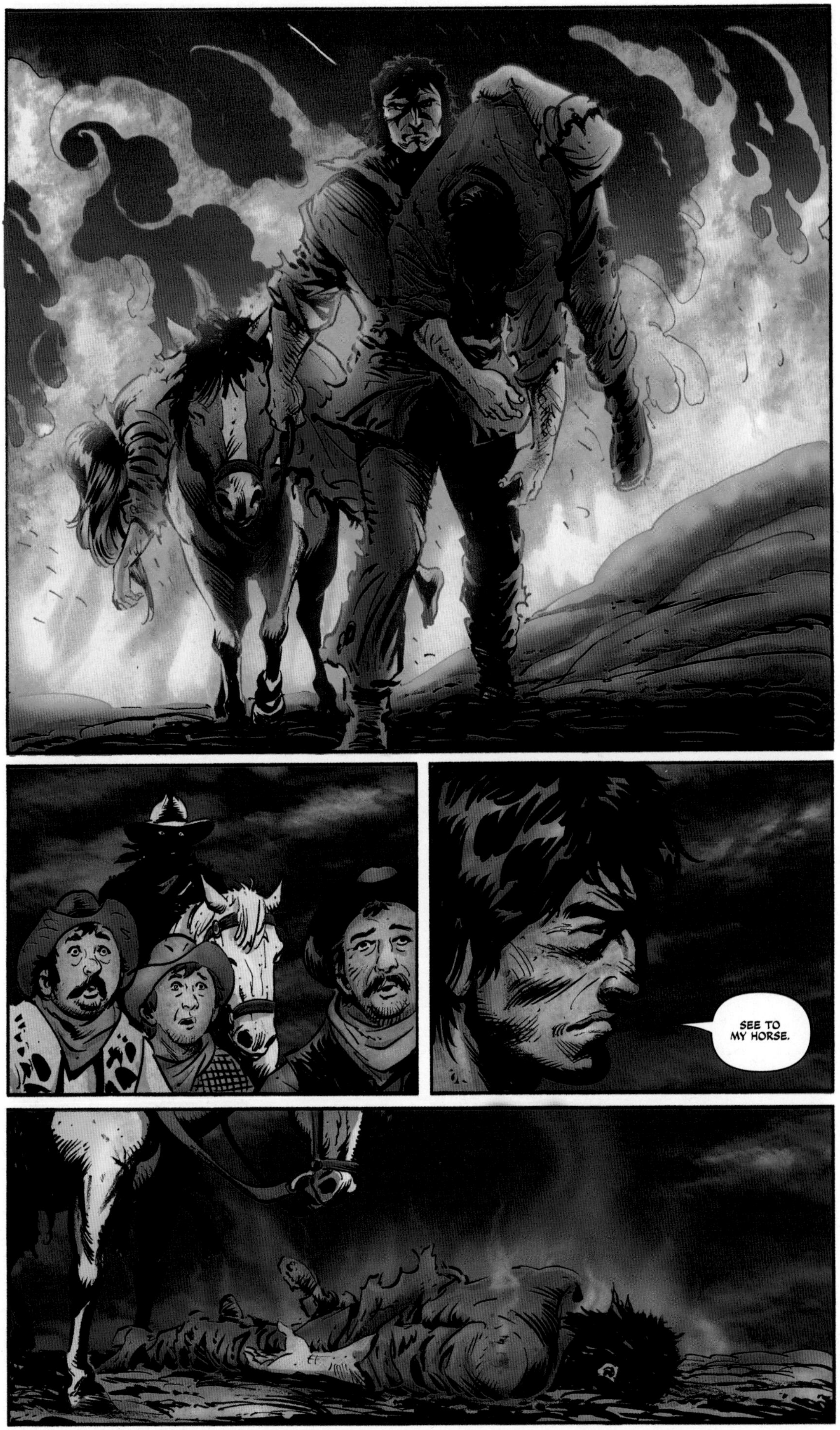
SEE TO
MY HORSE.

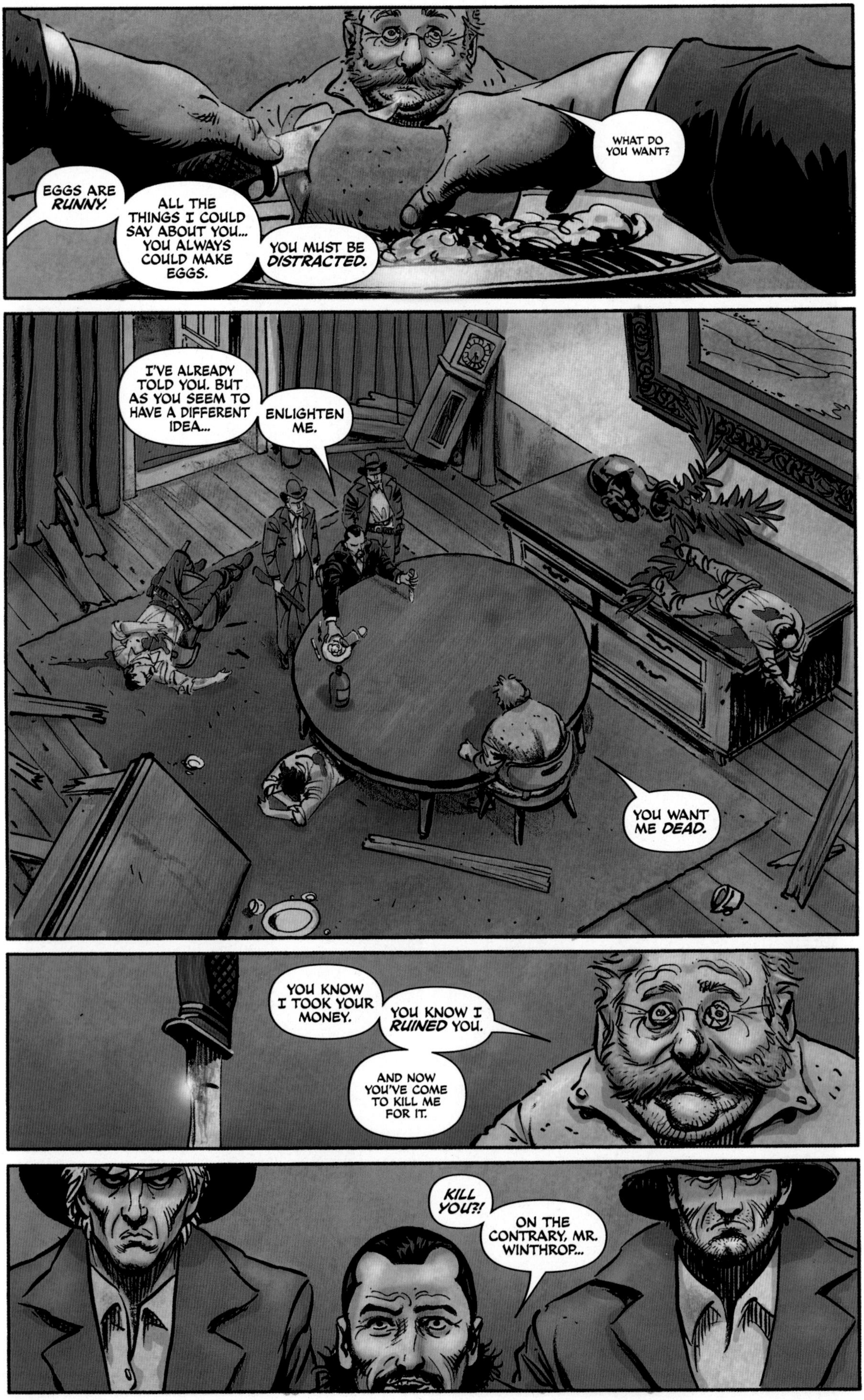
EGGS ARE RUNNY.
ALL THE THINGS I COULD SAY ABOUT YOU... YOU ALWAYS COULD MAKE EGGS.
YOU MUST BE DISTRACTED.
WHAT DO YOU WANT?
I'VE ALREADY TOLD YOU. BUT AS YOU SEEM TO HAVE A DIFFERENT IDEA...
ENLIGHTEN ME.
YOU WANT ME DEAD.
YOU KNOW I TOOK YOUR MONEY.
YOU KNOW I RUINED YOU.
AND NOW YOU'VE COME TO KILL ME FOR IT.
KILL YOU?!
ON THE CONTRARY, MR. WINTHROP...

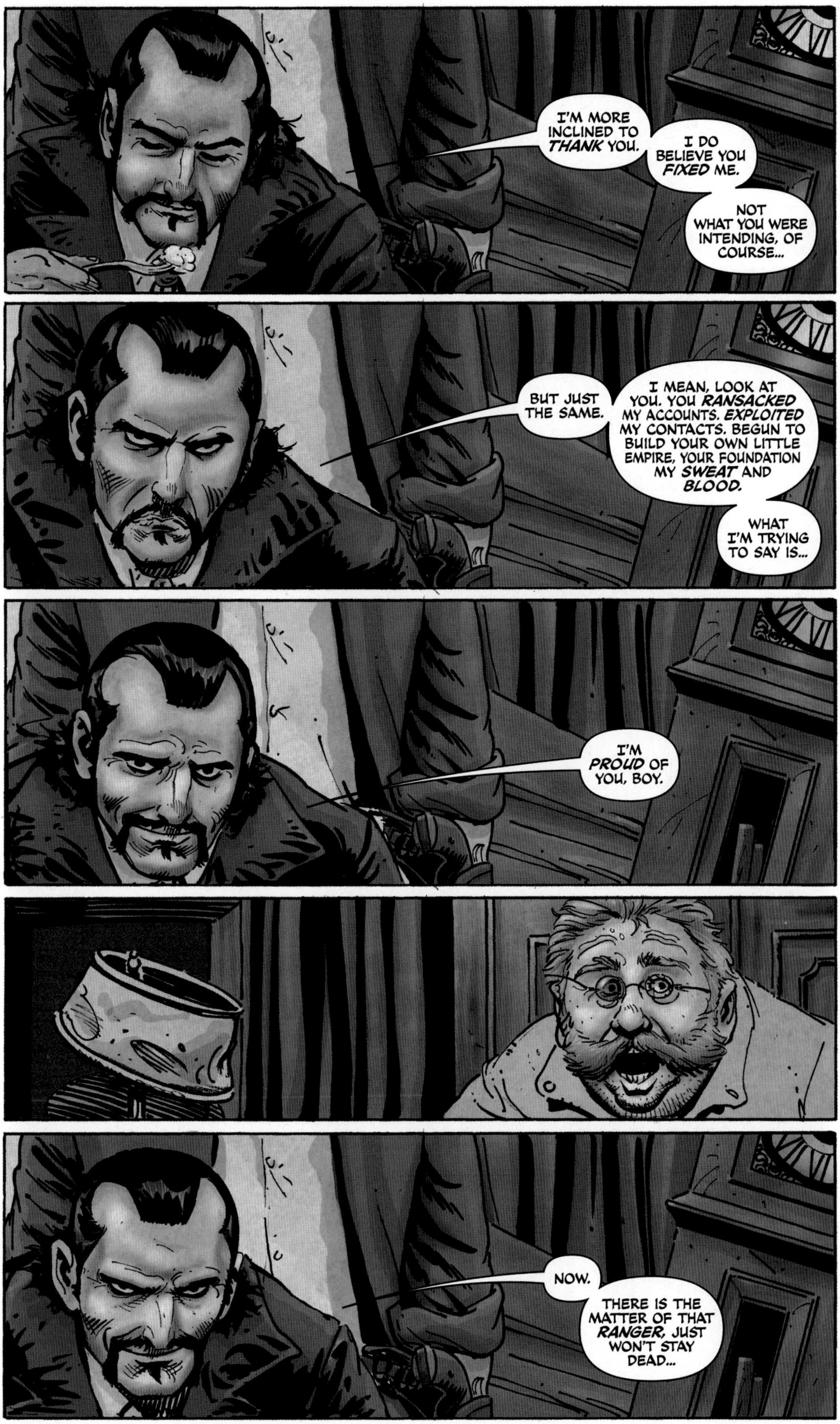
I'M MORE INCLINED TO *THANK* YOU.
I DO BELIEVE YOU *FIXED* ME.
NOT WHAT YOU WERE INTENDING, OF COURSE...
BUT JUST THE SAME.
I MEAN, LOOK AT YOU. YOU *RANSACKED* MY ACCOUNTS. *EXPLOITED* MY CONTACTS. BEGUN TO BUILD YOUR OWN LITTLE EMPIRE, YOUR FOUNDATION MY *SWEAT* AND *BLOOD.*
WHAT I'M TRYING TO SAY IS...
I'M *PROUD* OF YOU, BOY.
NOW.
THERE IS THE MATTER OF THAT *RANGER,* JUST WON'T STAY DEAD...

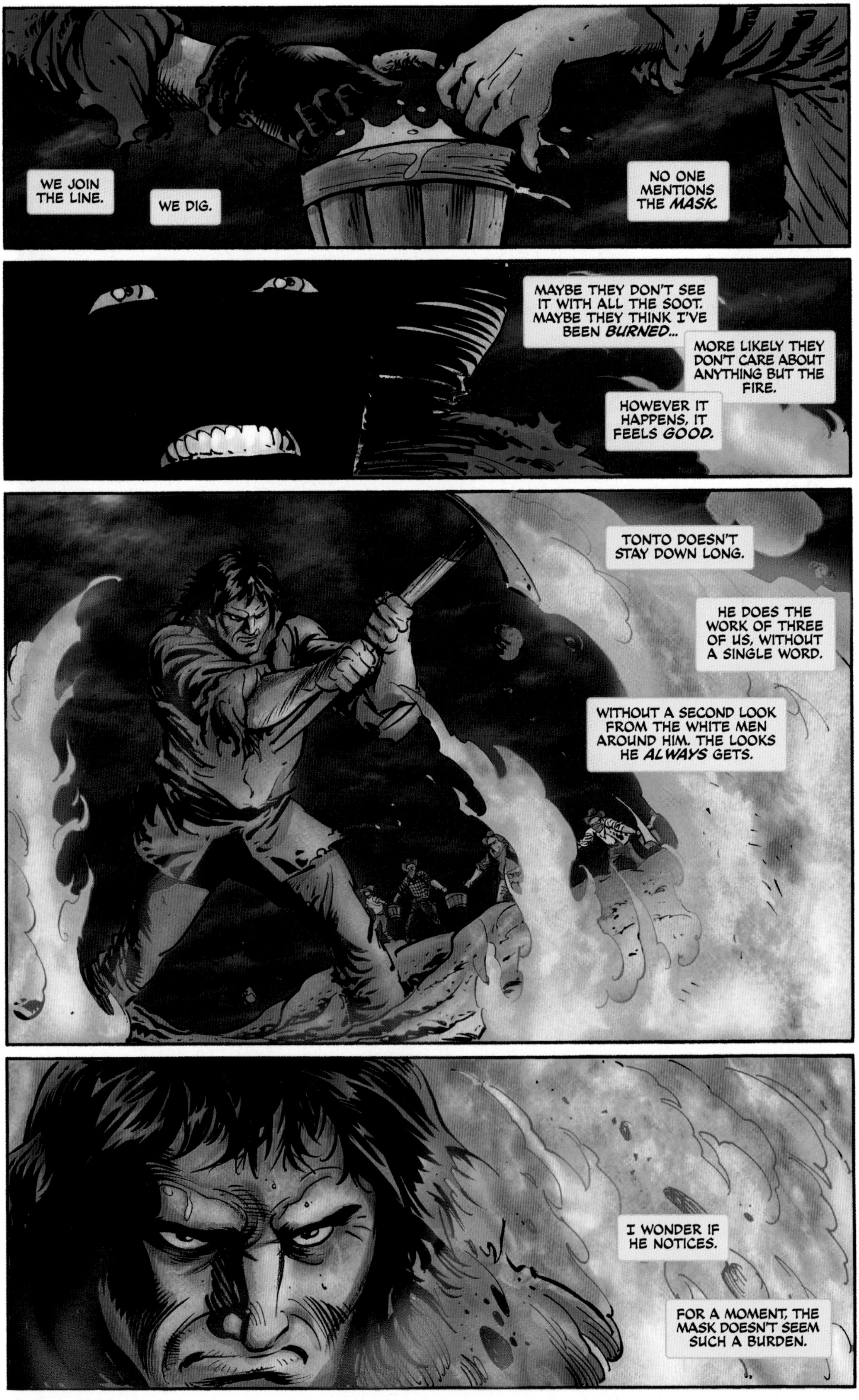
WE JOIN THE LINE.
WE DIG.
NO ONE MENTIONS THE MASK.
MAYBE THEY DON'T SEE IT WITH ALL THE SOOT. MAYBE THEY THINK I'VE BEEN BURNED...
MORE LIKELY THEY DON'T CARE ABOUT ANYTHING BUT THE FIRE.
HOWEVER IT HAPPENS, IT FEELS GOOD.
TONTO DOESN'T STAY DOWN LONG.
HE DOES THE WORK OF THREE OF US, WITHOUT A SINGLE WORD.
WITHOUT A SECOND LOOK FROM THE WHITE MEN AROUND HIM. THE LOOKS HE ALWAYS GETS.
I WONDER IF HE NOTICES.
FOR A MOMENT, THE MASK DOESN'T SEEM SUCH A BURDEN.

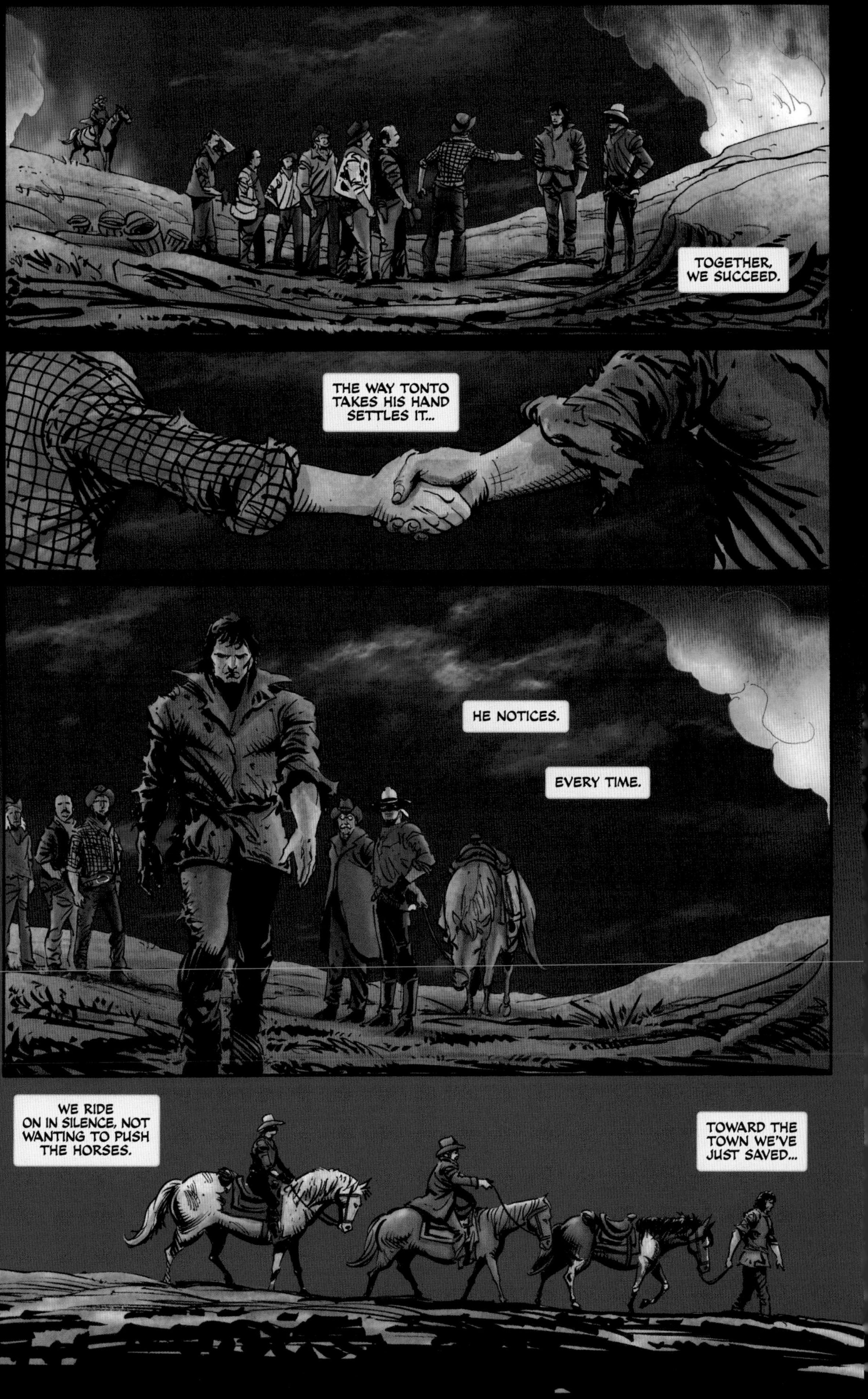
TOGETHER, WE SUCCEED.
THE WAY TONTO TAKES HIS HAND SETTLES IT...
HE NOTICES.
EVERY TIME.
WE RIDE ON IN SILENCE, NOT WANTING TO PUSH THE HORSES.
TOWARD THE TOWN WE'VE JUST SAVED...

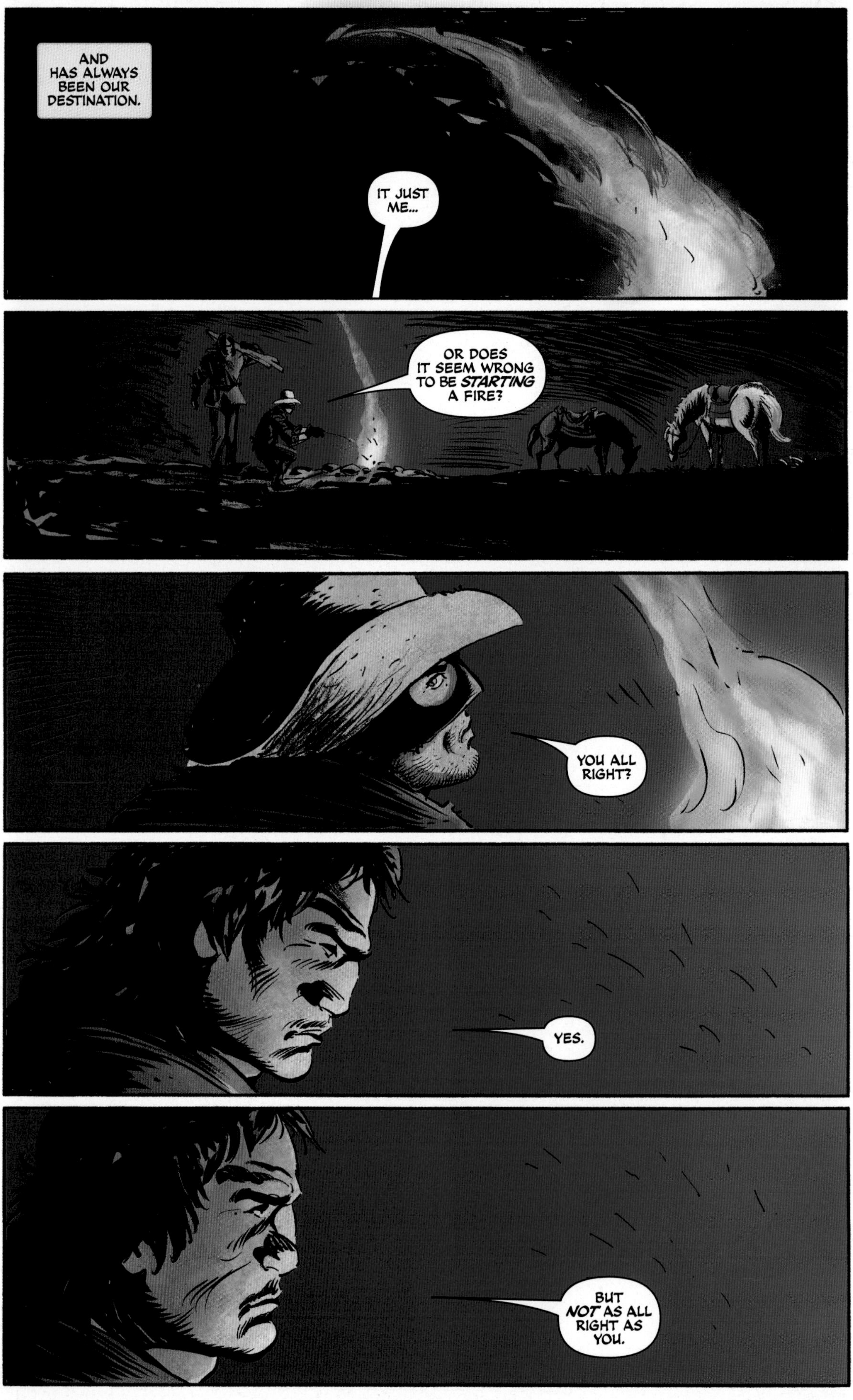
AND HAS ALWAYS BEEN OUR DESTINATION.
IT JUST ME...
OR DOES IT SEEM WRONG TO BE *STARTING* A FIRE?
YOU ALL RIGHT?
YES.
BUT *NOT* AS ALL RIGHT AS YOU.

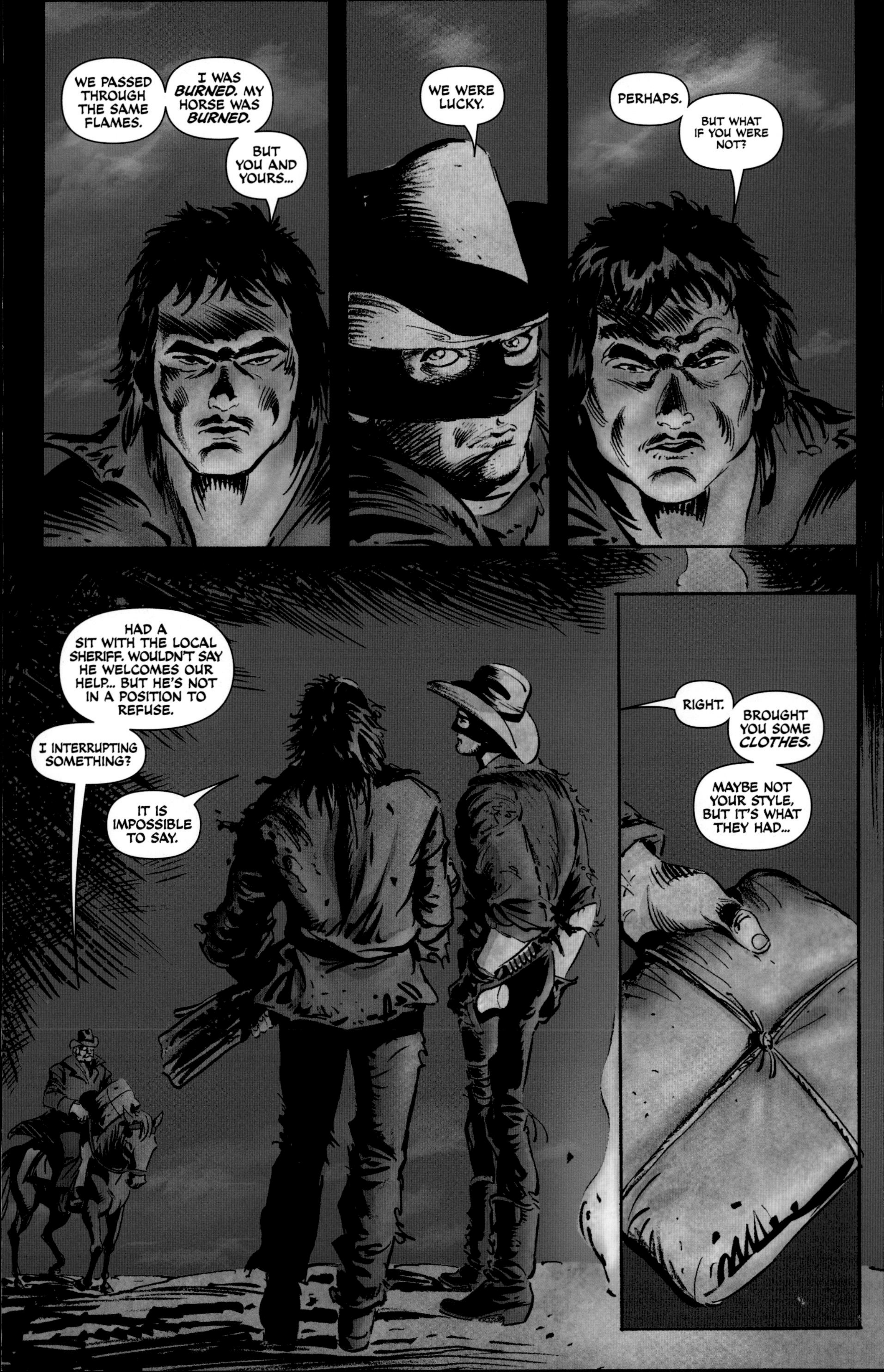
WE PASSED THROUGH THE SAME FLAMES.
I WAS BURNED. MY HORSE WAS BURNED.
BUT YOU AND YOURS...
WE WERE LUCKY.
PERHAPS.
BUT WHAT IF YOU WERE NOT?
IT IS IMPOSSIBLE TO SAY.
I INTERRUPTING SOMETHING?
HAD A SIT WITH THE LOCAL SHERIFF. WOULDN'T SAY HE WELCOMES OUR HELP... BUT HE'S NOT IN A POSITION TO REFUSE.
RIGHT.
BROUGHT YOU SOME CLOTHES.
MAYBE NOT YOUR STYLE, BUT IT'S WHAT THEY HAD...

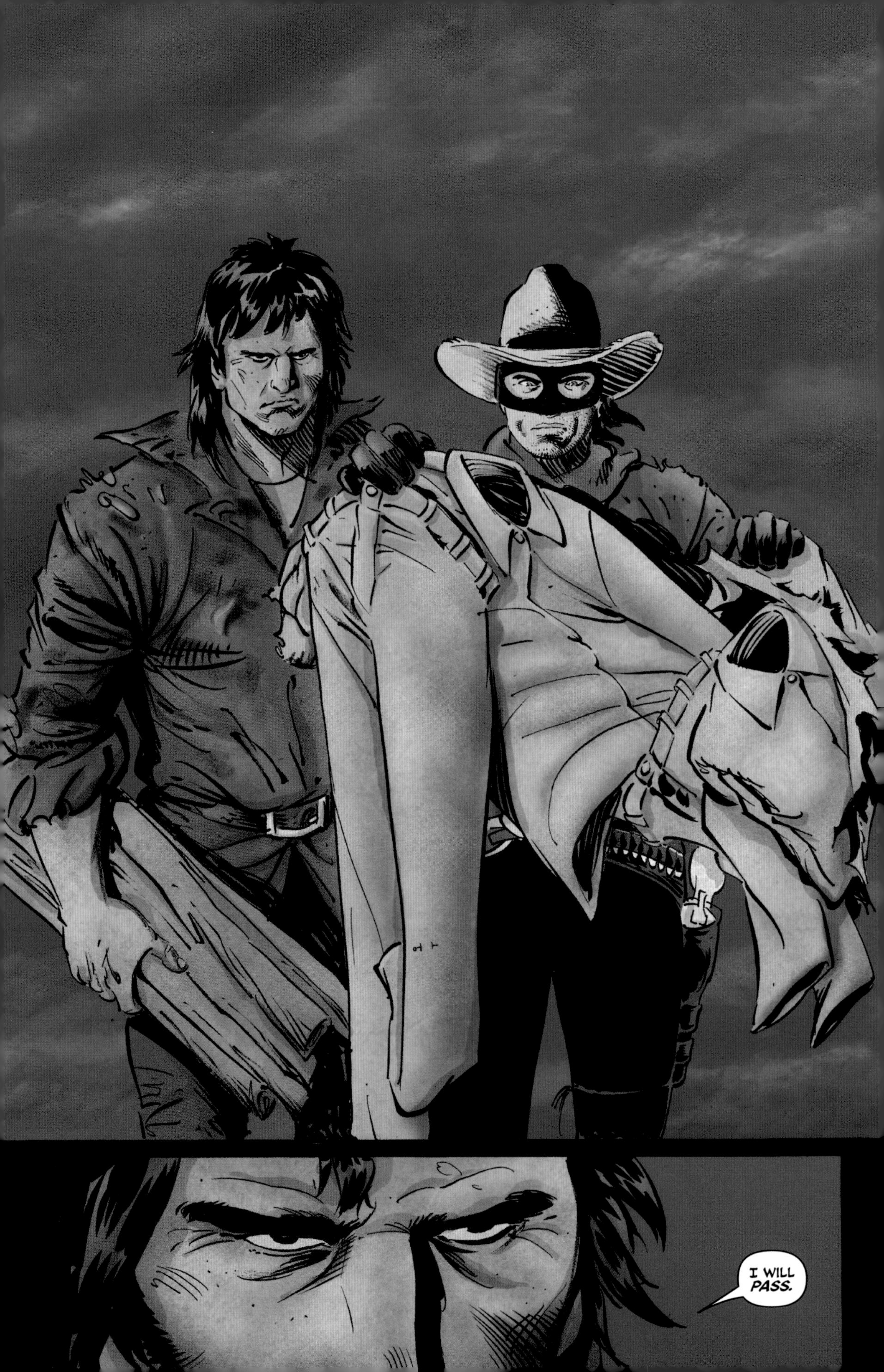
I WILL PASS.

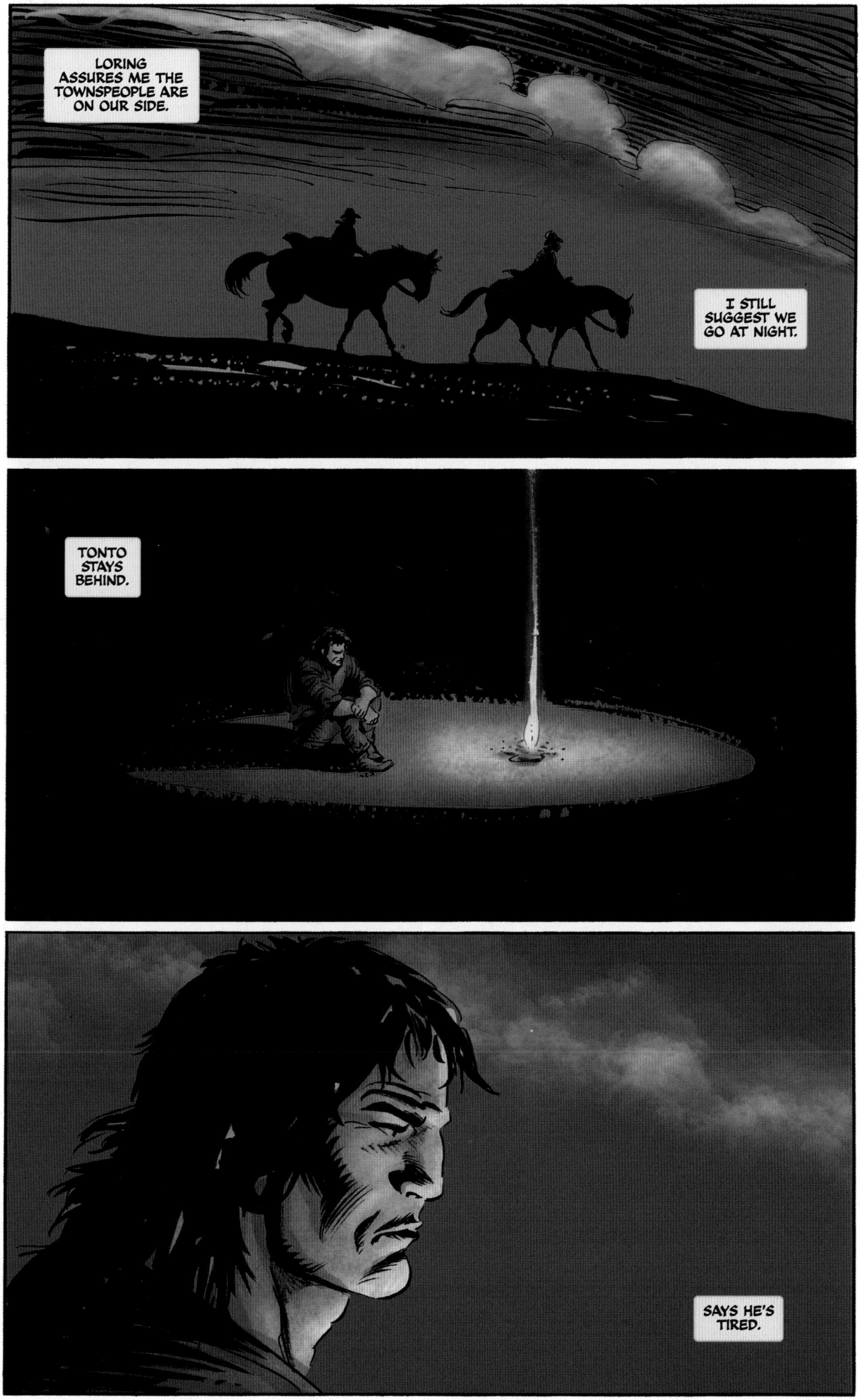
LORING ASSURES ME THE TOWNSPEOPLE ARE ON OUR SIDE.
I STILL SUGGEST WE GO AT NIGHT.
TONTO STAYS BEHIND.
SAYS HE'S TIRED.

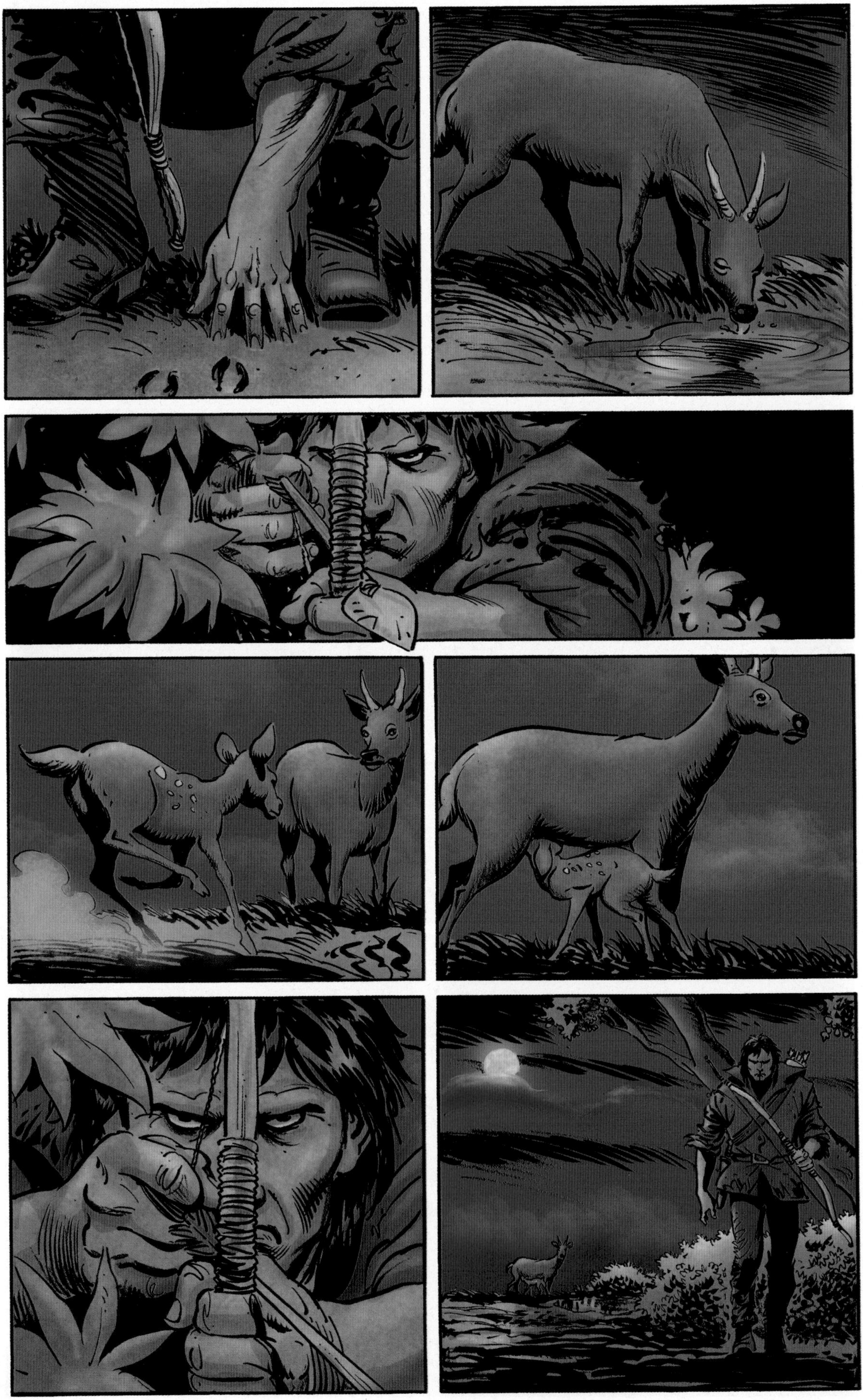

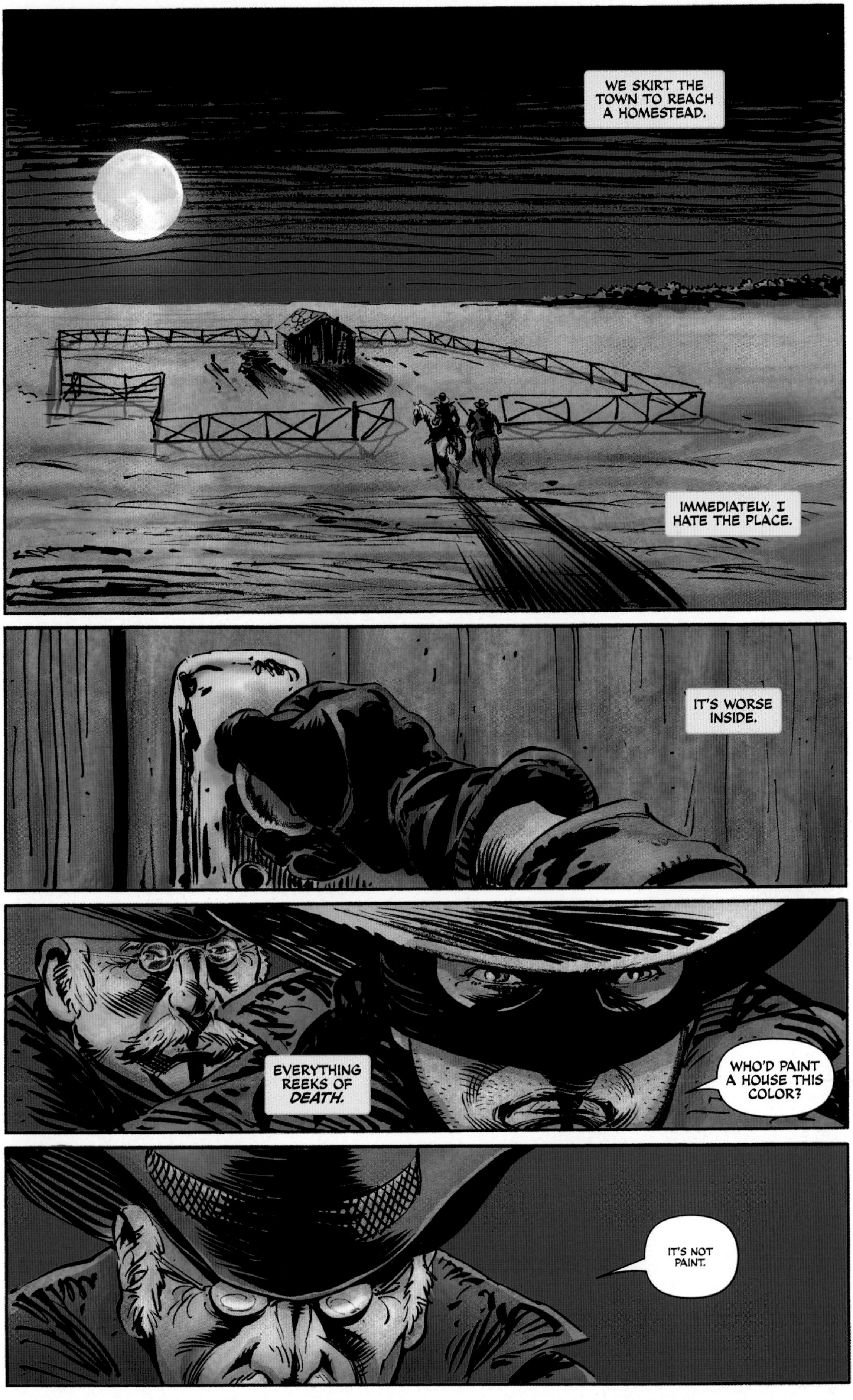
WE SKIRT THE TOWN TO REACH A HOMESTEAD.
IMMEDIATELY, I HATE THE PLACE.
IT'S WORSE INSIDE.
EVERYTHING REEKS OF *DEATH.*
WHO'D PAINT A HOUSE THIS COLOR?
IT'S NOT PAINT.

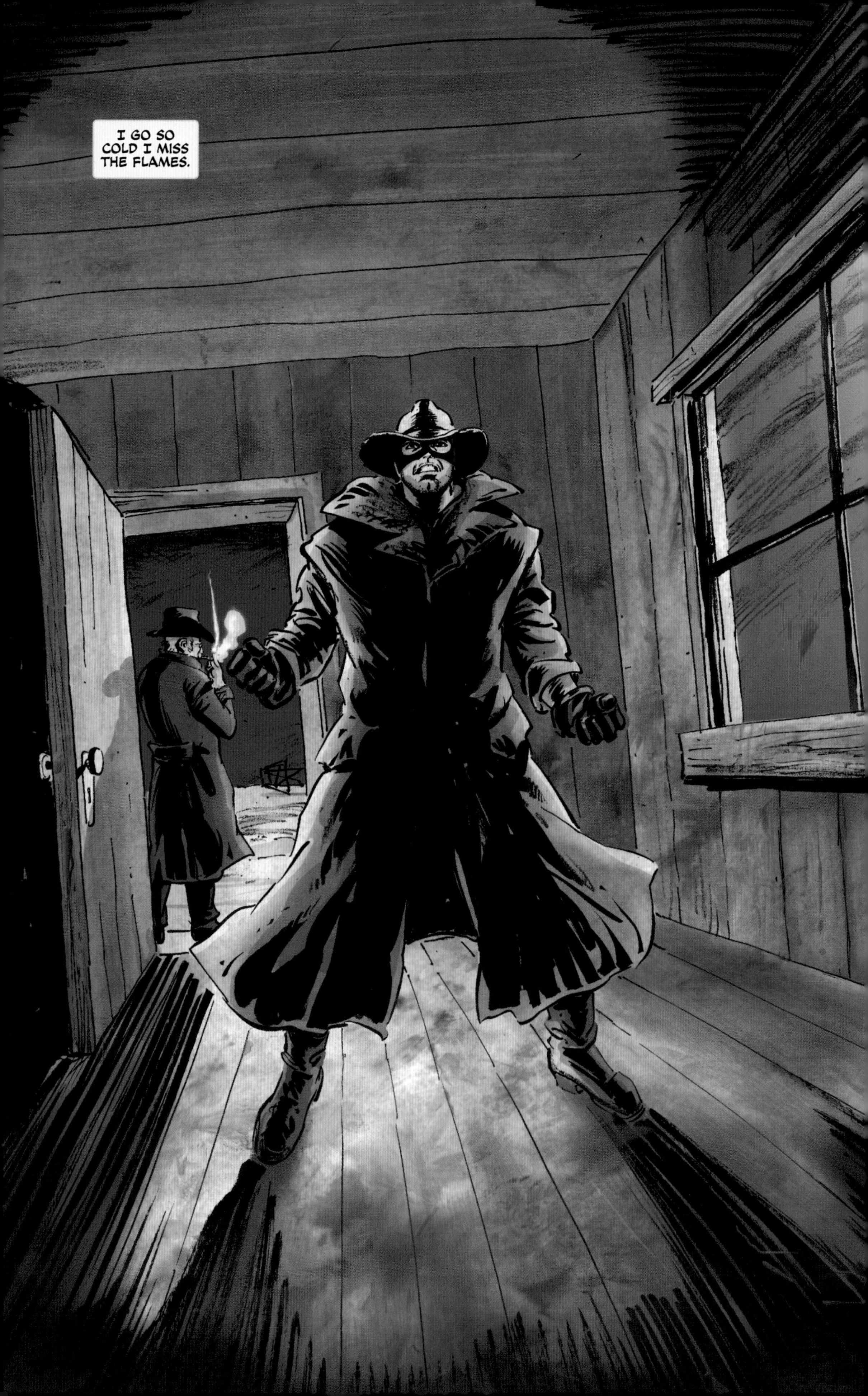
I GO SO COLD I MISS THE FLAMES.

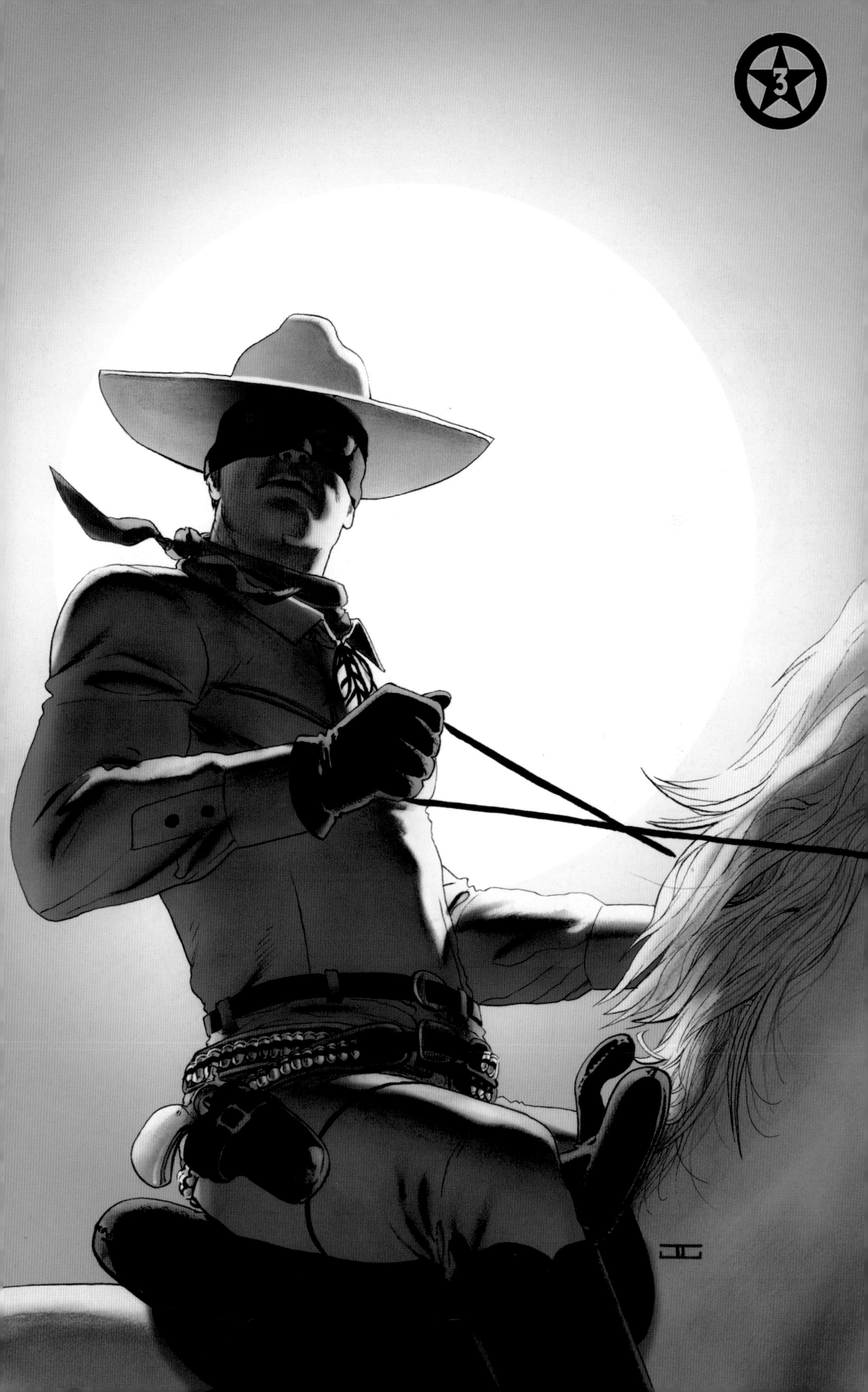
3

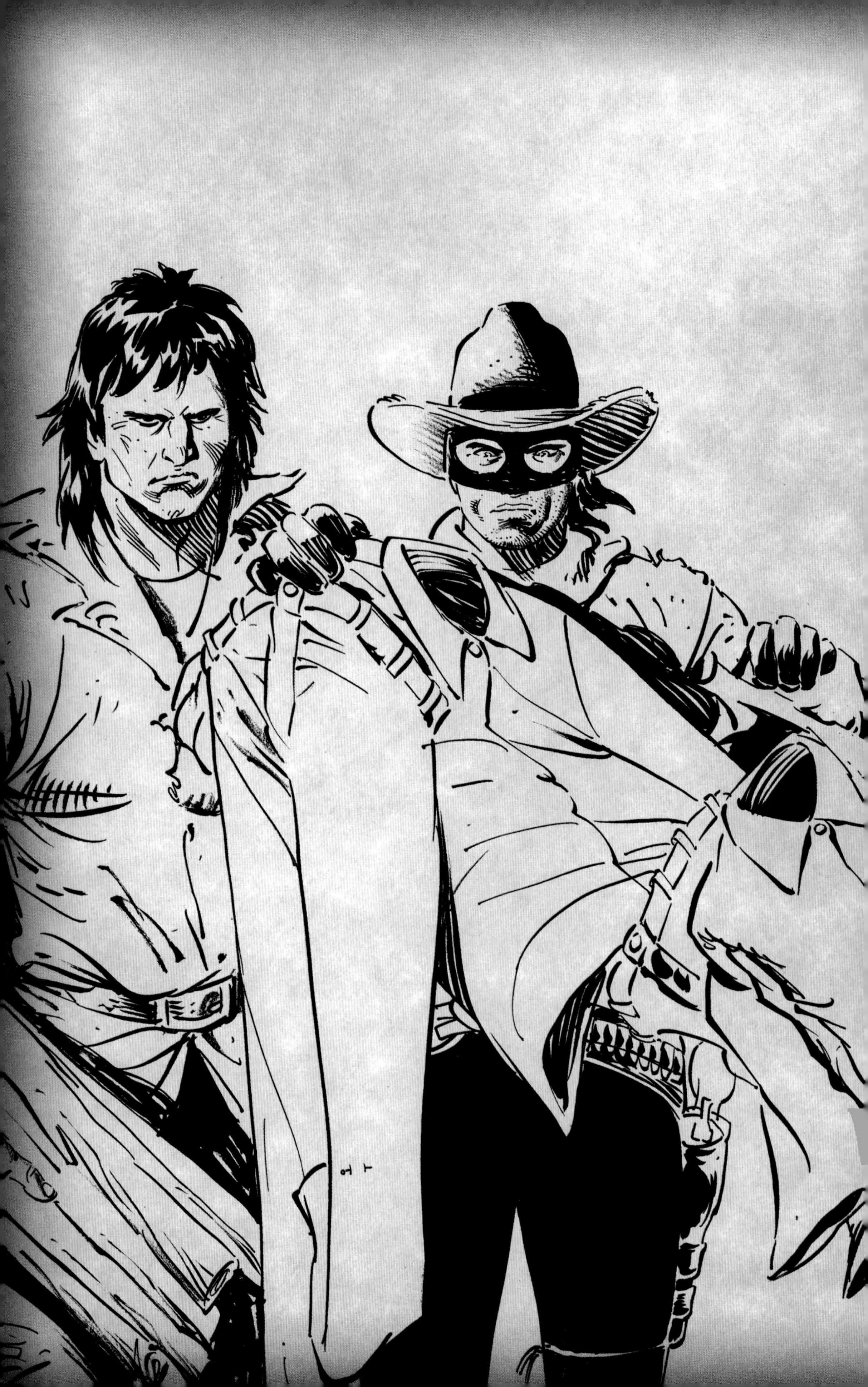

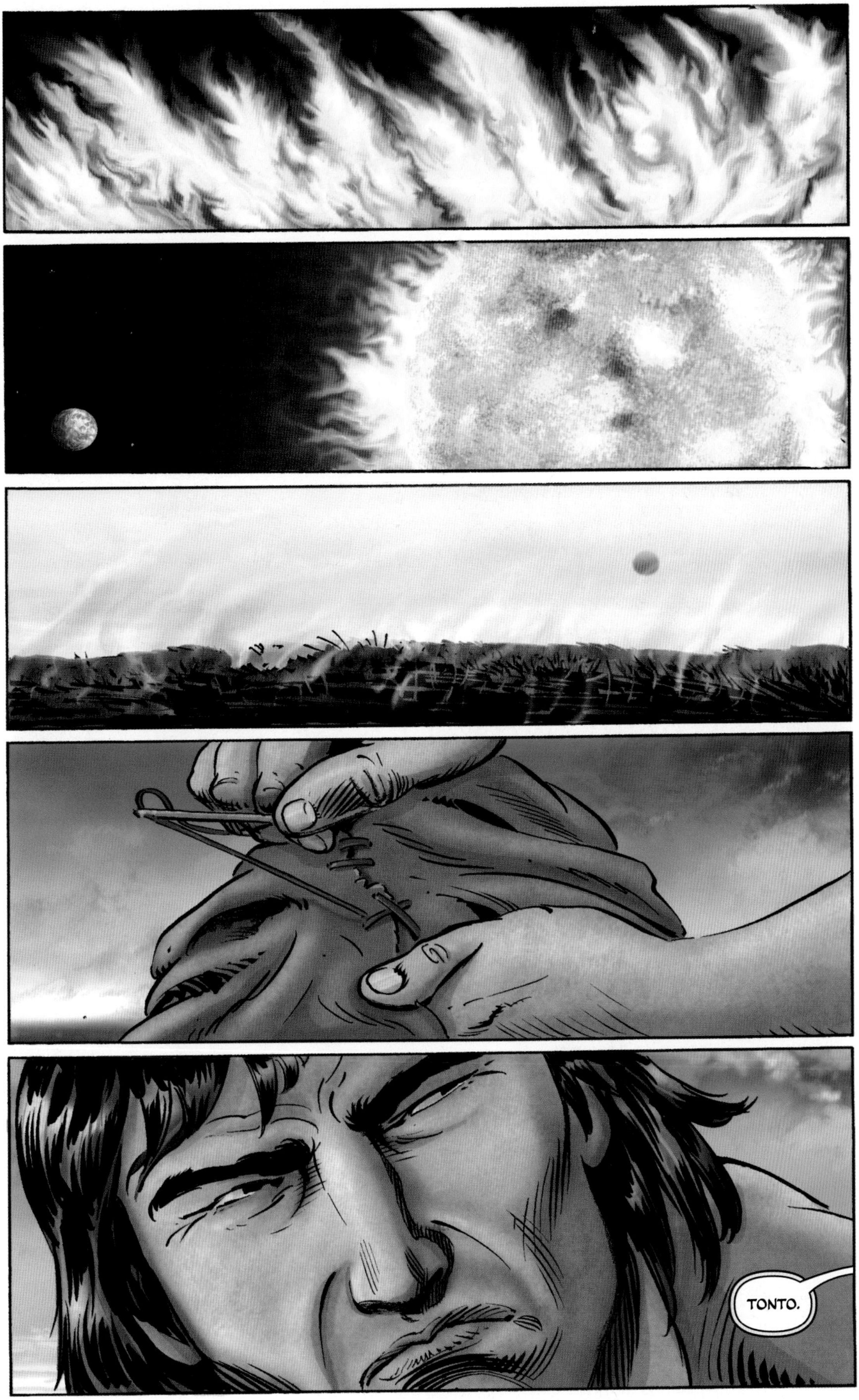
TONTO.

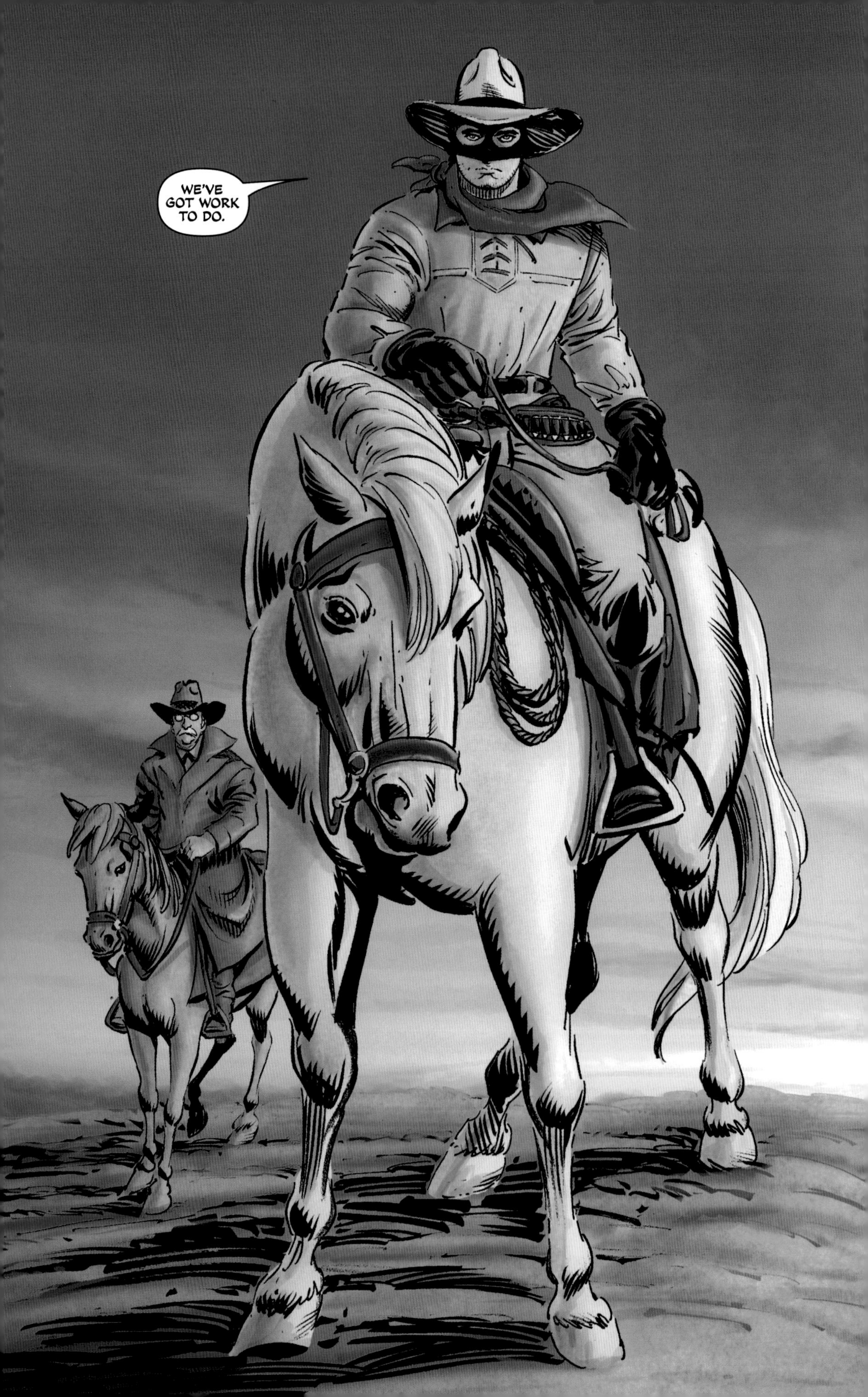
WE'VE GOT WORK TO DO.

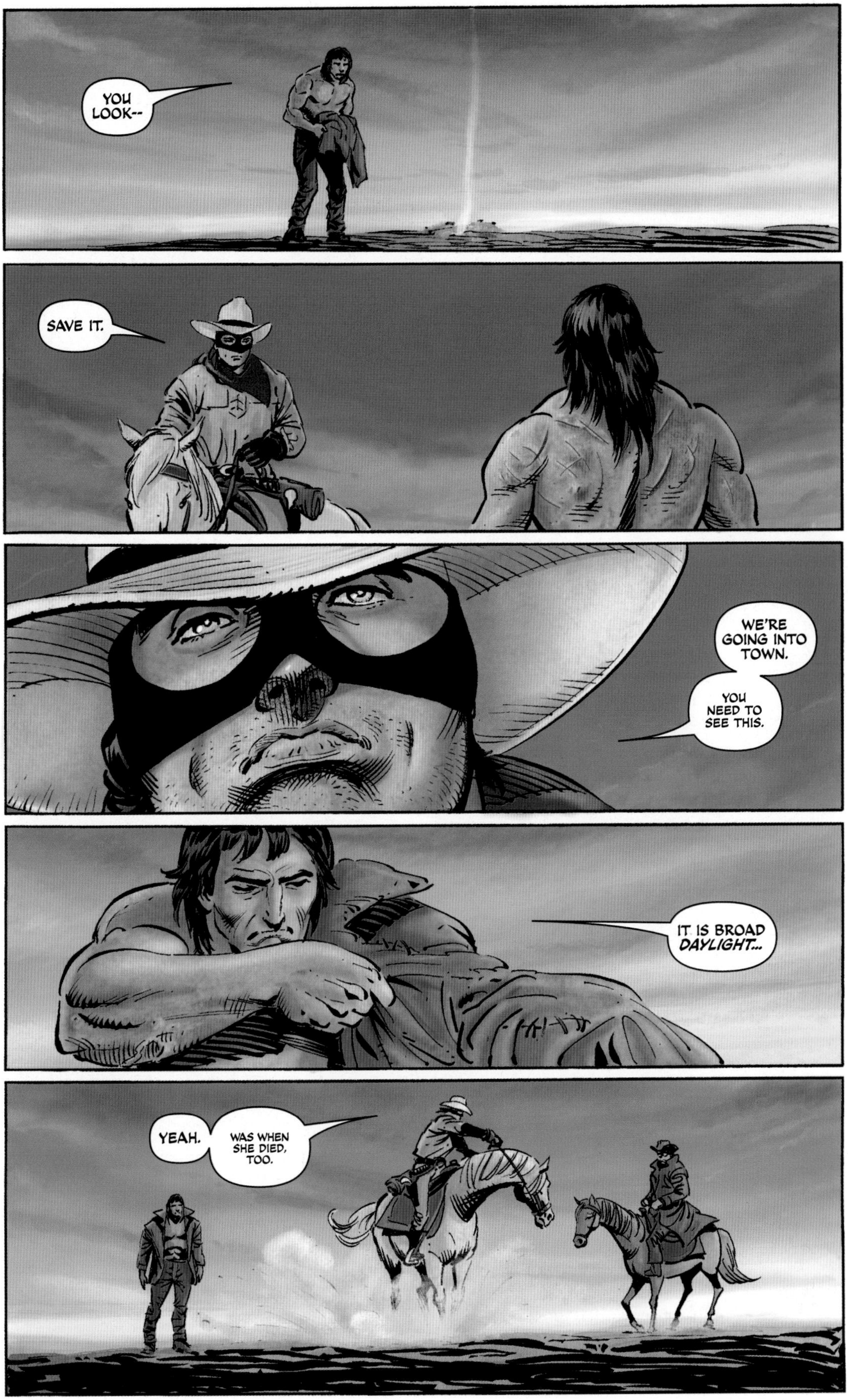
YOU LOOK--
SAVE IT.
WE'RE GOING INTO TOWN.
YOU NEED TO SEE THIS.
IT IS BROAD *DAYLIGHT...*
YEAH.
WAS WHEN SHE DIED, TOO.

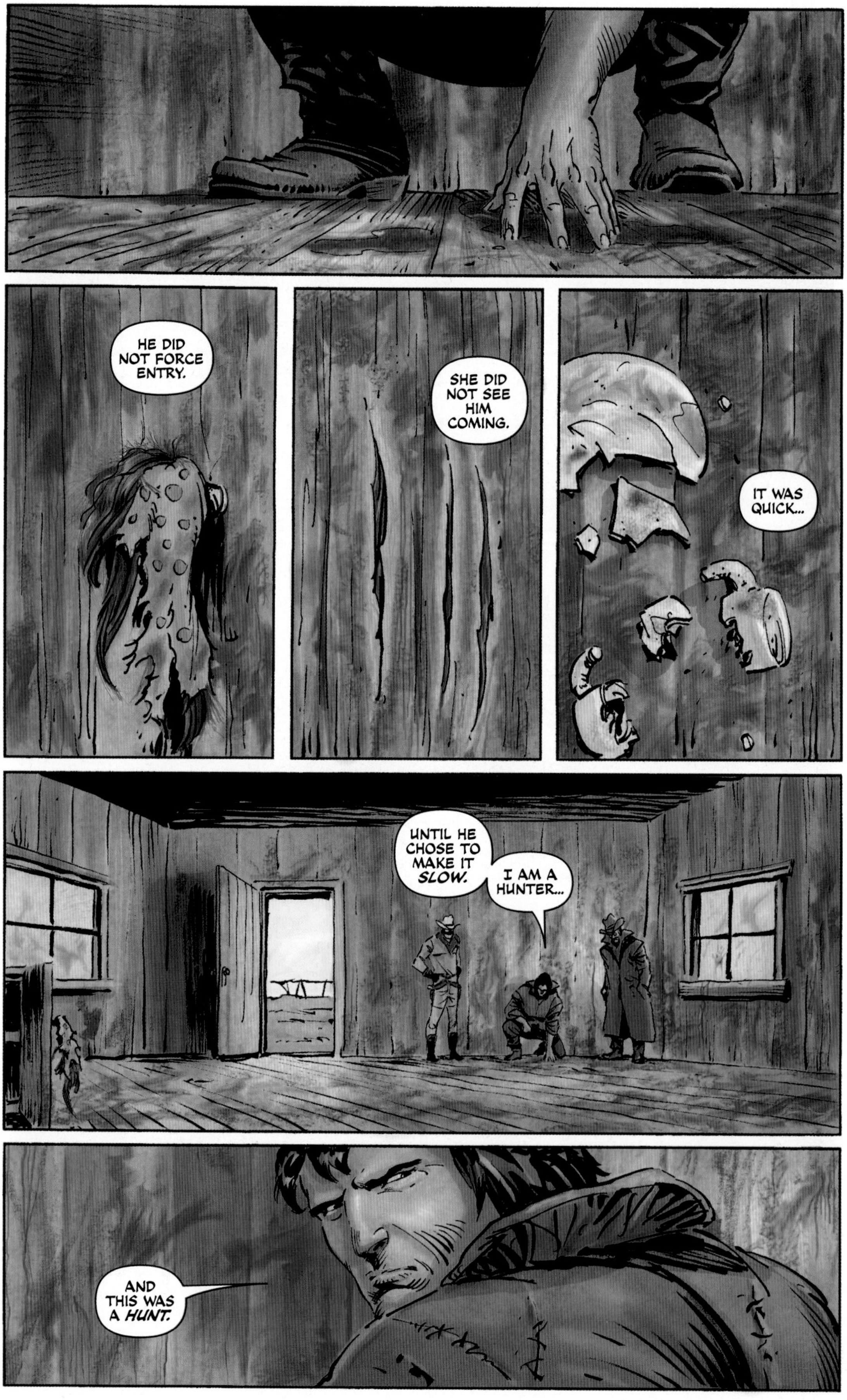
HE DID NOT FORCE ENTRY.
SHE DID NOT SEE HIM COMING.
IT WAS QUICK...
UNTIL HE CHOSE TO MAKE IT *SLOW.*
I AM A HUNTER...
AND THIS WAS A *HUNT.*

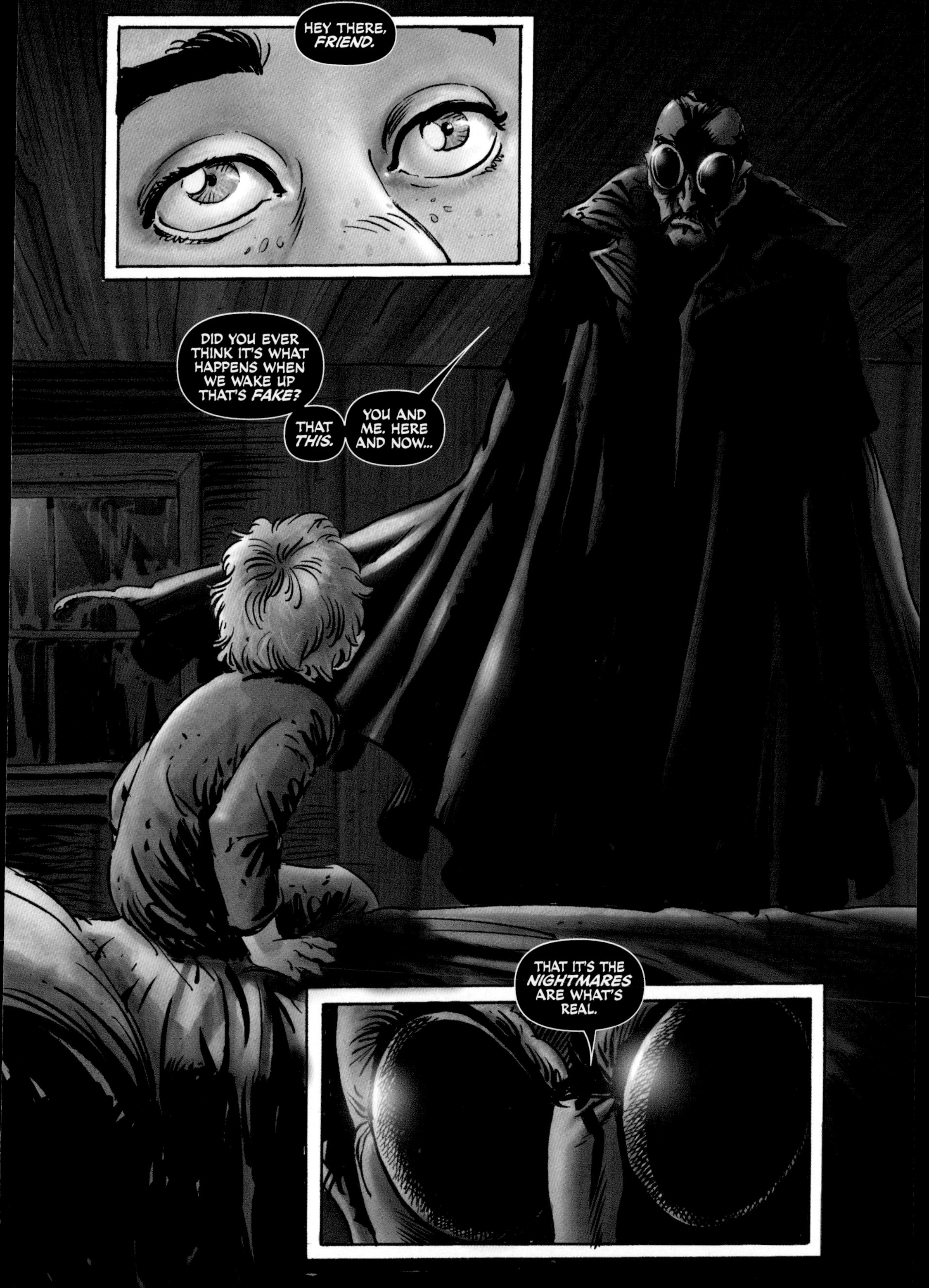
HEY THERE, *FRIEND.*
DID YOU EVER THINK IT'S WHAT HAPPENS WHEN WE WAKE UP THAT'S *FAKE?*
THAT *THIS.*
YOU AND ME. HERE AND NOW...
THAT IT'S THE *NIGHTMARES* ARE WHAT'S REAL.

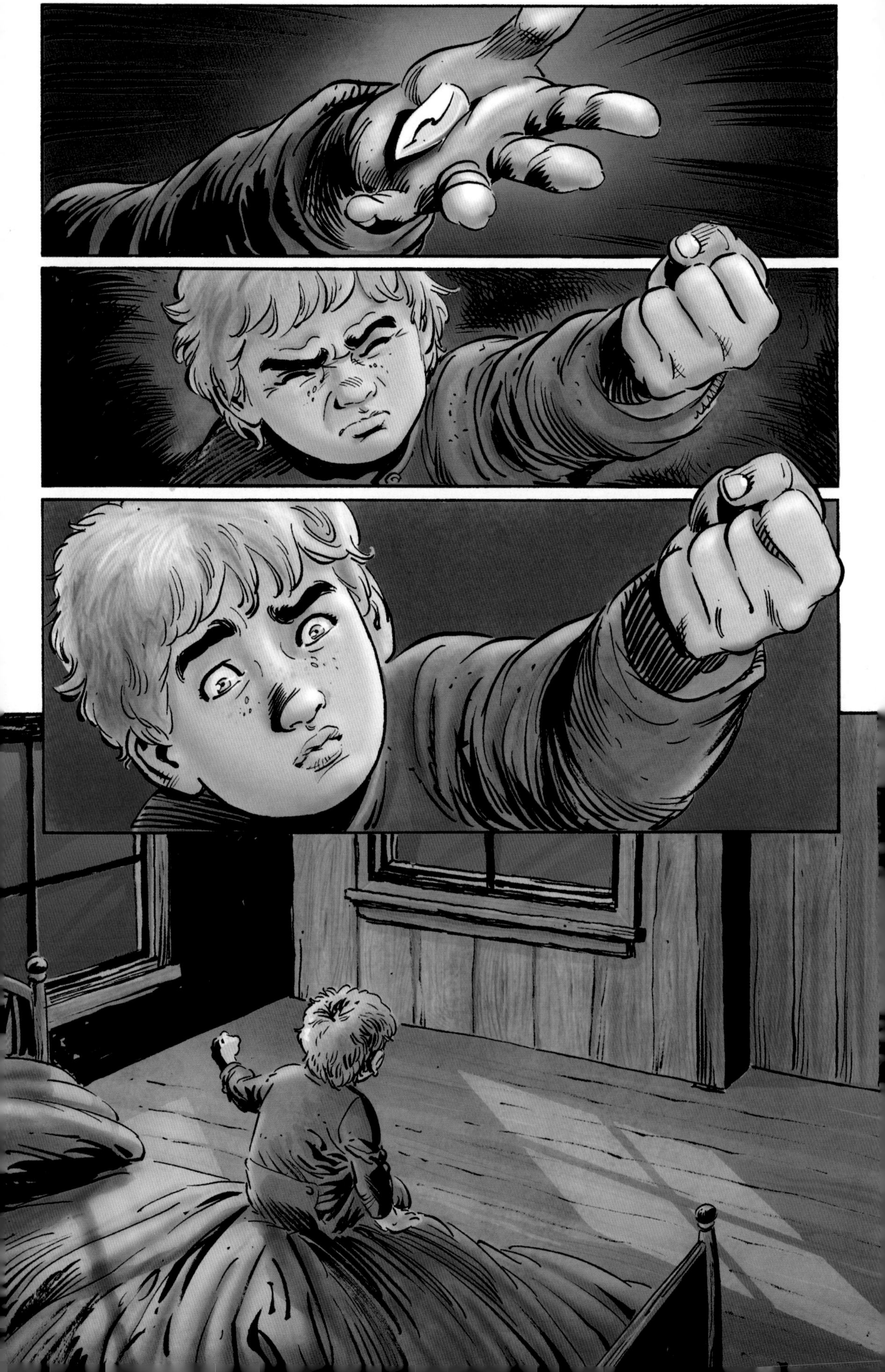

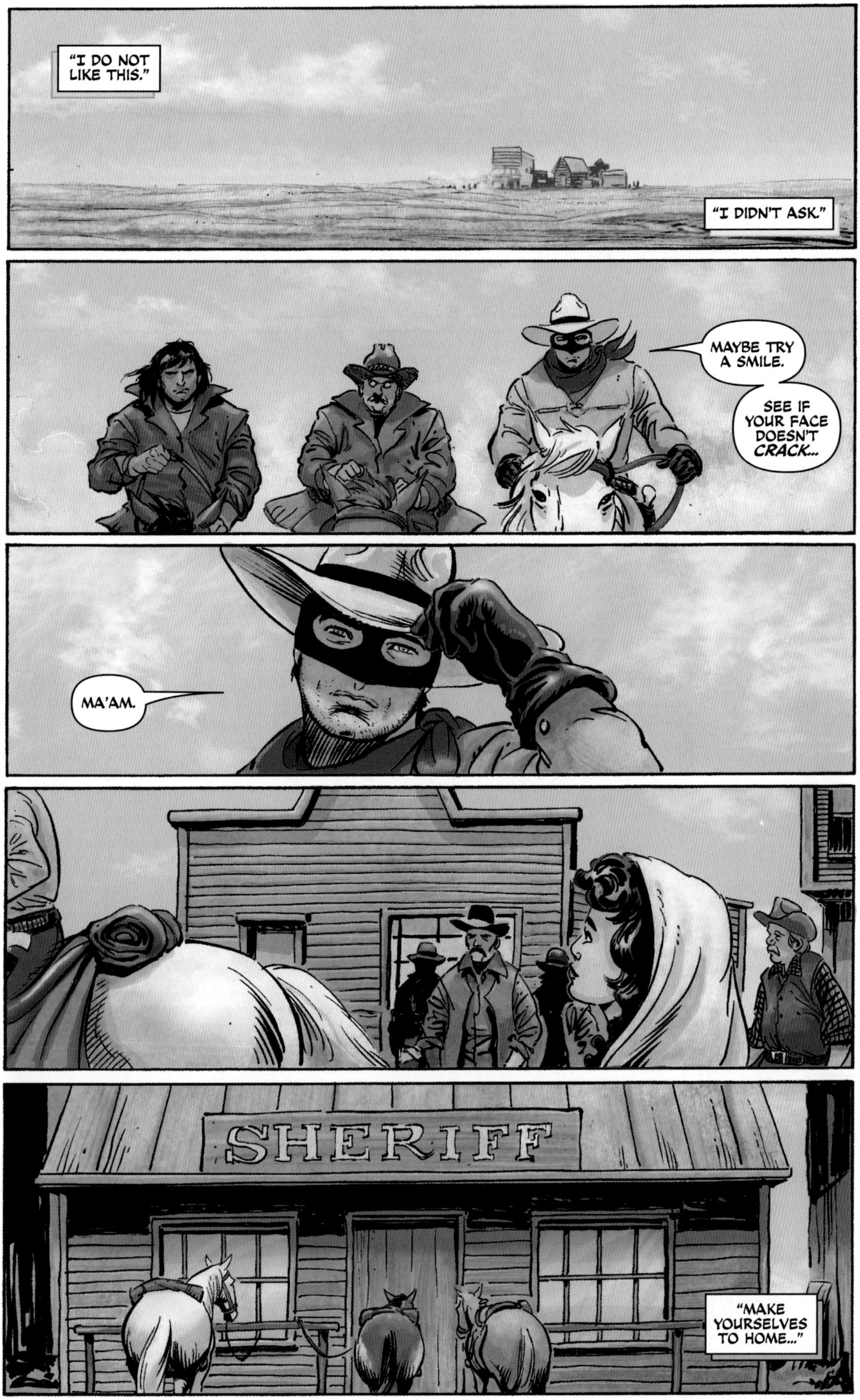
"I DO NOT LIKE THIS."
"I DIDN'T ASK."
MAYBE TRY A SMILE.
SEE IF YOUR FACE DOESN'T *CRACK...*
MA'AM.
SHERIFF
"MAKE YOURSELVES TO HOME..."

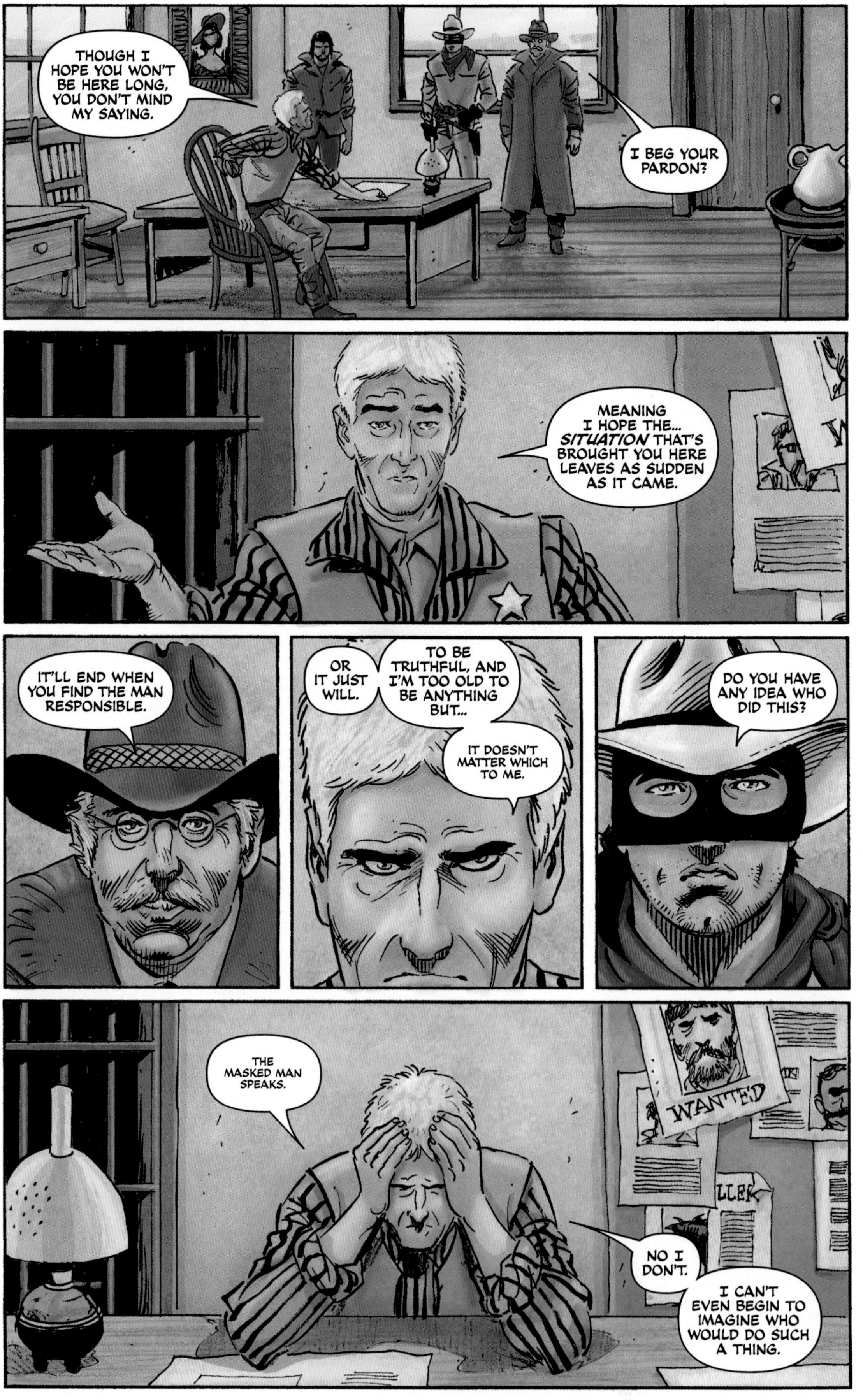
THOUGH I HOPE YOU WON'T BE HERE LONG, YOU DON'T MIND MY SAYING.
I BEG YOUR PARDON?
MEANING I HOPE THE... *SITUATION* THAT'S BROUGHT YOU HERE LEAVES AS SUDDEN AS IT CAME.
IT'LL END WHEN YOU FIND THE MAN RESPONSIBLE.
OR IT JUST WILL.
TO BE TRUTHFUL, AND I'M TOO OLD TO BE ANYTHING BUT...
IT DOESN'T MATTER WHICH TO ME.
DO YOU HAVE ANY IDEA WHO DID THIS?
THE MASKED MAN SPEAKS.
WANTED
NO I DON'T.
I CAN'T EVEN BEGIN TO IMAGINE WHO WOULD DO SUCH A THING.

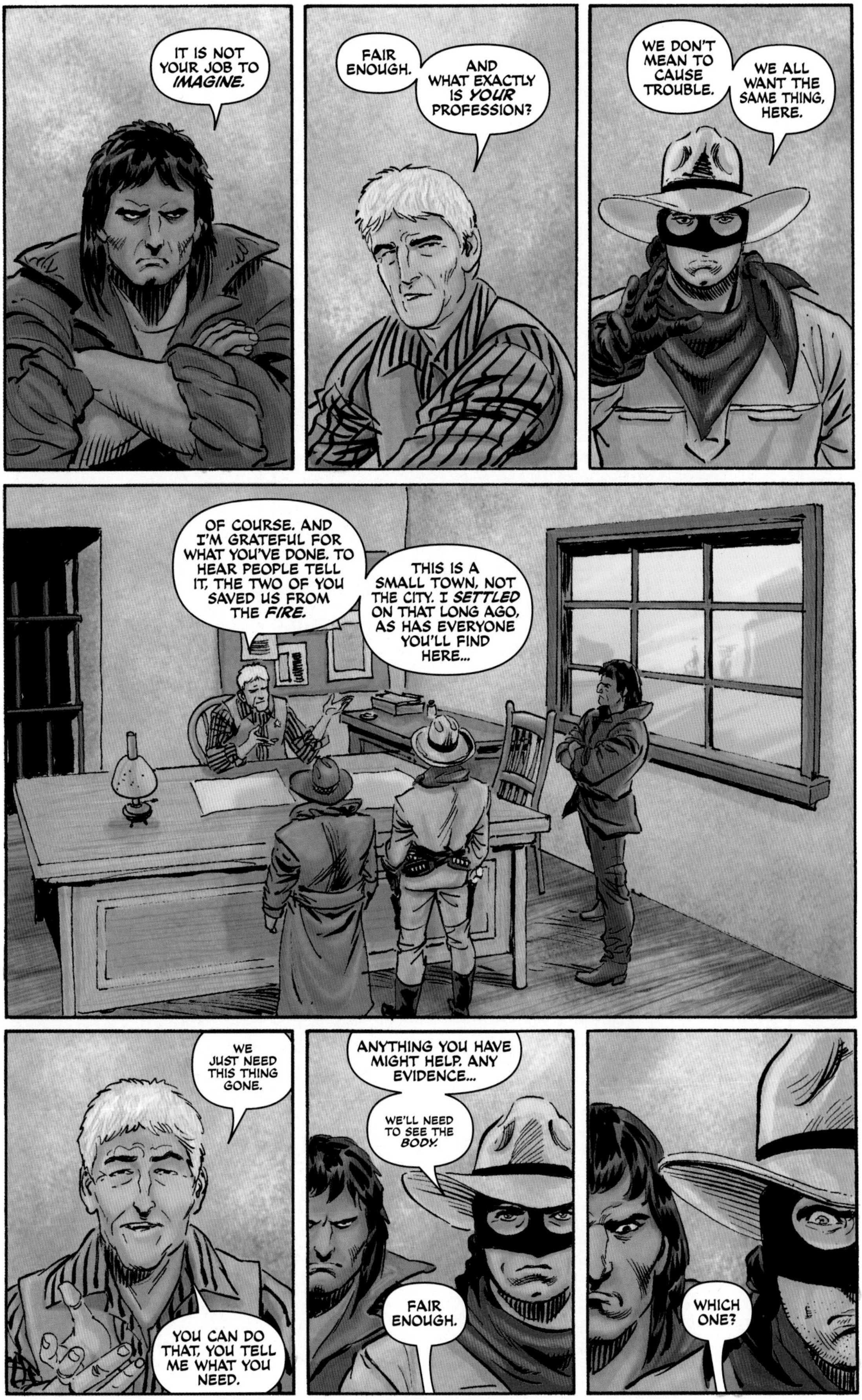
IT IS NOT YOUR JOB TO *IMAGINE.*
FAIR ENOUGH.
AND WHAT EXACTLY IS *YOUR* PROFESSION?
WE DON'T MEAN TO CAUSE TROUBLE.
WE ALL WANT THE SAME THING, HERE.
OF COURSE. AND I'M GRATEFUL FOR WHAT YOU'VE DONE. TO HEAR PEOPLE TELL IT, THE TWO OF YOU SAVED US FROM THE *FIRE.*
THIS IS A SMALL TOWN, NOT THE CITY. I *SETTLED* ON THAT LONG AGO, AS HAS EVERYONE YOU'LL FIND HERE...
WE JUST NEED THIS THING GONE.
YOU CAN DO THAT, YOU TELL ME WHAT YOU NEED.
ANYTHING YOU HAVE MIGHT HELP. ANY EVIDENCE...
WE'LL NEED TO SEE THE *BODY.*
FAIR ENOUGH.
WHICH ONE?

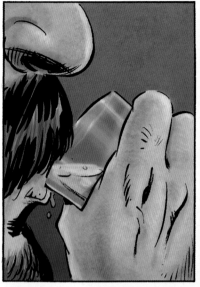
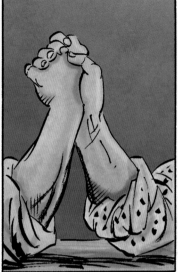

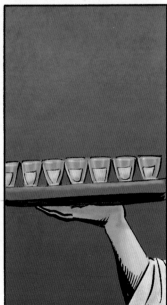

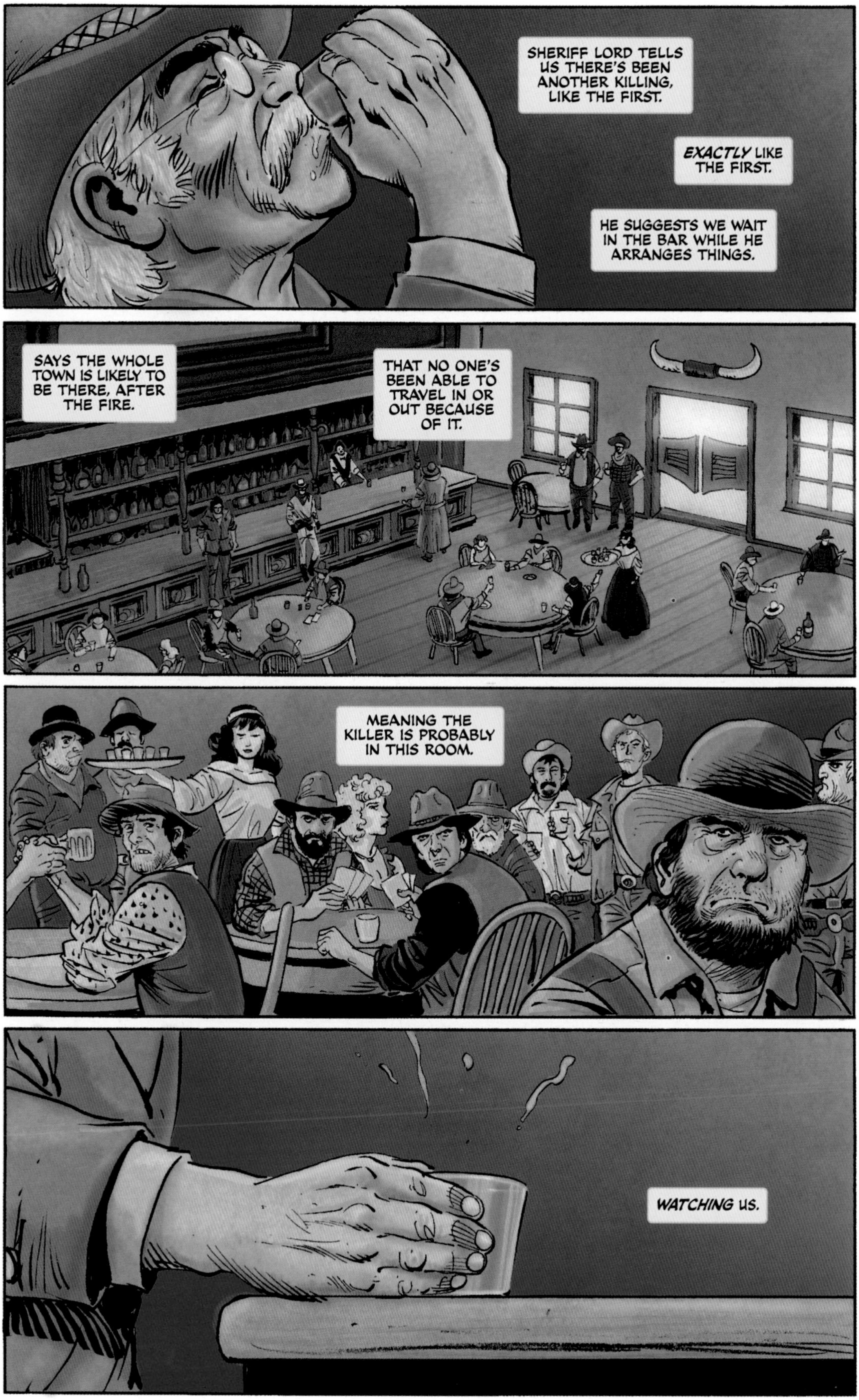
SHERIFF LORD TELLS US THERE'S BEEN ANOTHER KILLING, LIKE THE FIRST.
EXACTLY LIKE THE FIRST.
HE SUGGESTS WE WAIT IN THE BAR WHILE HE ARRANGES THINGS.
SAYS THE WHOLE TOWN IS LIKELY TO BE THERE, AFTER THE FIRE.
THAT NO ONE'S BEEN ABLE TO TRAVEL IN OR OUT BECAUSE OF IT.
MEANING THE KILLER IS PROBABLY IN THIS ROOM.
WATCHING US.

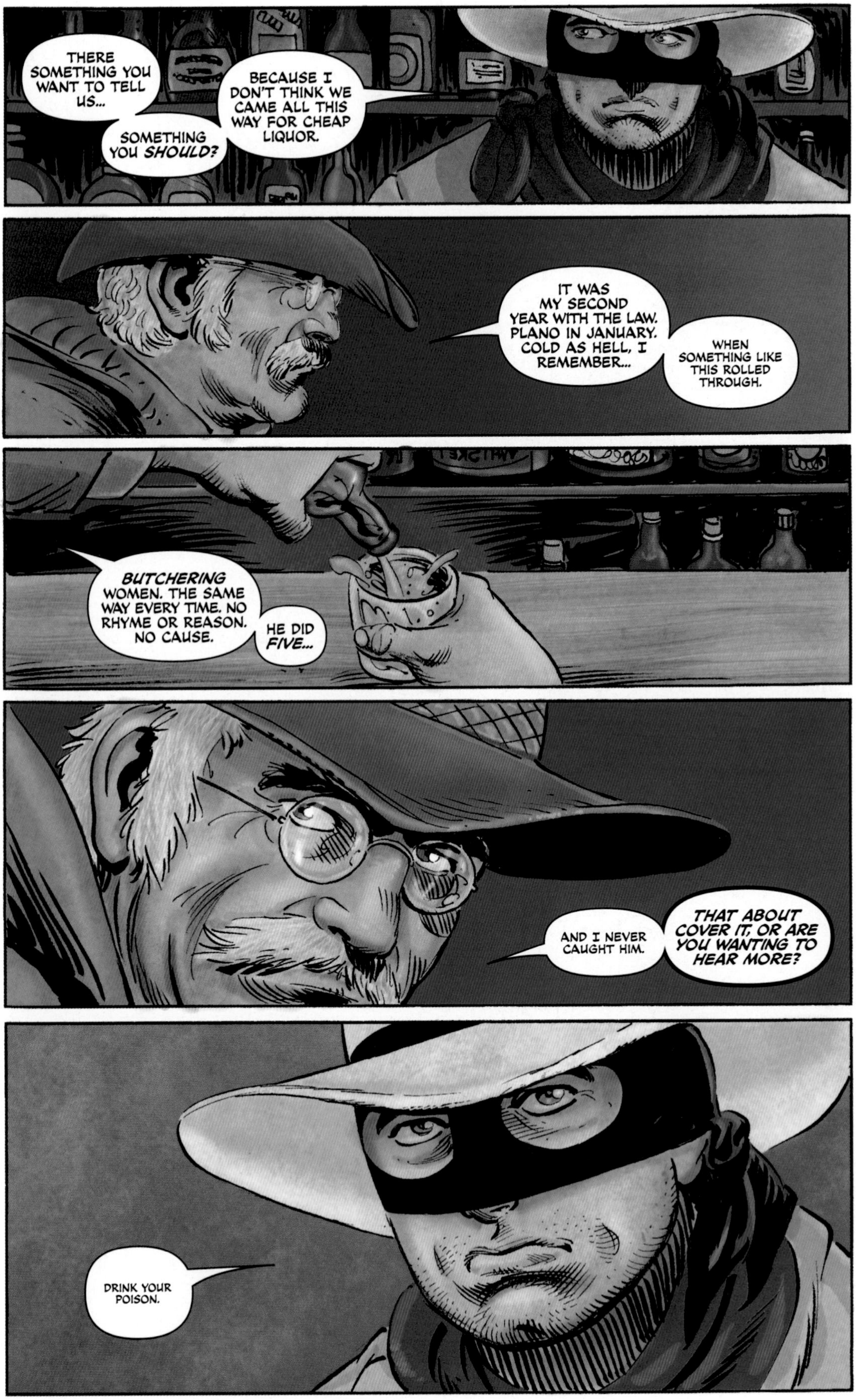
THERE SOMETHING YOU WANT TO TELL US...
SOMETHING YOU *SHOULD?*
BECAUSE I DON'T THINK WE CAME ALL THIS WAY FOR CHEAP LIQUOR.
IT WAS MY SECOND YEAR WITH THE LAW. PLANO IN JANUARY. COLD AS HELL, I REMEMBER...
WHEN SOMETHING LIKE THIS ROLLED THROUGH.
BUTCHERING WOMEN. THE SAME WAY EVERY TIME. NO RHYME OR REASON. NO CAUSE.
HE DID *FIVE...*
AND I NEVER CAUGHT HIM.
THAT ABOUT COVER IT, OR ARE YOU WANTING TO HEAR MORE?
DRINK YOUR POISON.

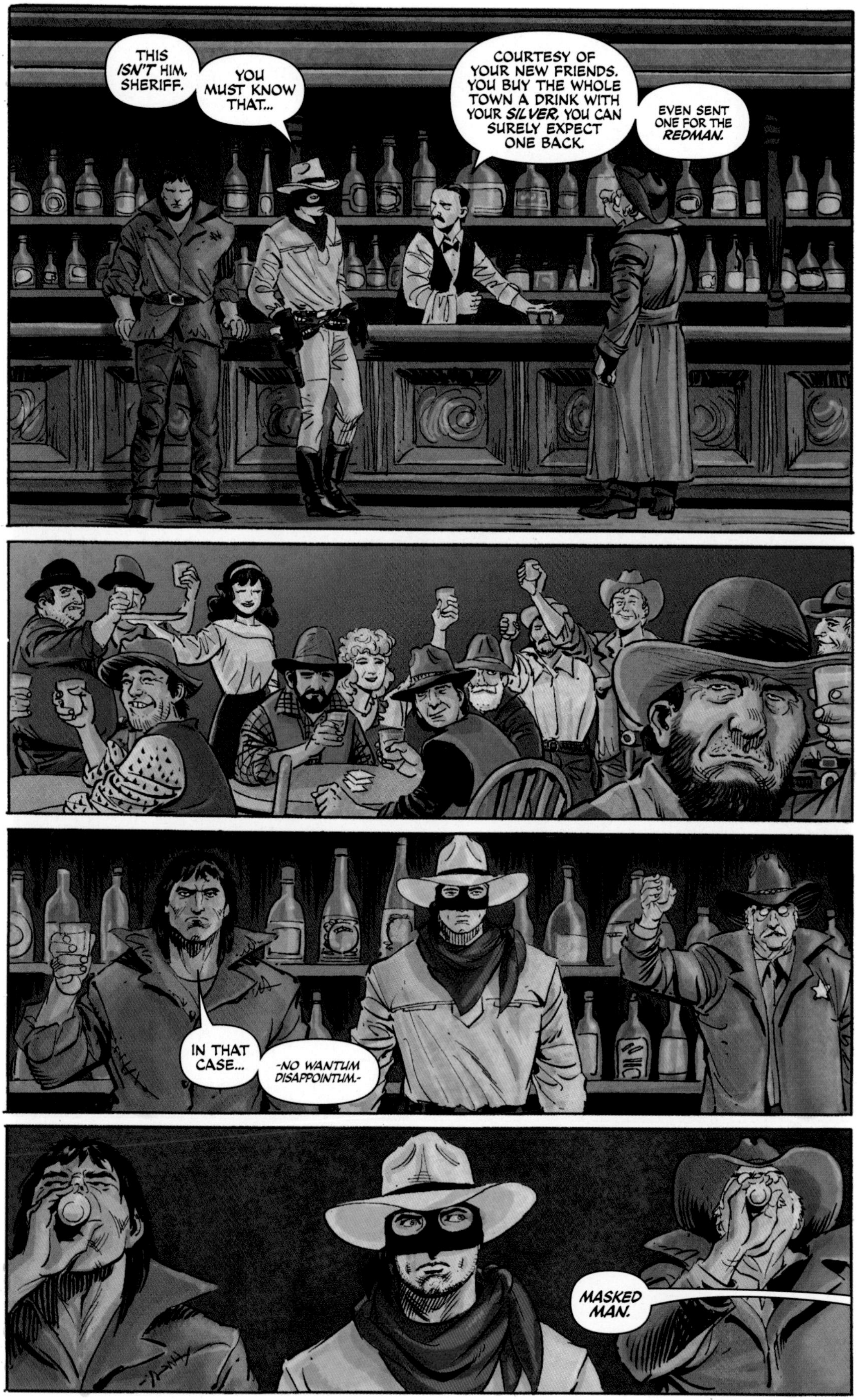
THIS ISN'T HIM, SHERIFF.
YOU MUST KNOW THAT...
COURTESY OF YOUR NEW FRIENDS. YOU BUY THE WHOLE TOWN A DRINK WITH YOUR SILVER, YOU CAN SURELY EXPECT ONE BACK.
EVEN SENT ONE FOR THE REDMAN.
IN THAT CASE...
-NO WANTUM DISAPPOINTUM.-
MASKED MAN.

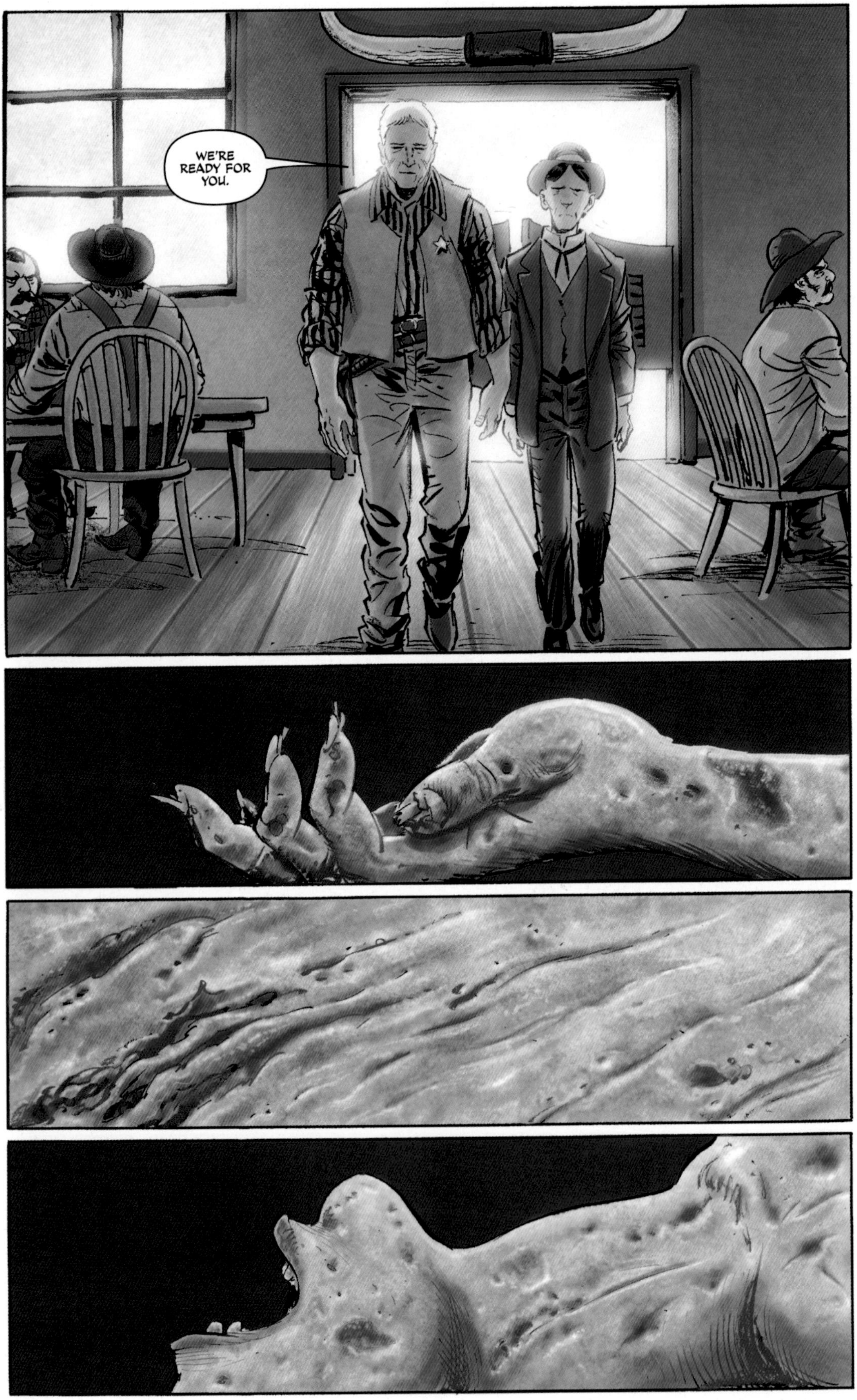
WE'RE READY FOR YOU.

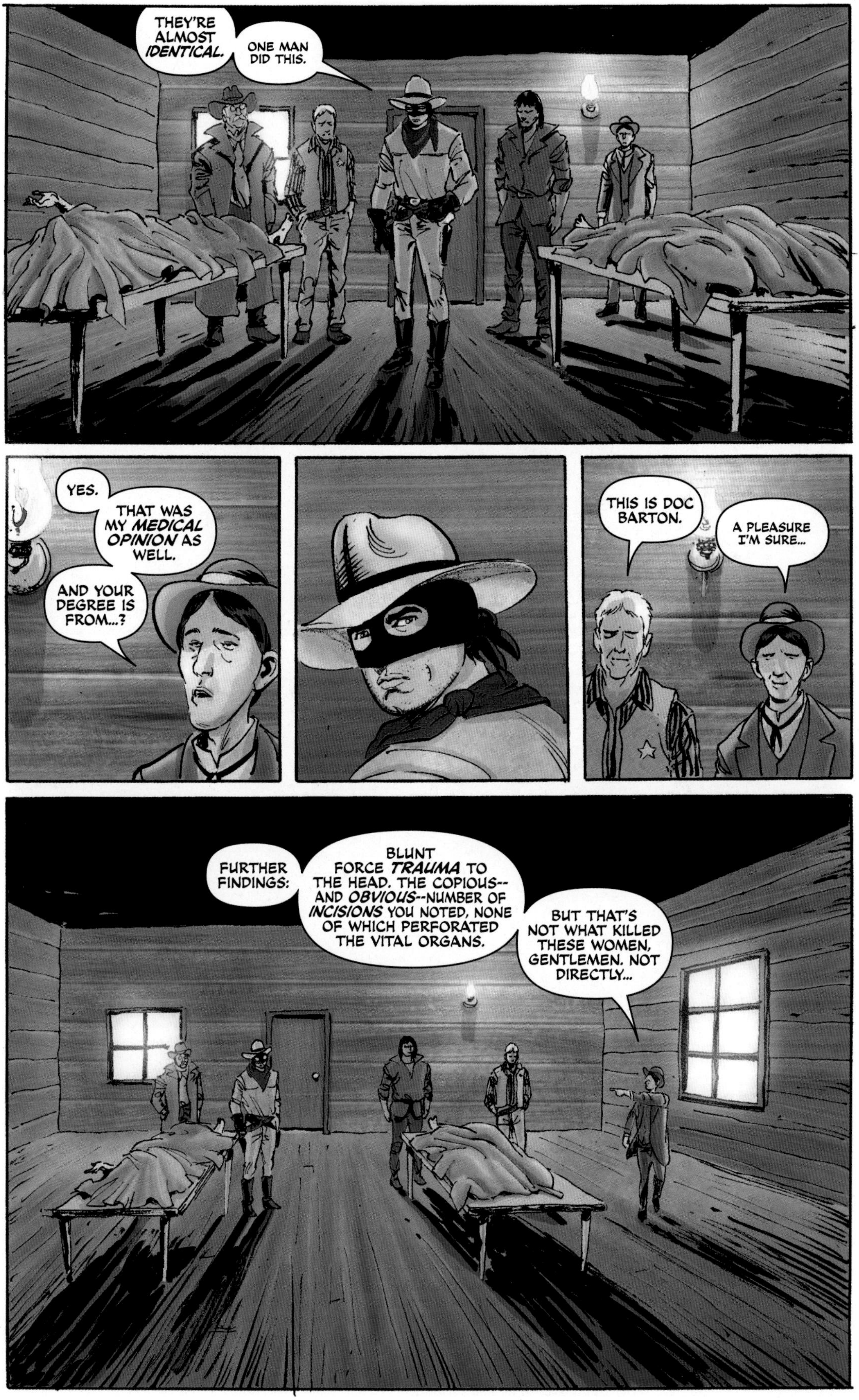
THEY'RE ALMOST IDENTICAL.
ONE MAN DID THIS.
YES.
THAT WAS MY MEDICAL OPINION AS WELL.
AND YOUR DEGREE IS FROM...?
THIS IS DOC BARTON.
A PLEASURE I'M SURE...
FURTHER FINDINGS:
BLUNT FORCE TRAUMA TO THE HEAD. THE COPIOUS-- AND OBVIOUS--NUMBER OF INCISIONS YOU NOTED, NONE OF WHICH PERFORATED THE VITAL ORGANS.
BUT THAT'S NOT WHAT KILLED THESE WOMEN, GENTLEMEN. NOT DIRECTLY...

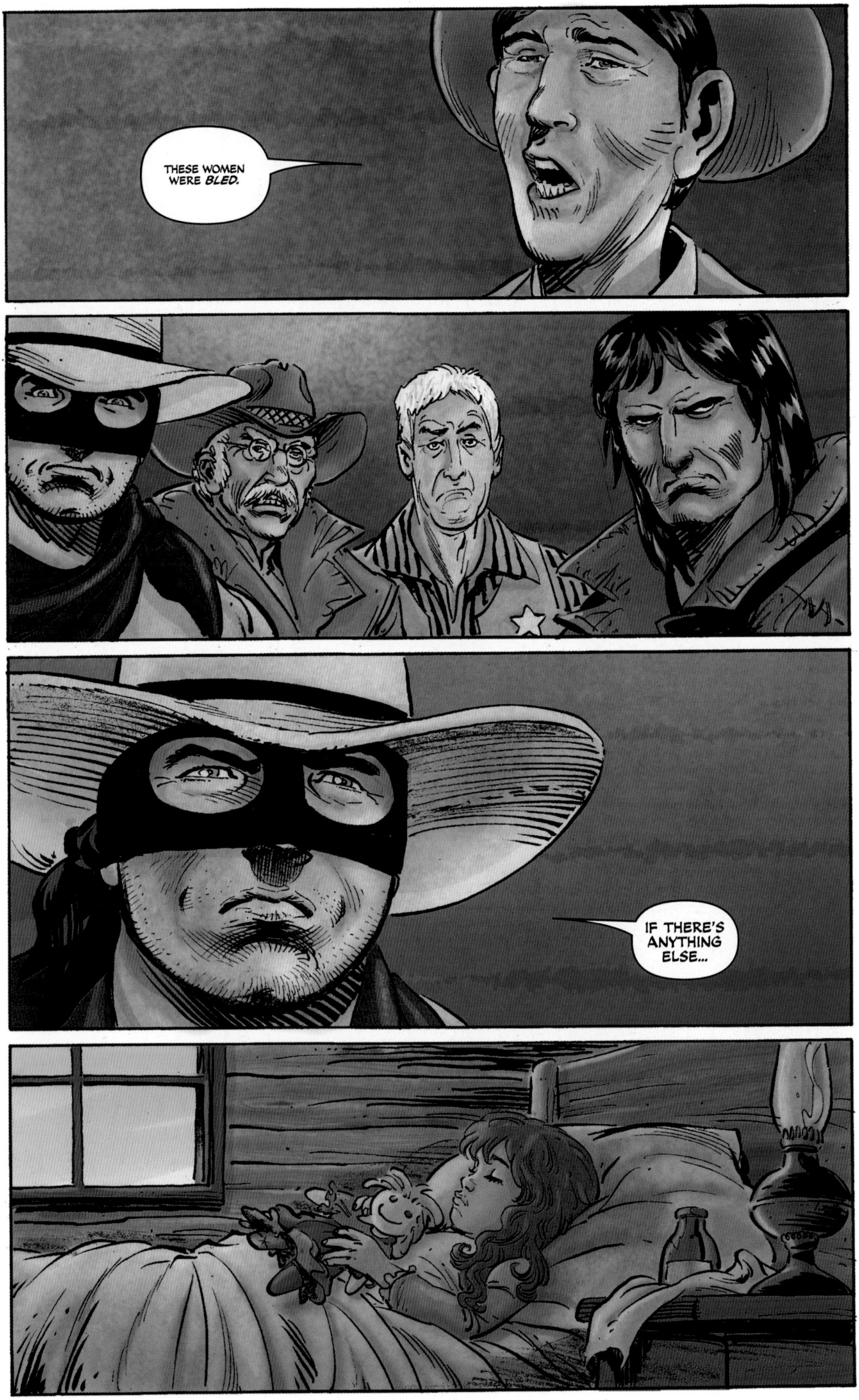
THESE WOMEN WERE *BLED.*
IF THERE'S ANYTHING ELSE...

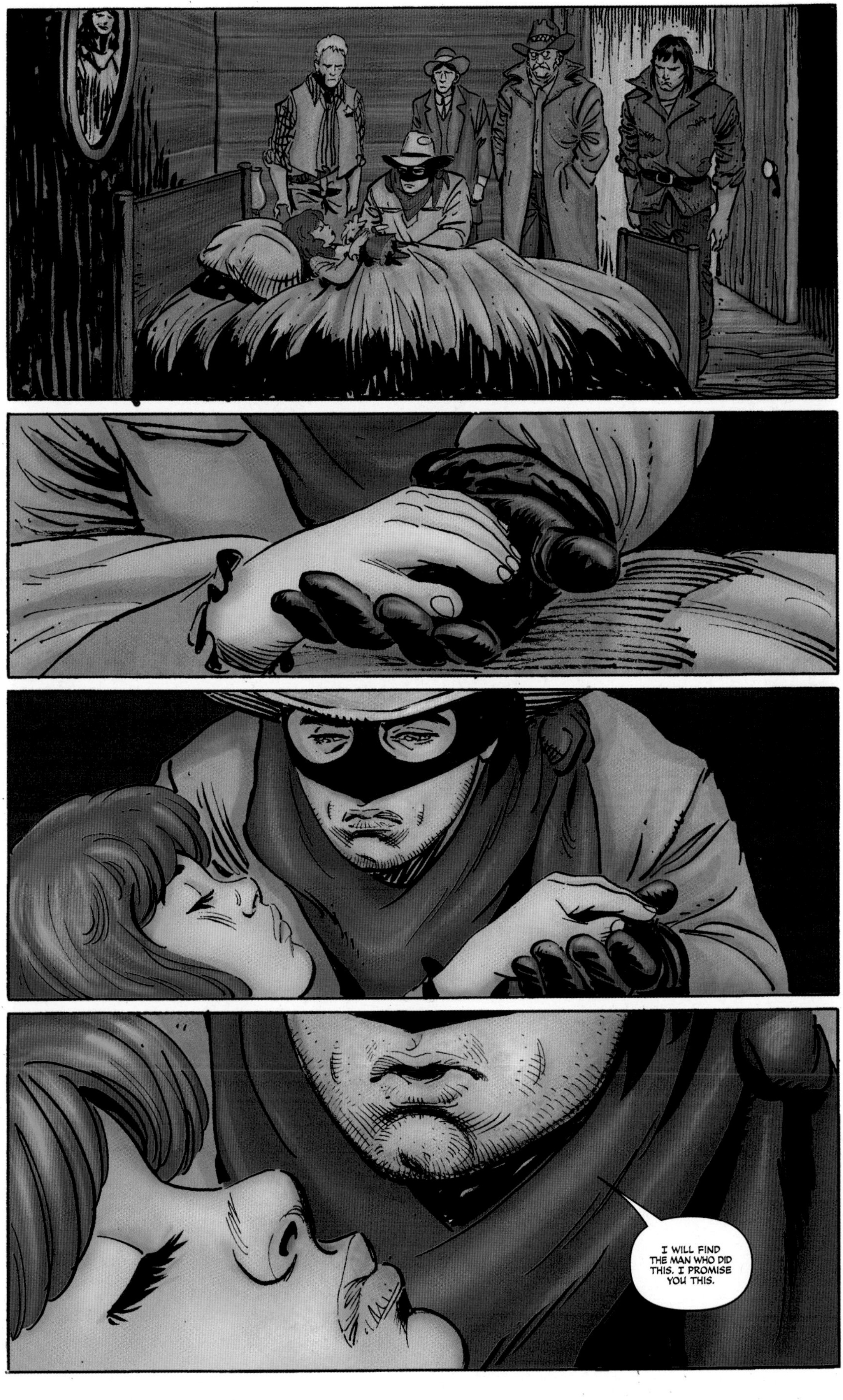
I WILL FIND THE MAN WHO DID THIS. I PROMISE YOU THIS.

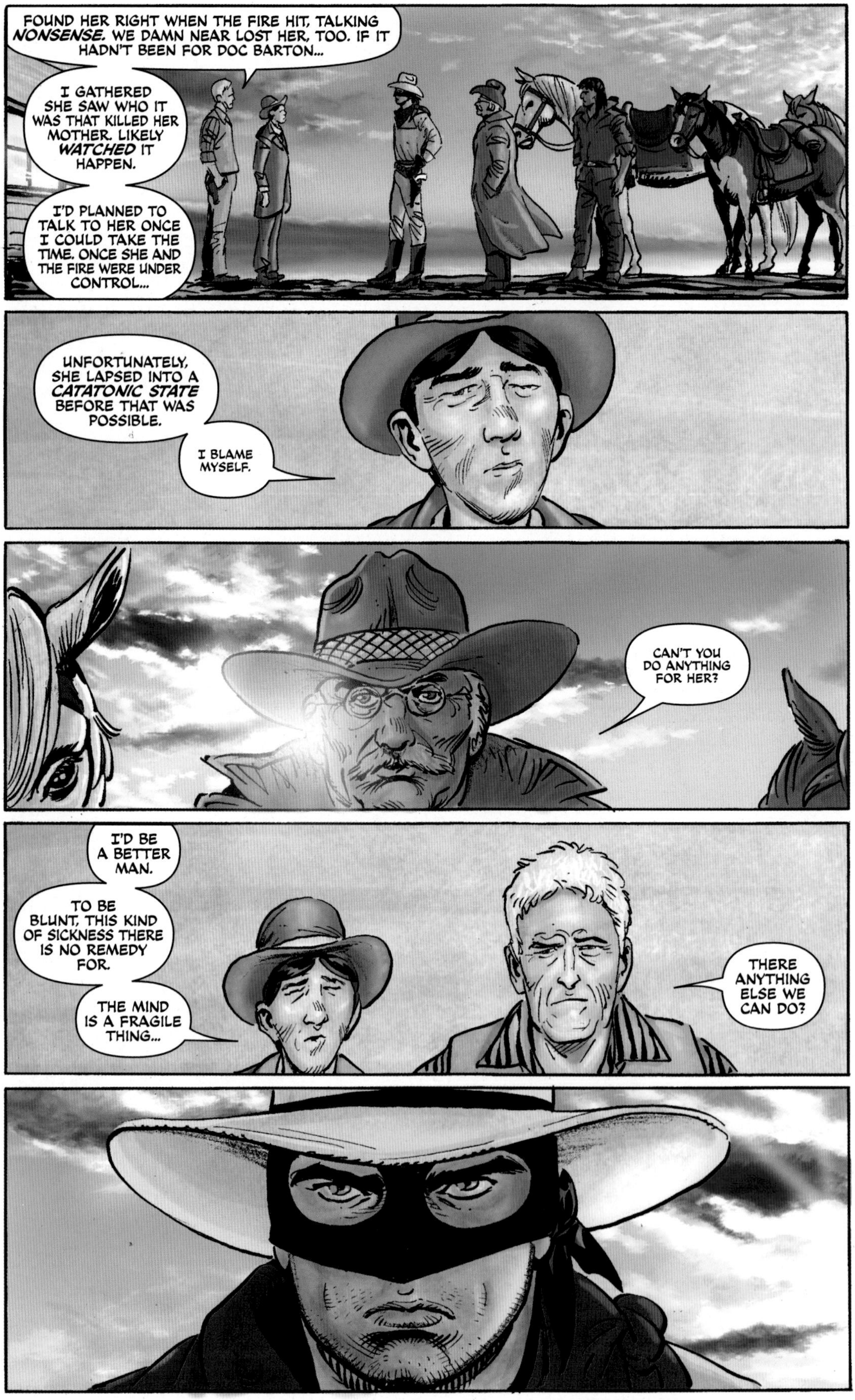
FOUND HER RIGHT WHEN THE FIRE HIT, TALKING *NONSENSE.* WE DAMN NEAR LOST HER, TOO. IF IT HADN'T BEEN FOR DOC BARTON...
I GATHERED SHE SAW WHO IT WAS THAT KILLED HER MOTHER. LIKELY *WATCHED* IT HAPPEN.
I'D PLANNED TO TALK TO HER ONCE I COULD TAKE THE TIME. ONCE SHE AND THE FIRE WERE UNDER CONTROL...
UNFORTUNATELY, SHE LAPSED INTO A *CATATONIC STATE* BEFORE THAT WAS POSSIBLE.
I BLAME MYSELF.
CAN'T YOU DO ANYTHING FOR HER?
I'D BE A BETTER MAN.
TO BE BLUNT, THIS KIND OF SICKNESS THERE IS NO REMEDY FOR.
THE MIND IS A FRAGILE THING...
THERE ANYTHING ELSE WE CAN DO?

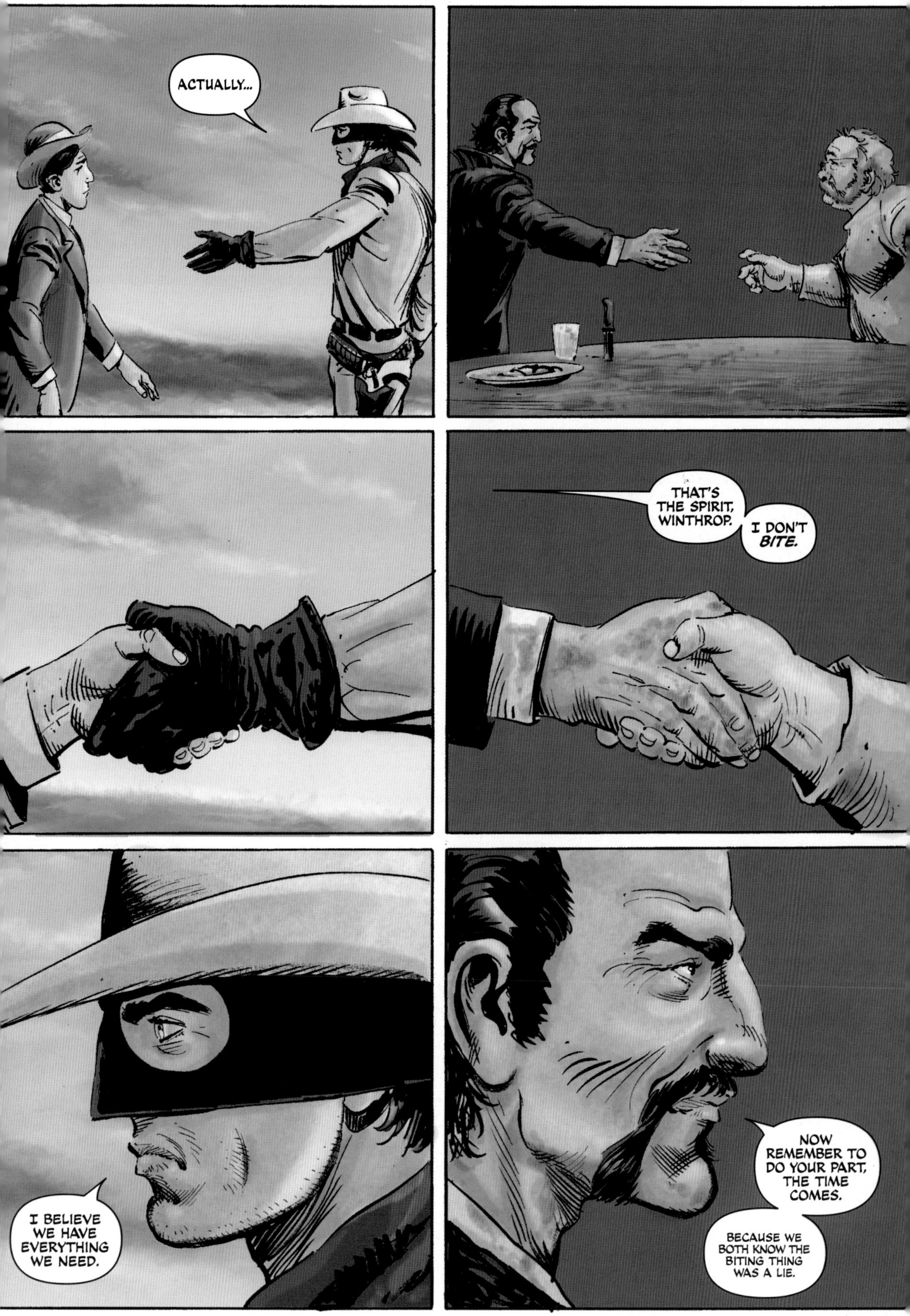
ACTUALLY...
THAT'S THE SPIRIT, WINTHROP.
I DON'T *BITE.*
I BELIEVE WE HAVE EVERYTHING WE NEED.
NOW REMEMBER TO DO YOUR PART, THE TIME COMES.
BECAUSE WE BOTH KNOW THE BITING THING WAS A LIE.

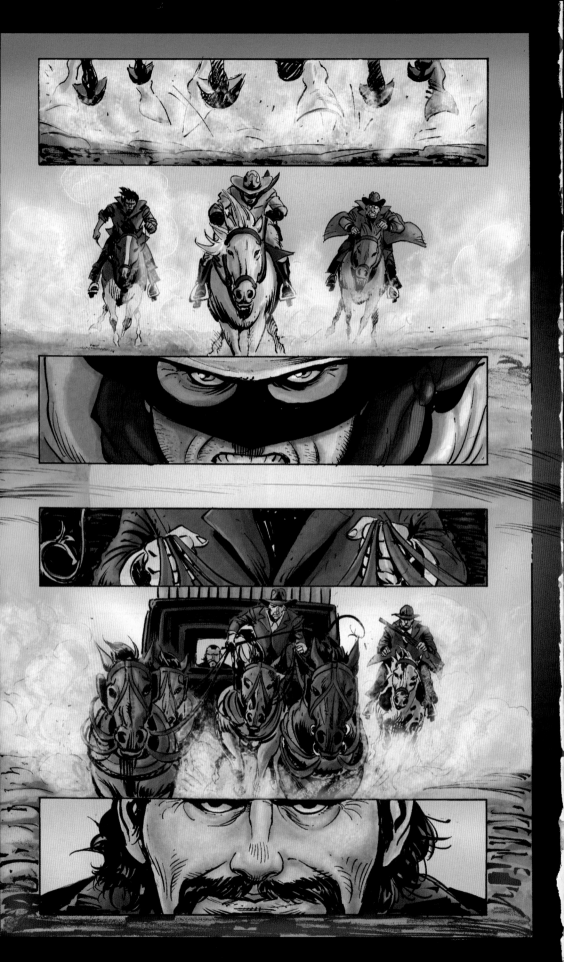

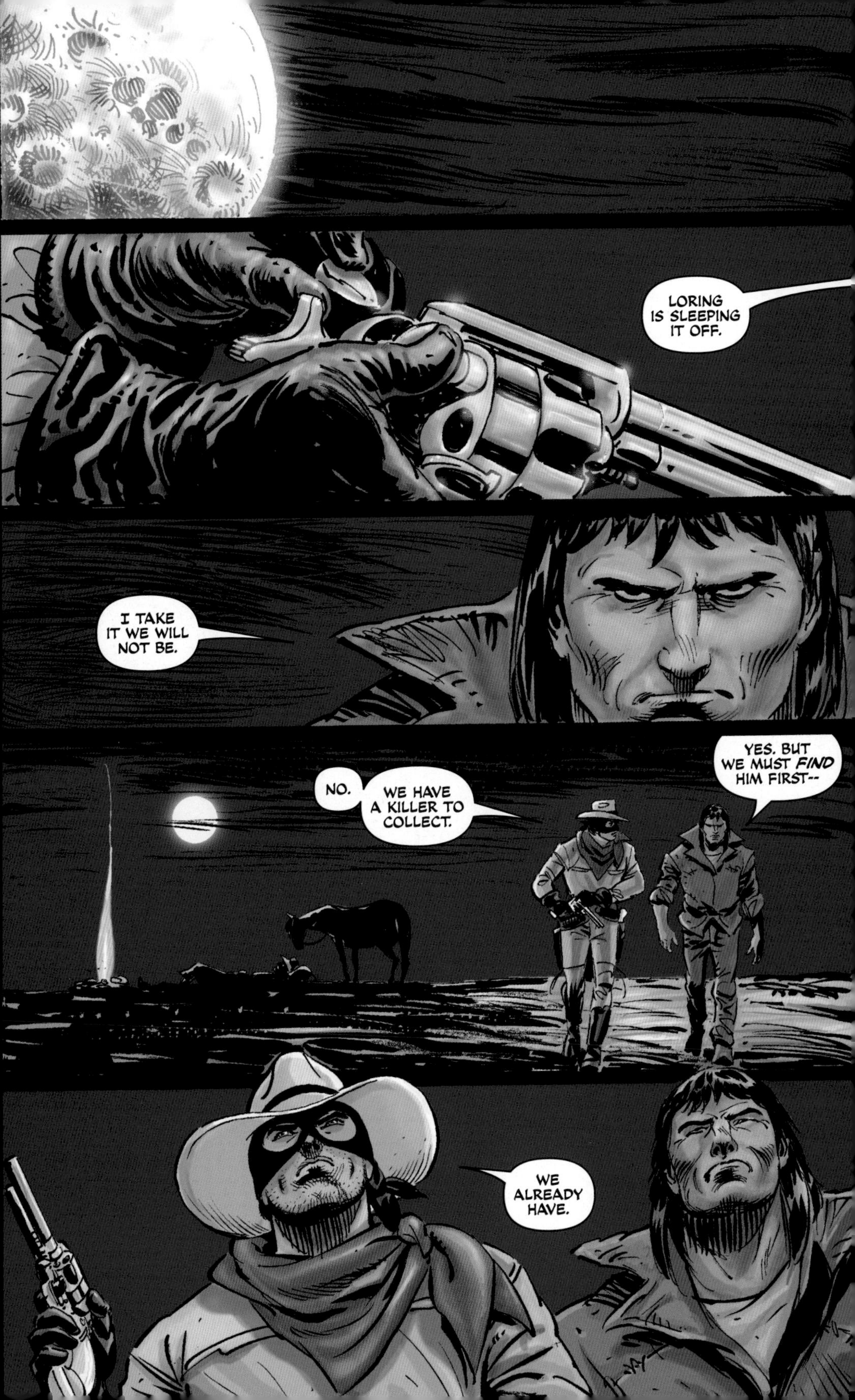
LORING IS SLEEPING IT OFF.
I TAKE IT WE WILL NOT BE.
NO.
WE HAVE A KILLER TO COLLECT.
YES. BUT WE MUST FIND HIM FIRST--
WE ALREADY HAVE.

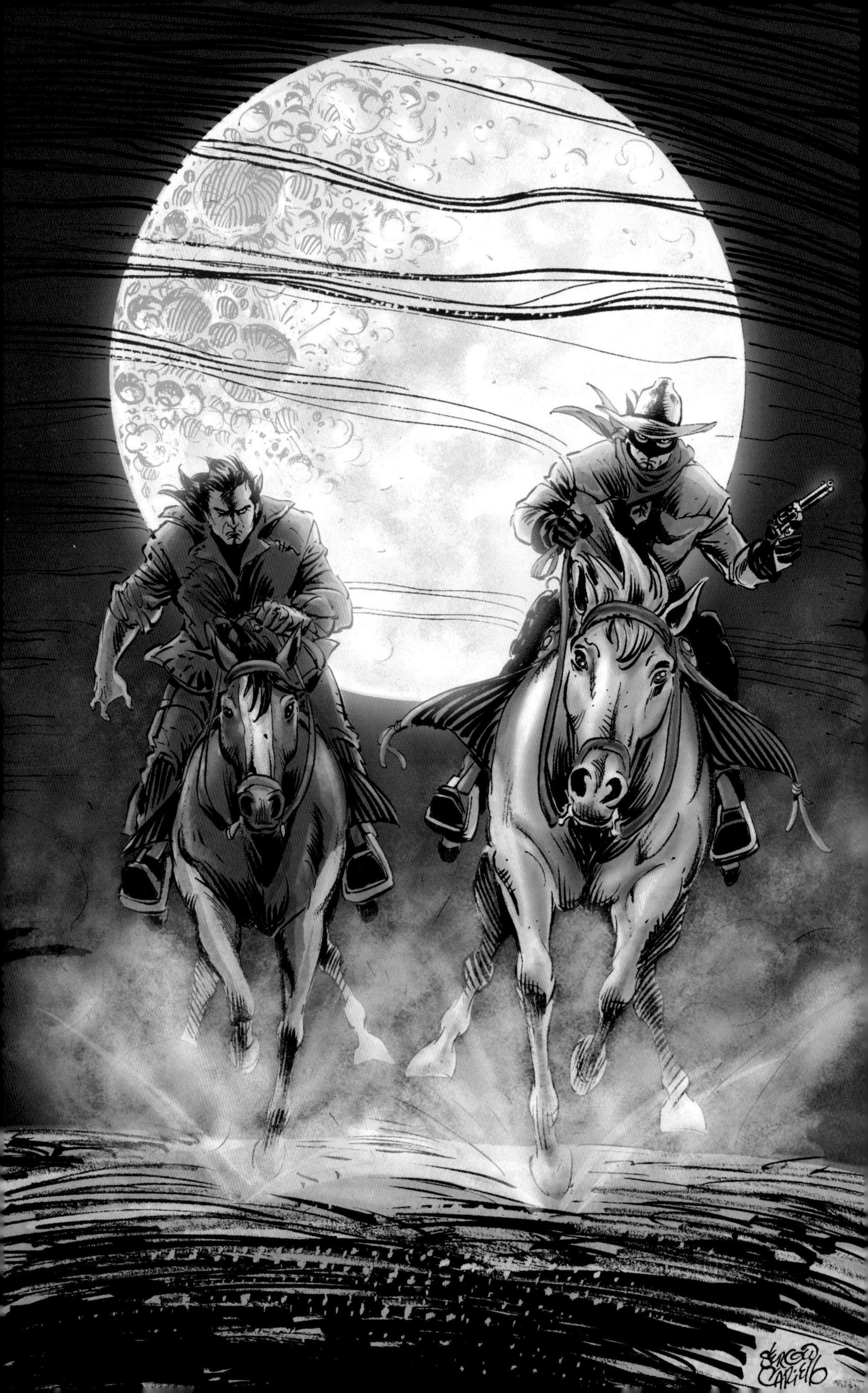

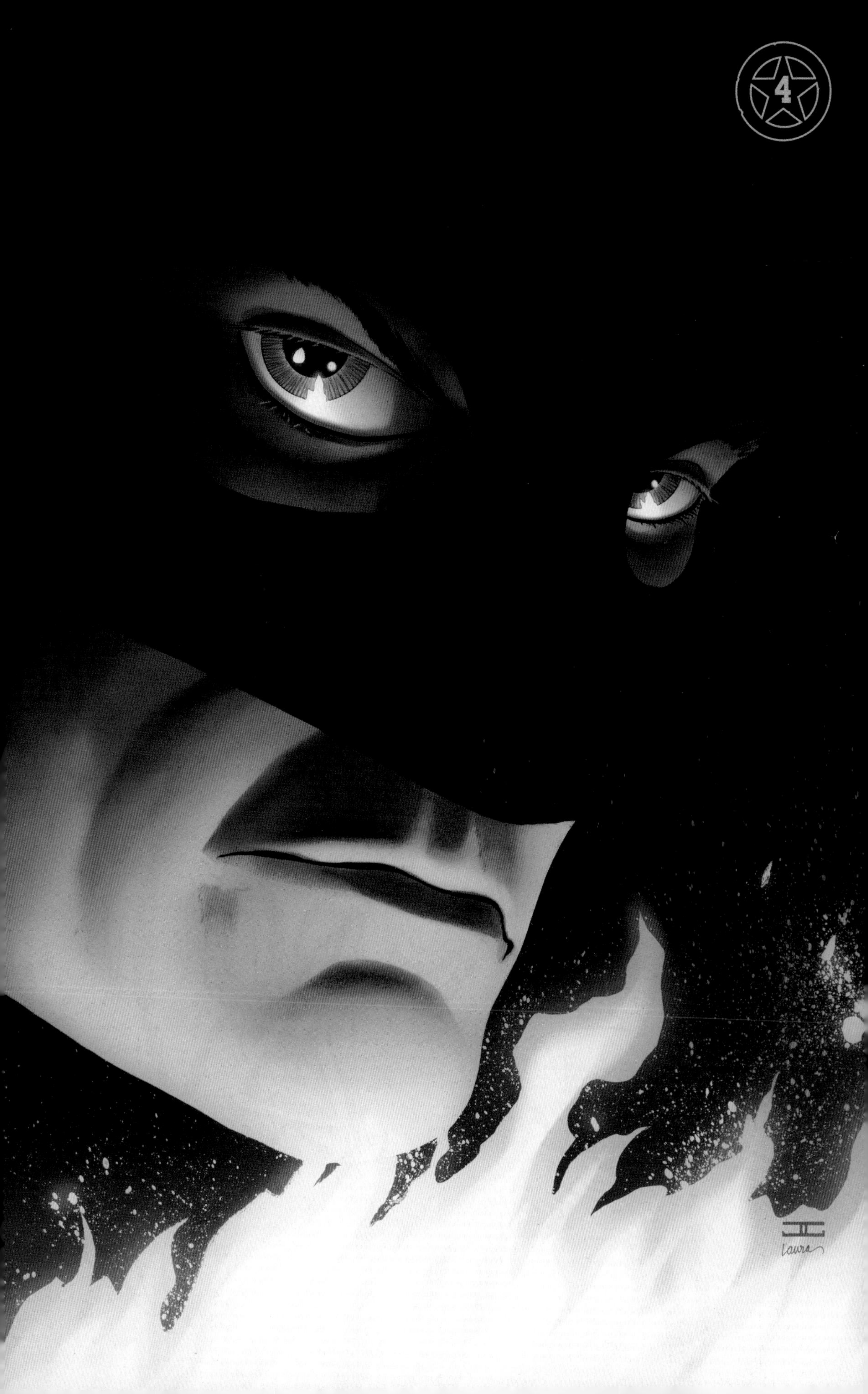
4

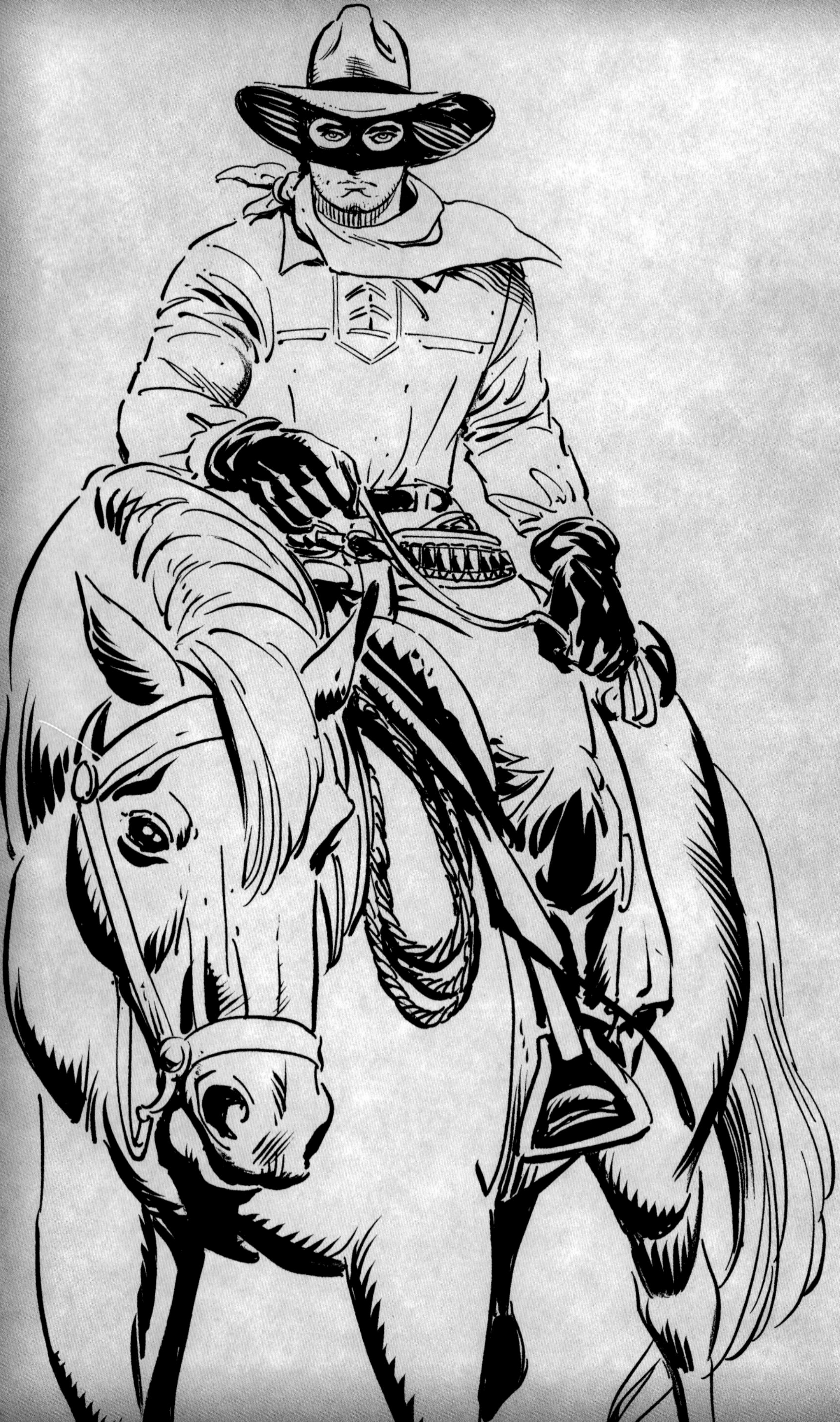

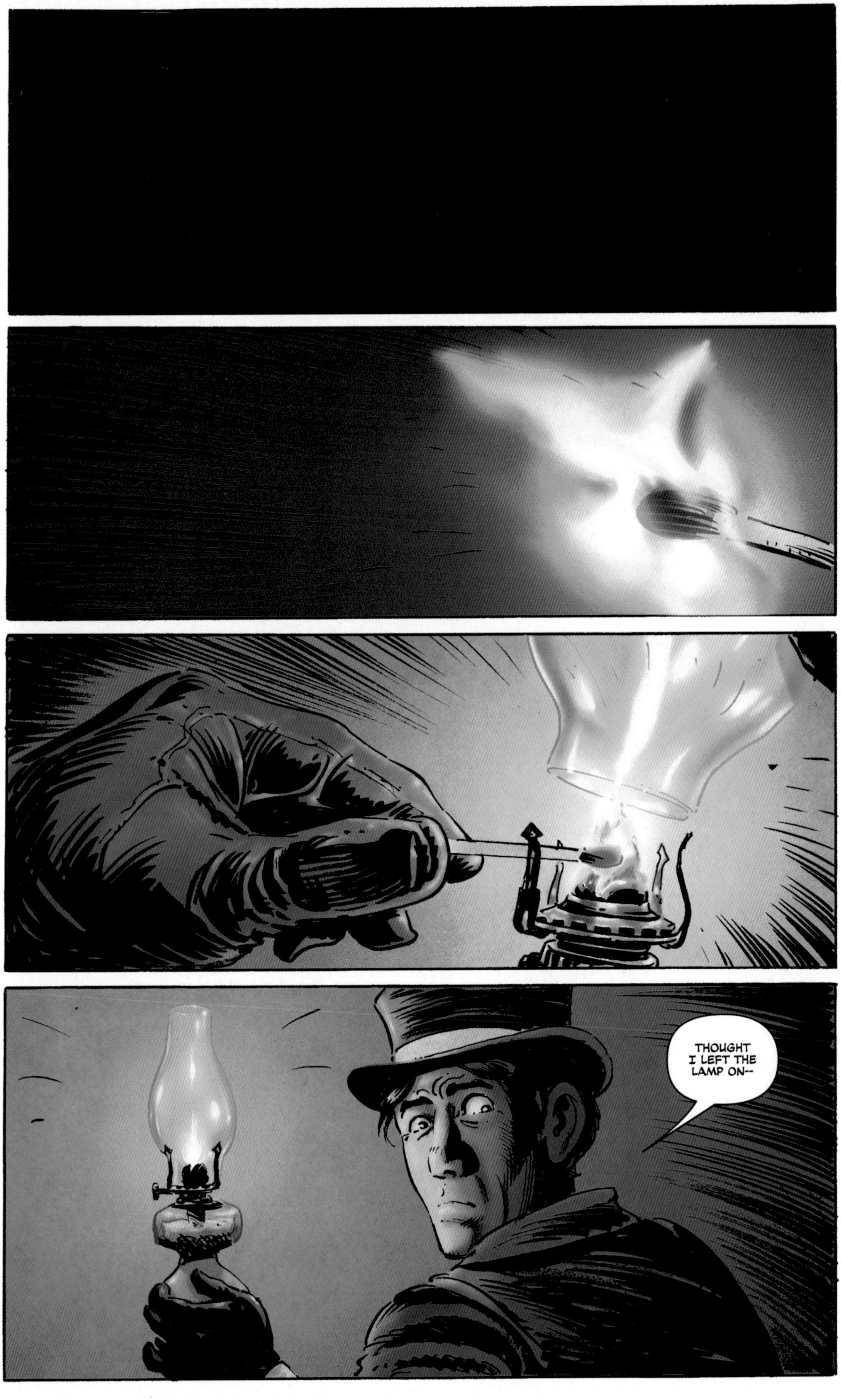
THOUGHT I LEFT THE LAMP ON--

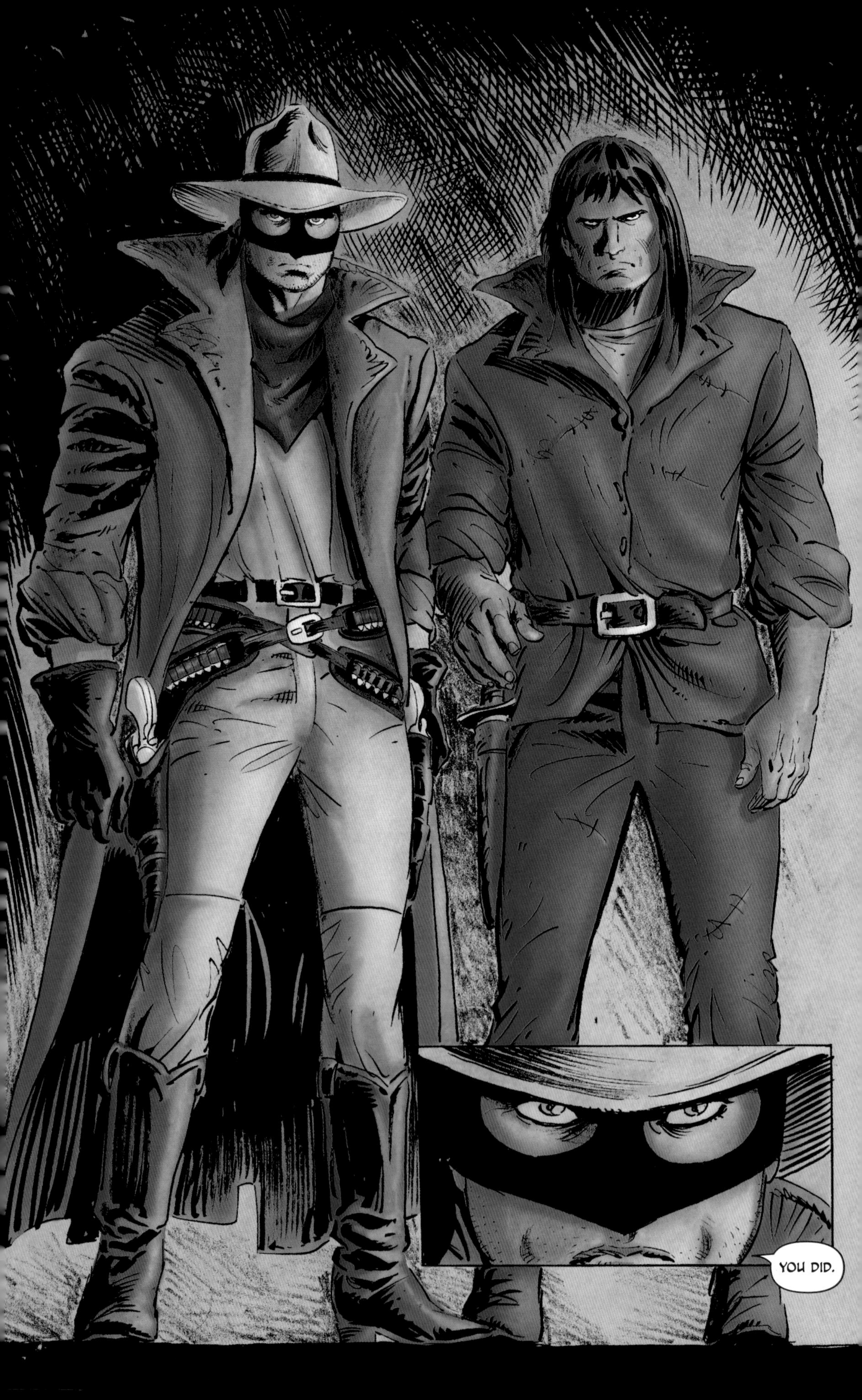
YOU DID.

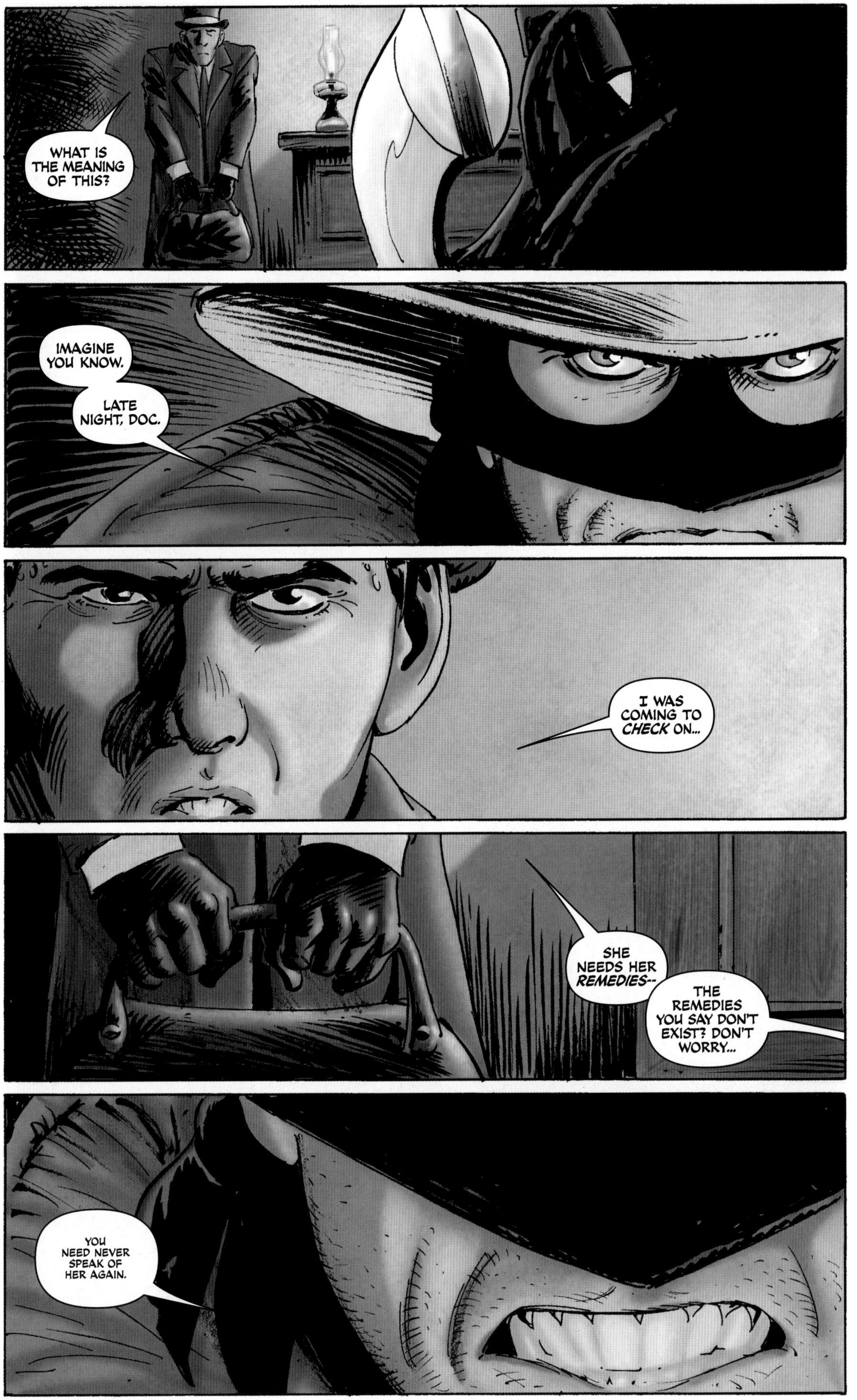
WHAT IS THE MEANING OF THIS?
IMAGINE YOU KNOW.
LATE NIGHT, DOC.
I WAS COMING TO *CHECK* ON...
SHE NEEDS HER *REMEDIES*--
THE REMEDIES YOU SAY DON'T EXIST? DON'T WORRY...
YOU NEED NEVER SPEAK OF HER AGAIN.

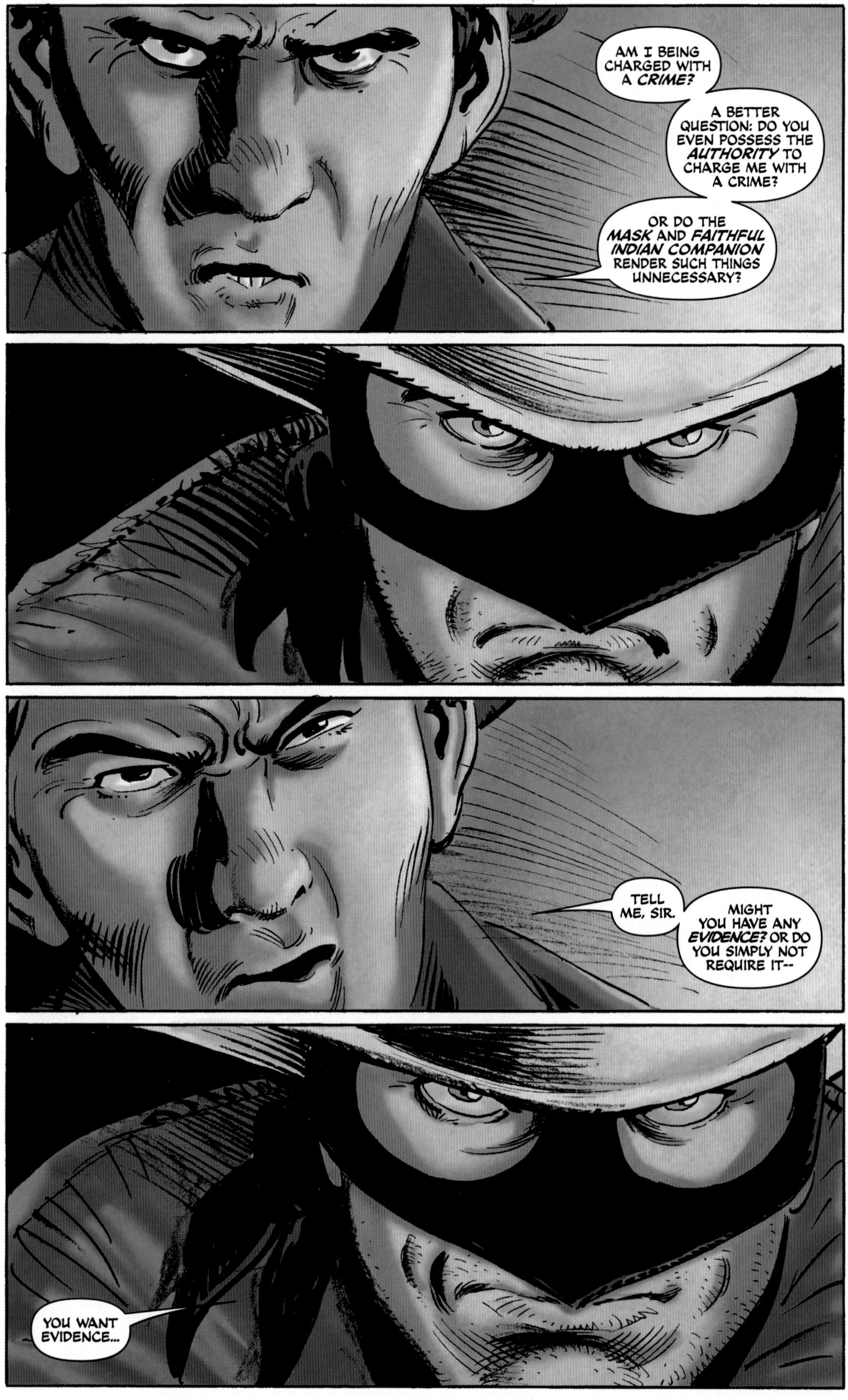
AM I BEING CHARGED WITH A *CRIME?*
A BETTER QUESTION: DO YOU EVEN POSSESS THE *AUTHORITY* TO CHARGE ME WITH A CRIME?
OR DO THE *MASK* AND *FAITHFUL INDIAN COMPANION* RENDER SUCH THINGS UNNECESSARY?
TELL ME, SIR.
MIGHT YOU HAVE ANY *EVIDENCE?* OR DO YOU SIMPLY NOT REQUIRE IT--
YOU WANT EVIDENCE...

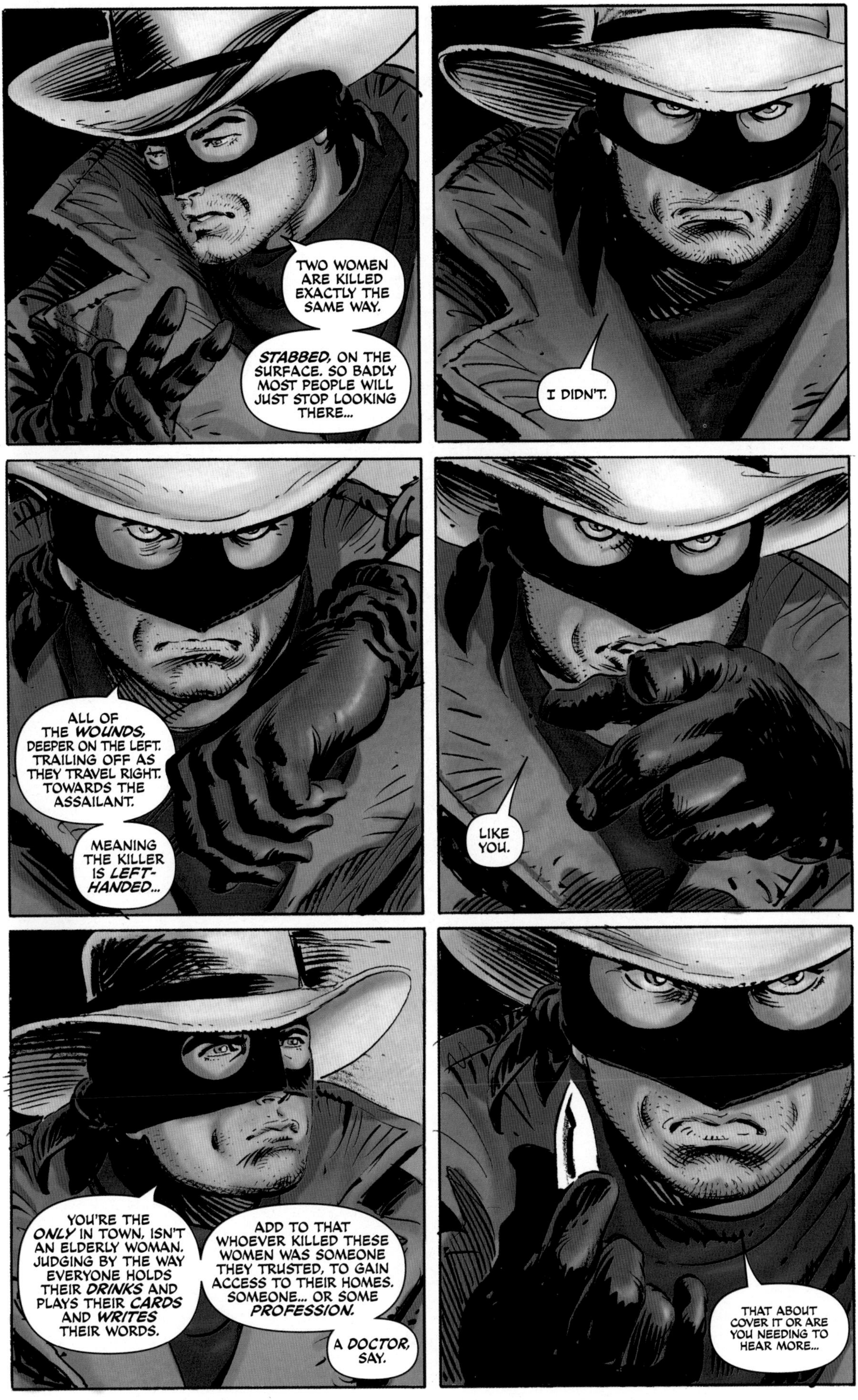
TWO WOMEN ARE KILLED EXACTLY THE SAME WAY.
STABBED, ON THE SURFACE. SO BADLY MOST PEOPLE WILL JUST STOP LOOKING THERE...
I DIDN'T.
ALL OF THE WOUNDS, DEEPER ON THE LEFT. TRAILING OFF AS THEY TRAVEL RIGHT. TOWARDS THE ASSAILANT.
MEANING THE KILLER IS LEFT-HANDED...
LIKE YOU.
YOU'RE THE ONLY IN TOWN, ISN'T AN ELDERLY WOMAN. JUDGING BY THE WAY EVERYONE HOLDS THEIR DRINKS AND PLAYS THEIR CARDS AND WRITES THEIR WORDS.
ADD TO THAT WHOEVER KILLED THESE WOMEN WAS SOMEONE THEY TRUSTED, TO GAIN ACCESS TO THEIR HOMES. SOMEONE... OR SOME PROFESSION.
A DOCTOR, SAY.
THAT ABOUT COVER IT OR ARE YOU NEEDING TO HEAR MORE...

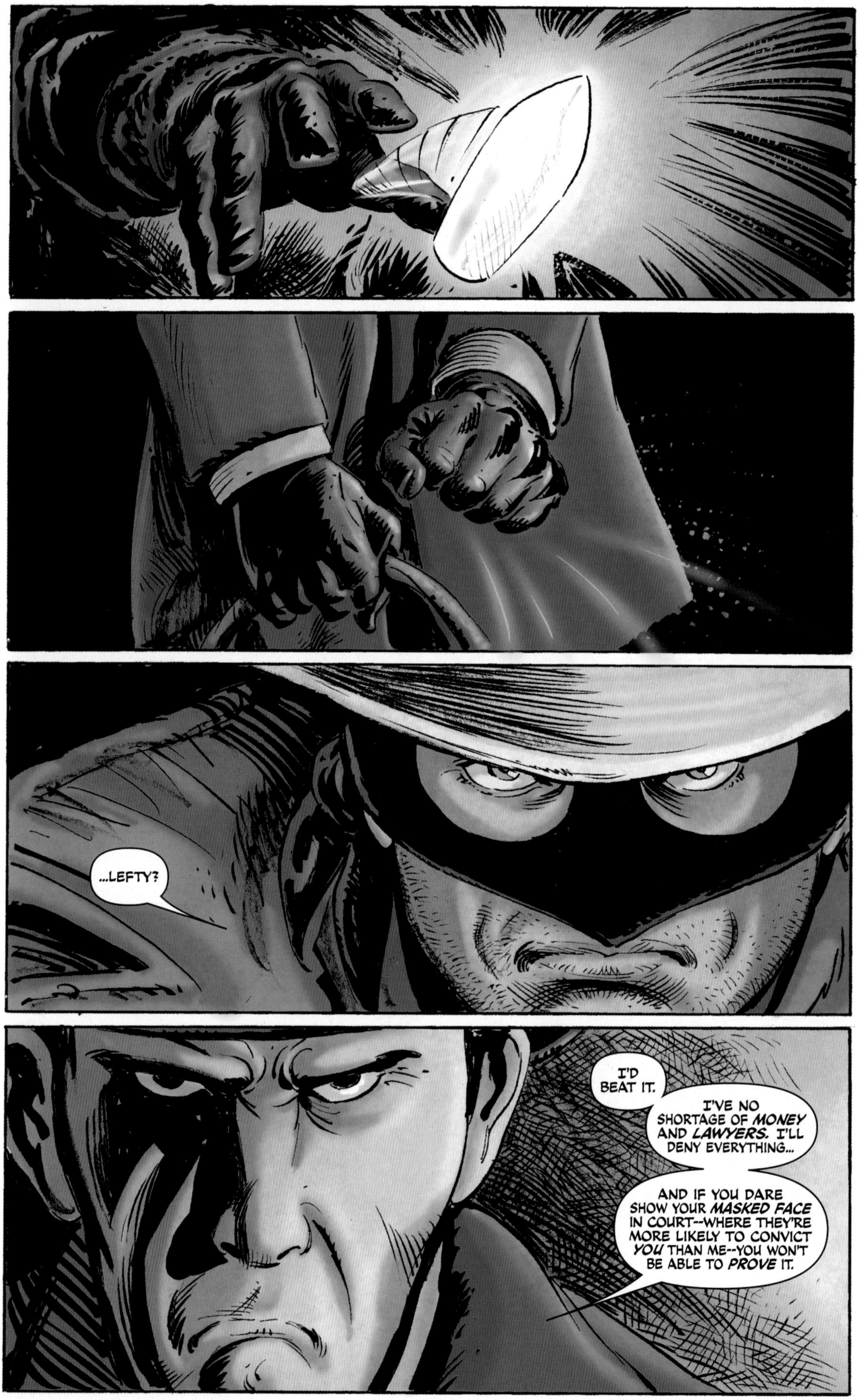
...LEFTY?
I'D BEAT IT.
I'VE NO SHORTAGE OF *MONEY* AND *LAWYERS.* I'LL DENY EVERYTHING...
AND IF YOU DARE SHOW YOUR *MASKED FACE* IN COURT--WHERE THEY'RE MORE LIKELY TO CONVICT *YOU* THAN ME--YOU WON'T BE ABLE TO *PROVE* IT.

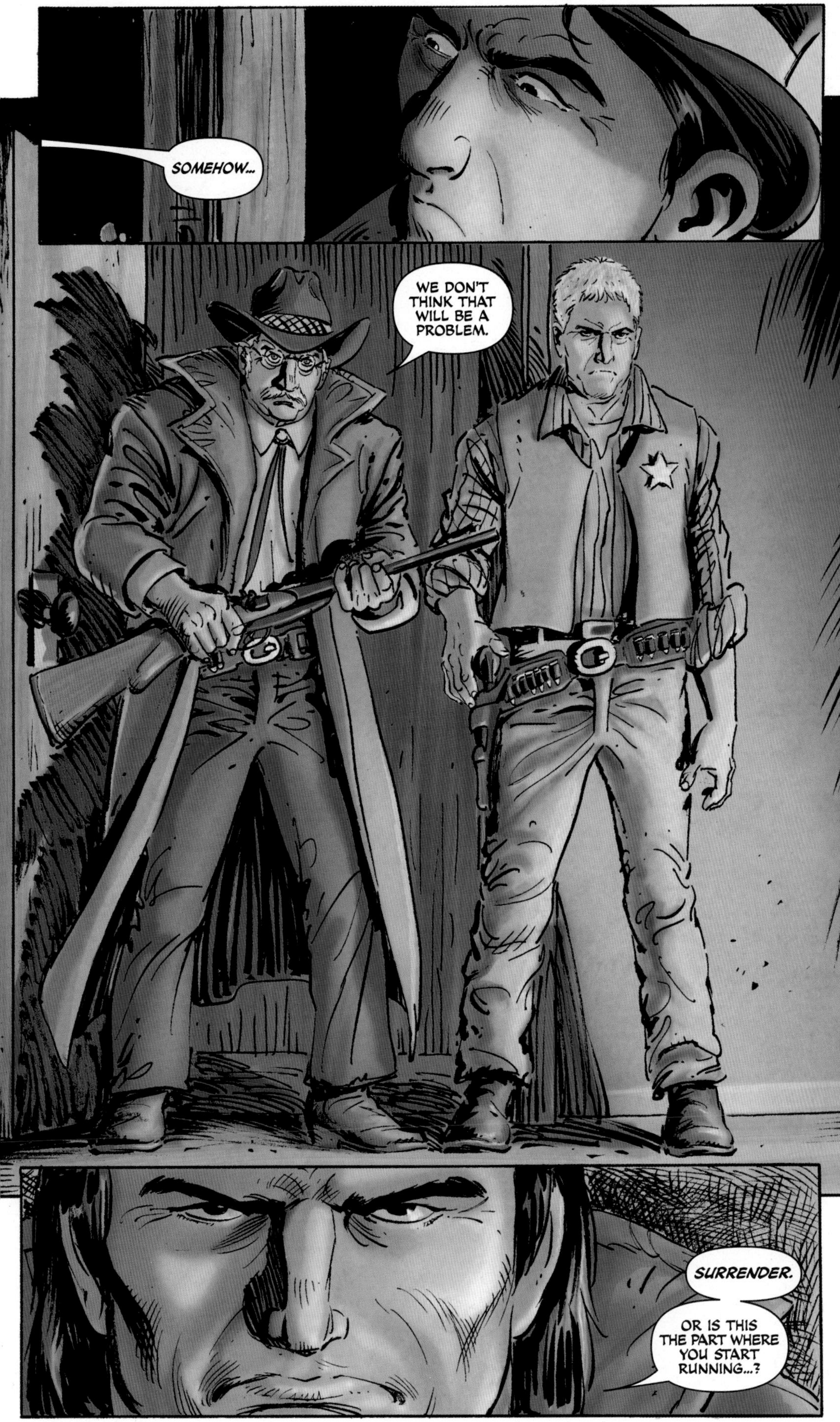
SOMEHOW...
WE DON'T THINK THAT WILL BE A PROBLEM.
SURRENDER.
OR IS THIS THE PART WHERE YOU START RUNNING...?

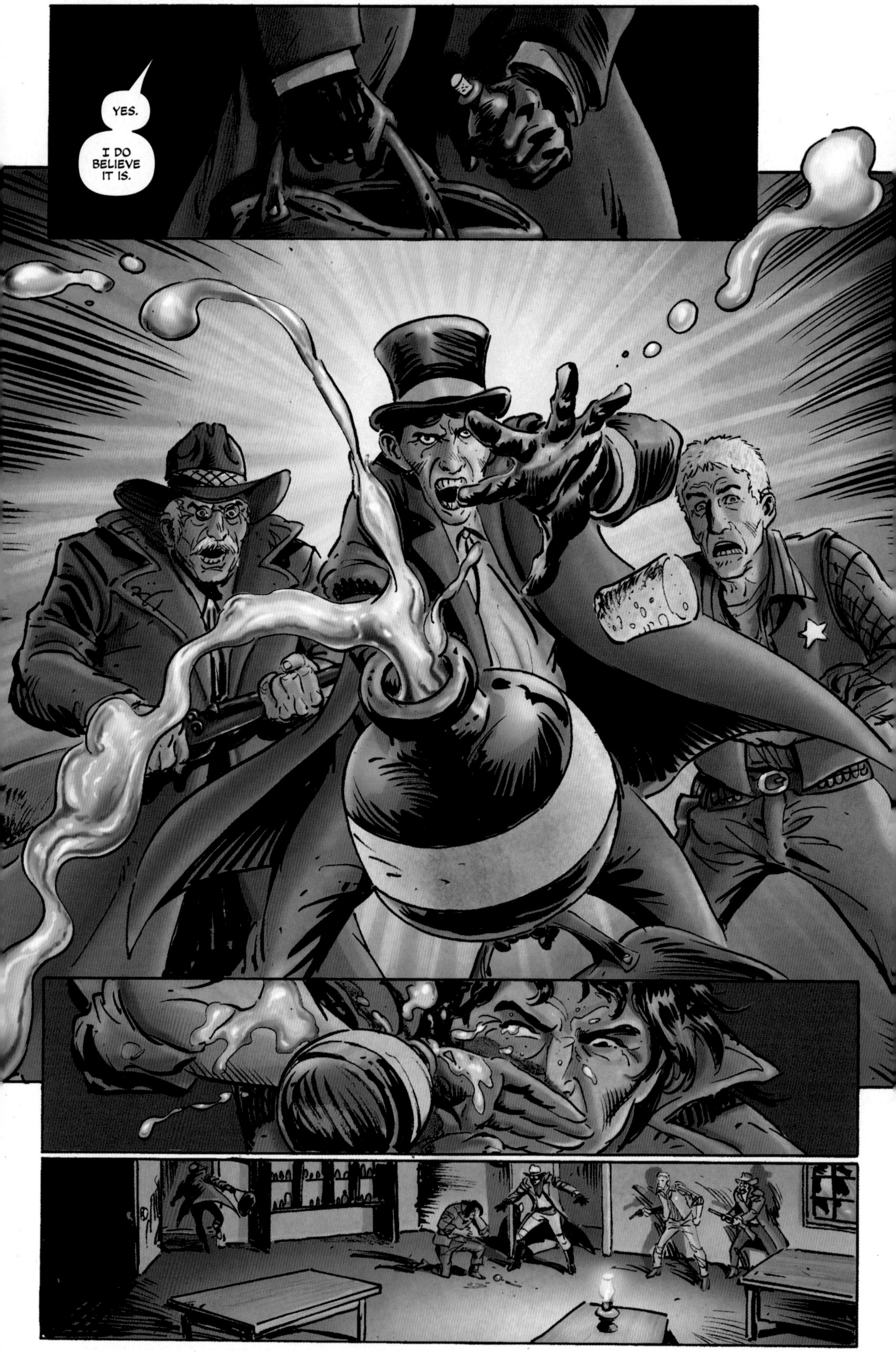
YES.
I DO BELIEVE IT IS.

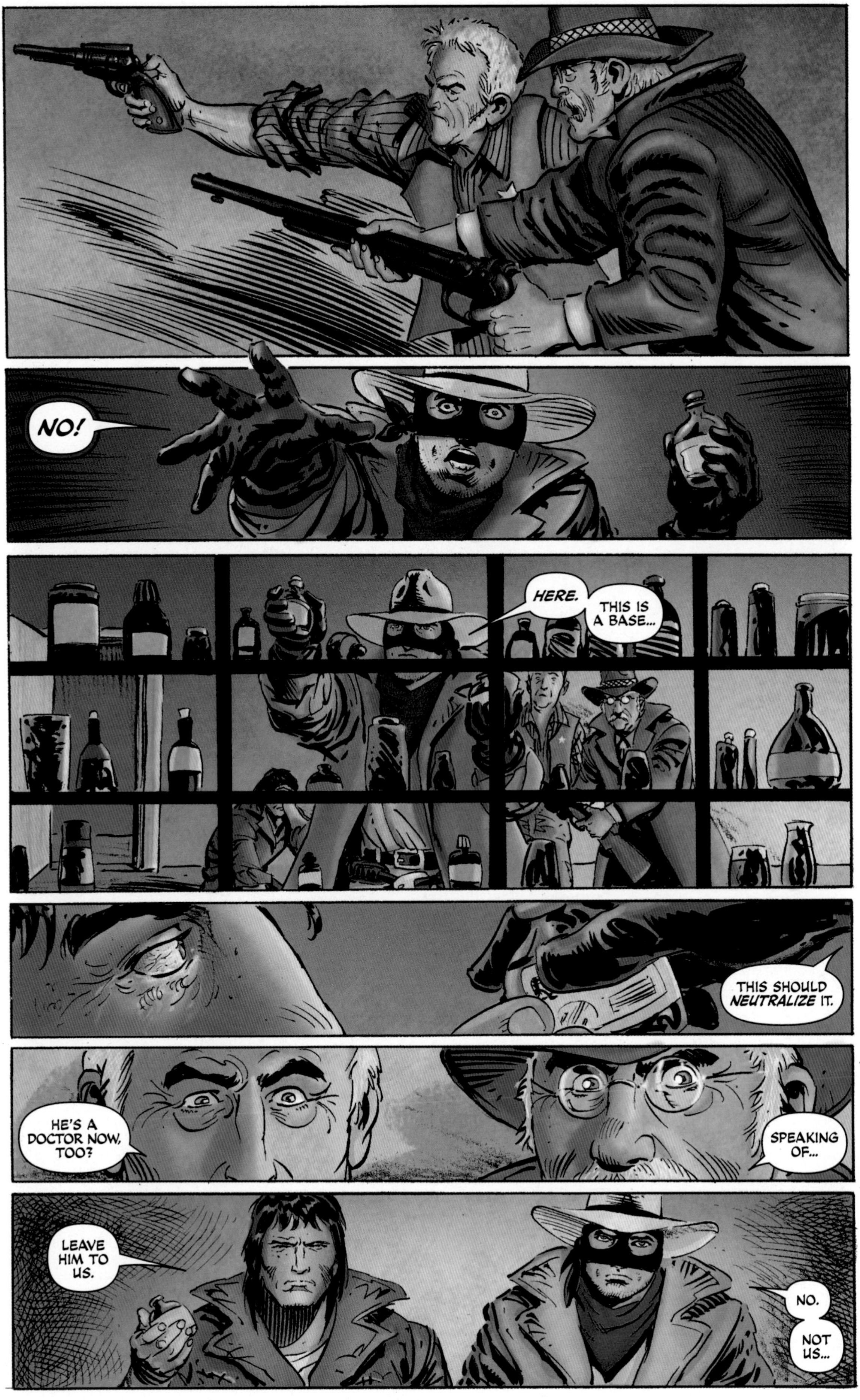
NO!
HERE.
THIS IS A BASE...
THIS SHOULD *NEUTRALIZE* IT.
HE'S A DOCTOR NOW, TOO?
SPEAKING OF...
LEAVE HIM TO US.
NO.
NOT US...

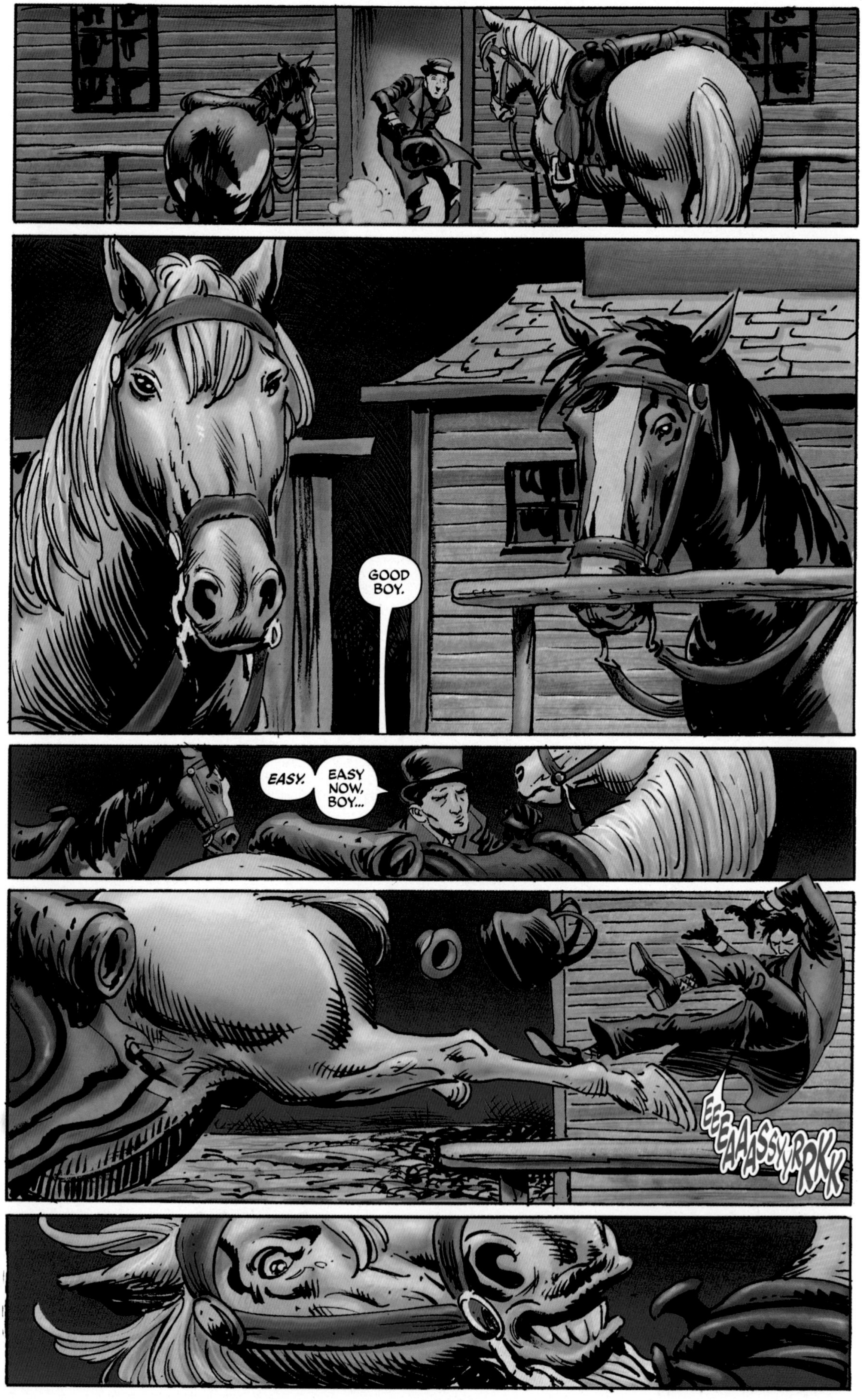
GOOD BOY.
EASY.
EASY NOW, BOY...
EEEAAASSYYRRKK

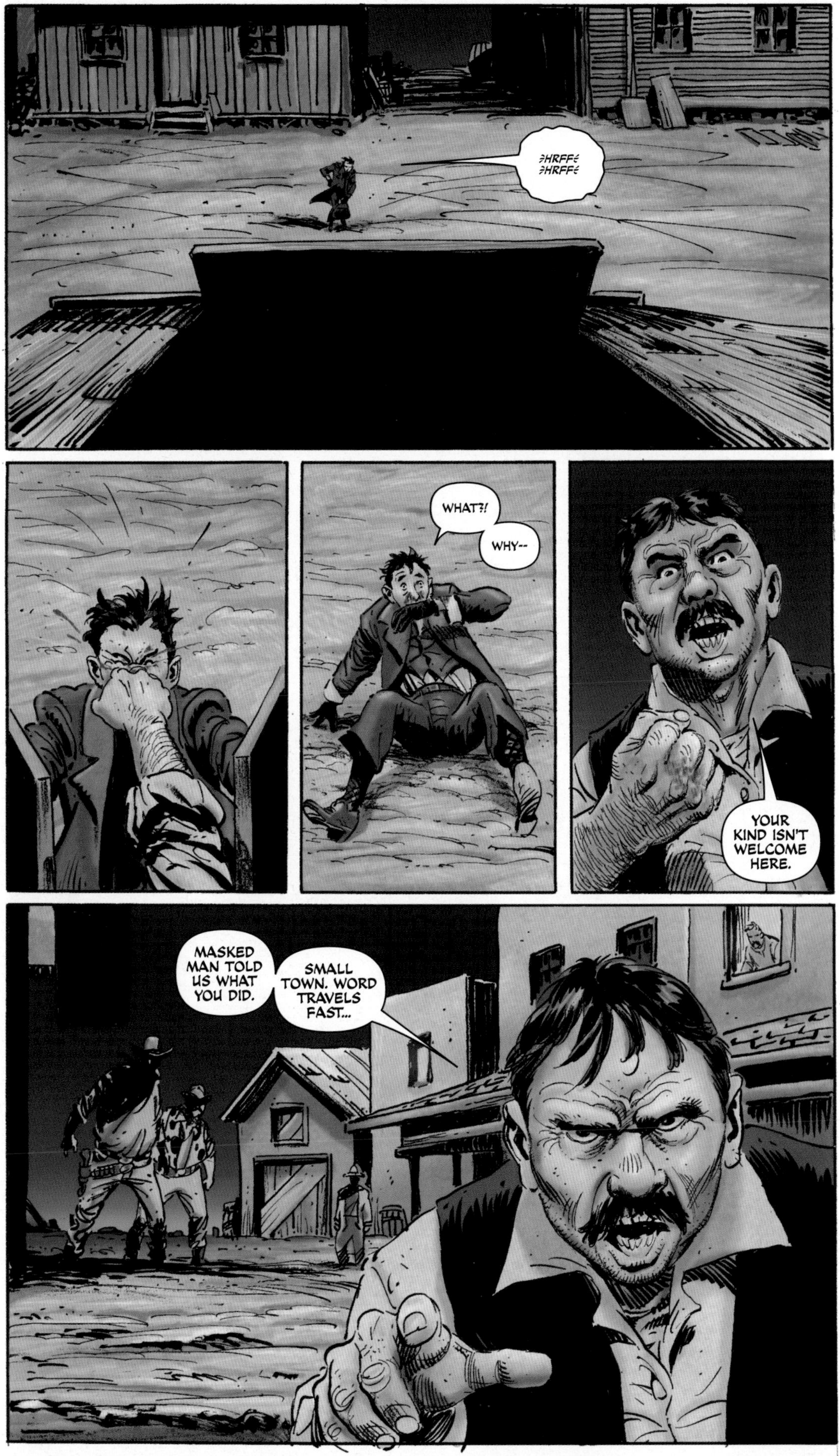

HRFF
HRFF
WHAT?!
WHY--
YOUR KIND ISN'T WELCOME HERE.
MASKED MAN TOLD US WHAT YOU DID.
SMALL TOWN. WORD TRAVELS FAST...

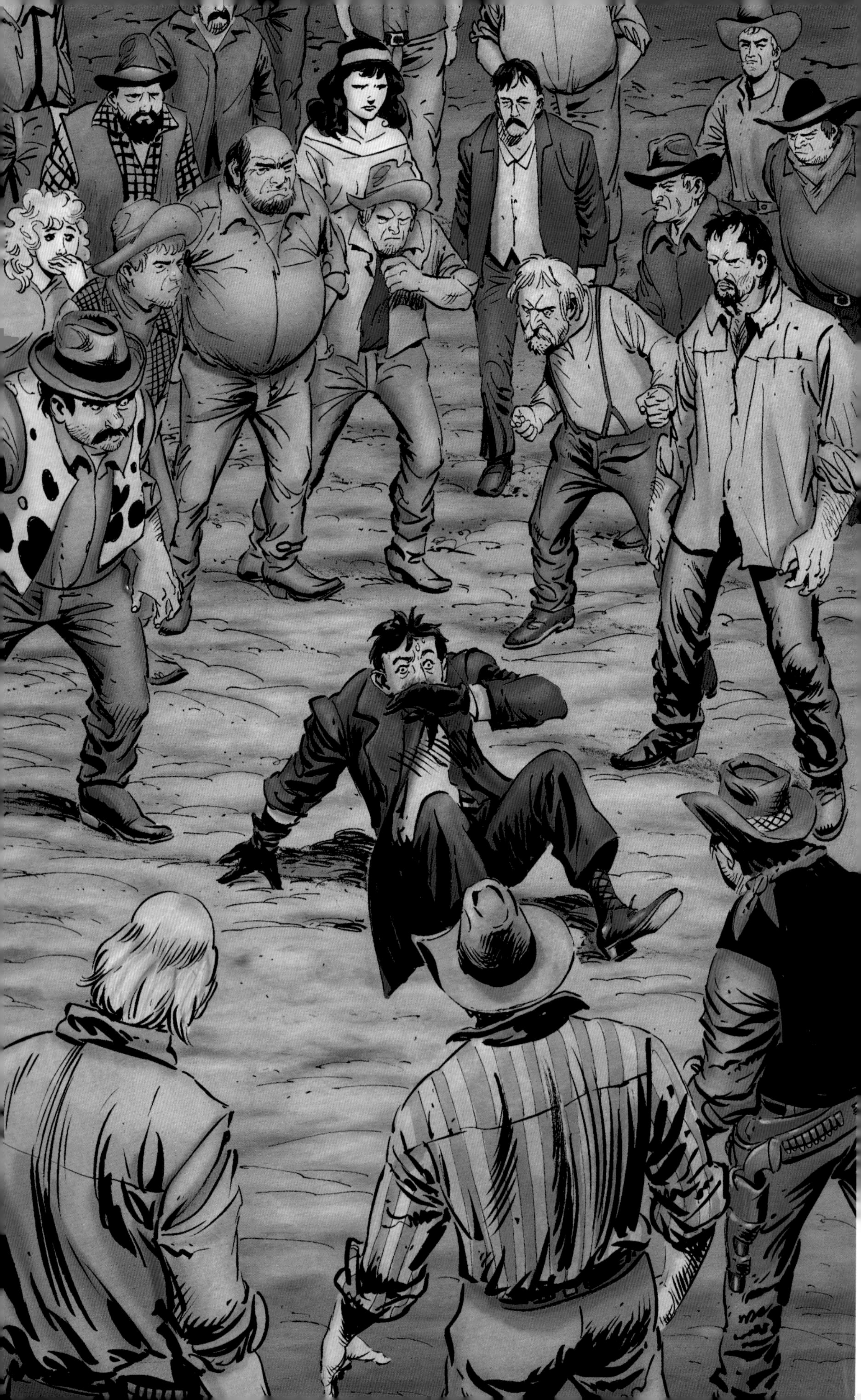

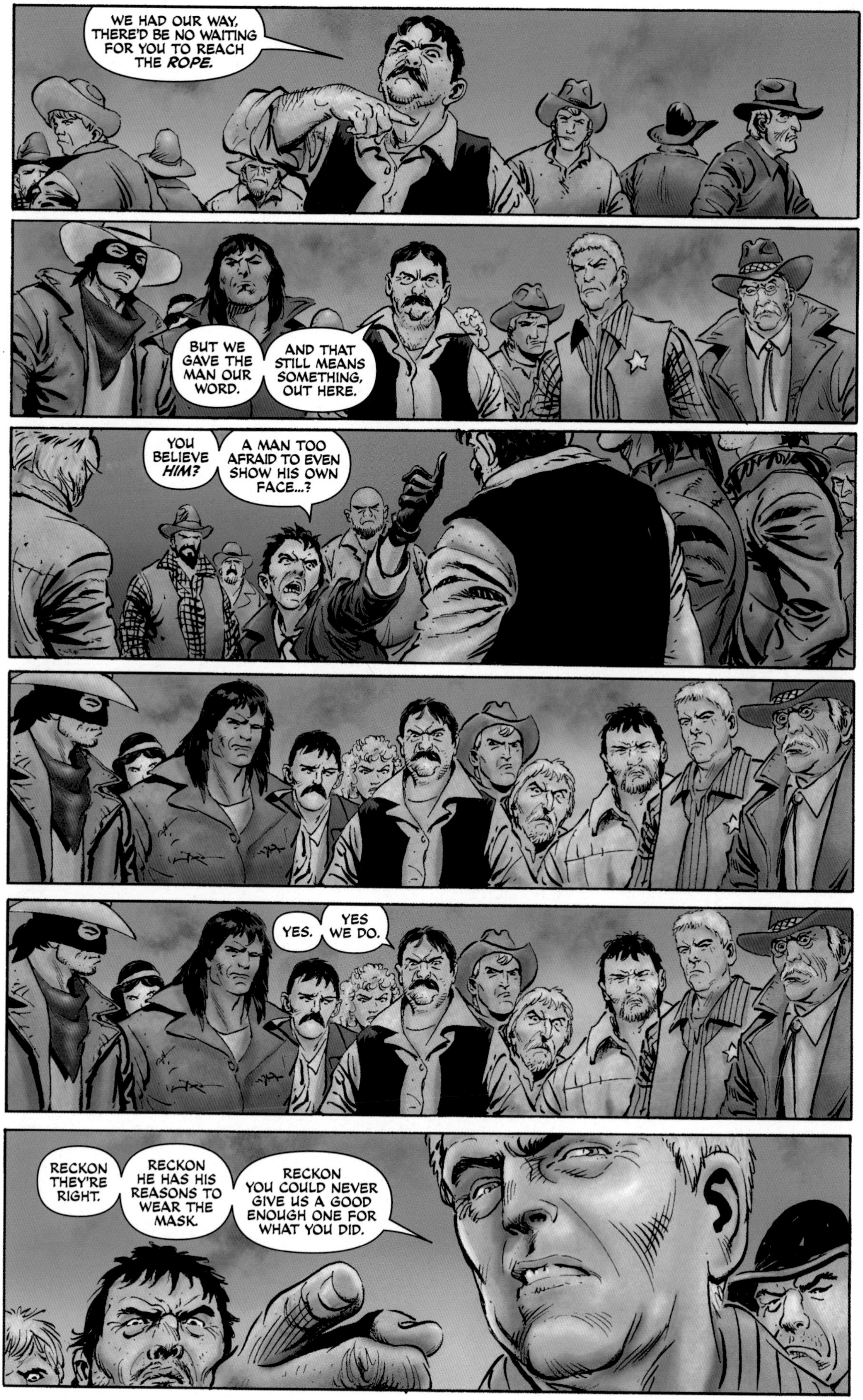
WE HAD OUR WAY, THERE'D BE NO WAITING FOR YOU TO REACH THE *ROPE.*
BUT WE GAVE THE MAN OUR WORD.
AND THAT STILL MEANS SOMETHING, OUT HERE.
YOU BELIEVE *HIM?*
A MAN TOO AFRAID TO EVEN SHOW HIS OWN FACE...?
YES.
YES WE DO.
RECKON THEY'RE RIGHT.
RECKON HE HAS HIS REASONS TO WEAR THE MASK.
RECKON YOU COULD NEVER GIVE US A GOOD ENOUGH ONE FOR WHAT YOU DID.

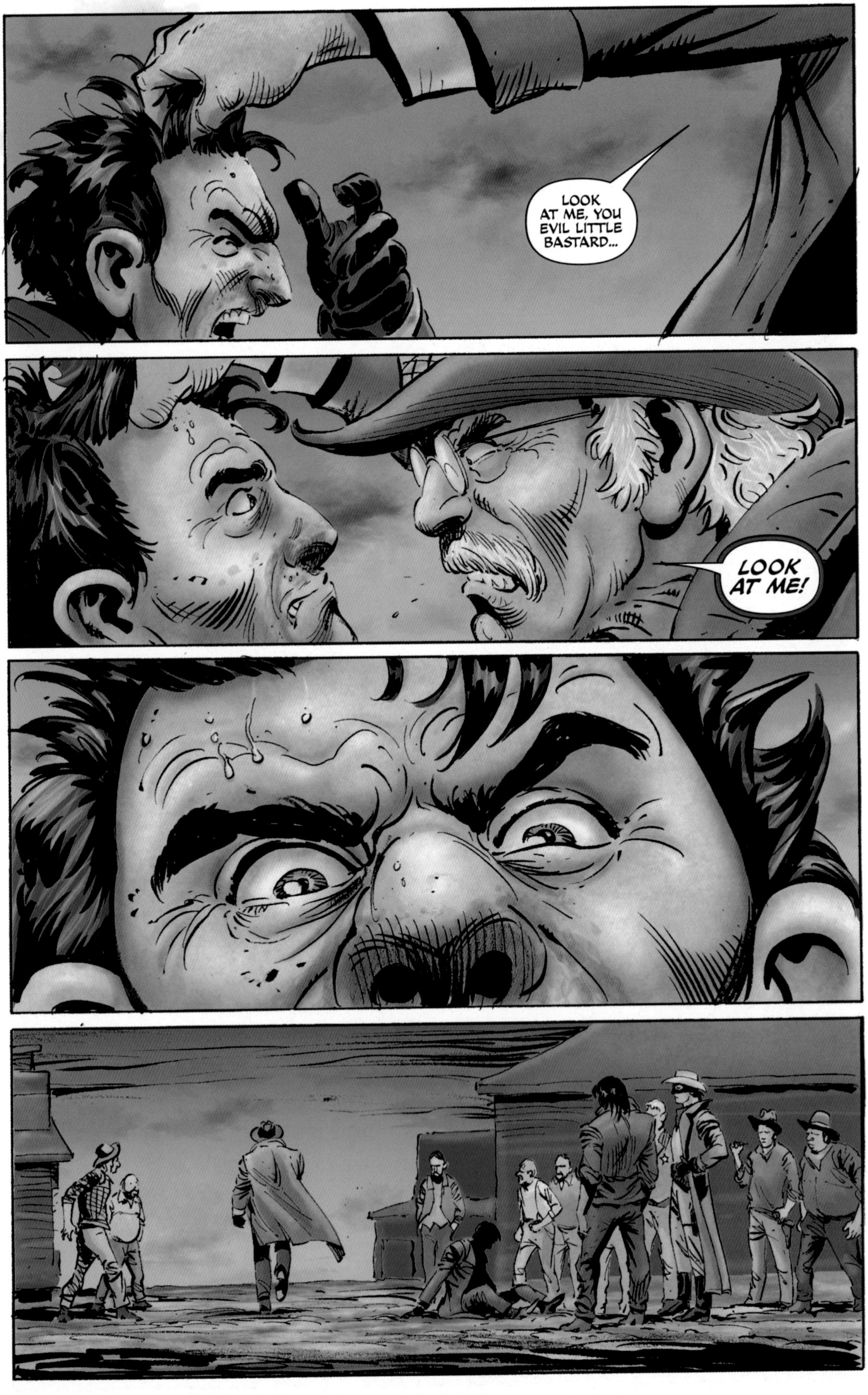
LOOK AT ME, YOU EVIL LITTLE BASTARD...
LOOK AT ME!

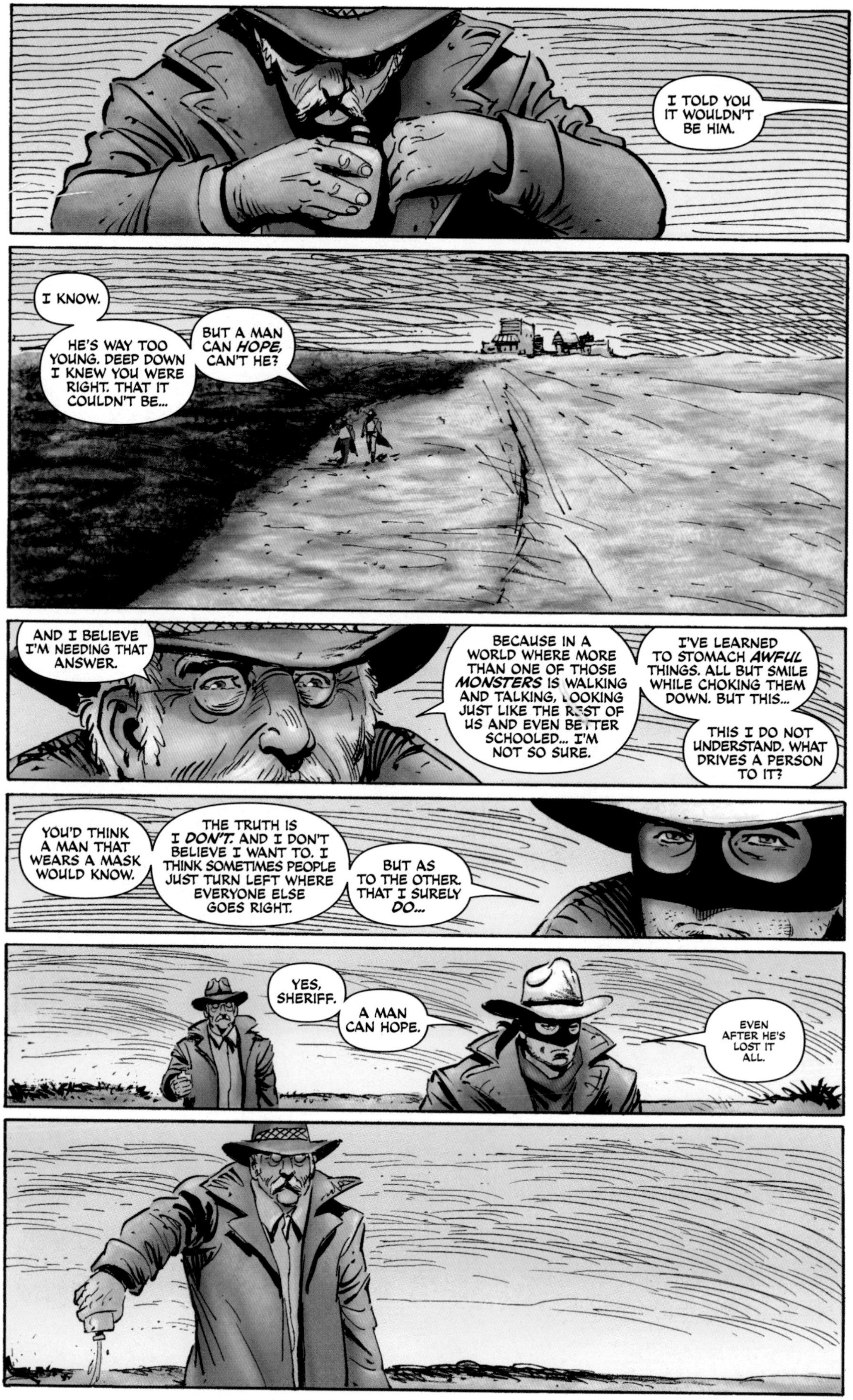
I TOLD YOU IT WOULDN'T BE HIM.
I KNOW.
HE'S WAY TOO YOUNG. DEEP DOWN I KNEW YOU WERE RIGHT. THAT IT COULDN'T BE...
BUT A MAN CAN *HOPE,* CAN'T HE?
AND I BELIEVE I'M NEEDING THAT ANSWER.
BECAUSE IN A WORLD WHERE MORE THAN ONE OF THOSE *MONSTERS* IS WALKING AND TALKING, LOOKING JUST LIKE THE REST OF US AND EVEN BETTER SCHOOLED... I'M NOT SO SURE.
I'VE LEARNED TO STOMACH *AWFUL* THINGS. ALL BUT SMILE WHILE CHOKING THEM DOWN. BUT THIS...
THIS I DO NOT UNDERSTAND. WHAT DRIVES A PERSON TO IT?
YOU'D THINK A MAN THAT WEARS A MASK WOULD KNOW.
THE TRUTH IS I *DON'T.* AND I DON'T BELIEVE I WANT TO. I THINK SOMETIMES PEOPLE JUST TURN LEFT WHERE EVERYONE ELSE GOES RIGHT.
BUT AS TO THE OTHER. THAT I SURELY *DO...*
YES, SHERIFF.
A MAN CAN HOPE.
EVEN AFTER HE'S LOST IT ALL.

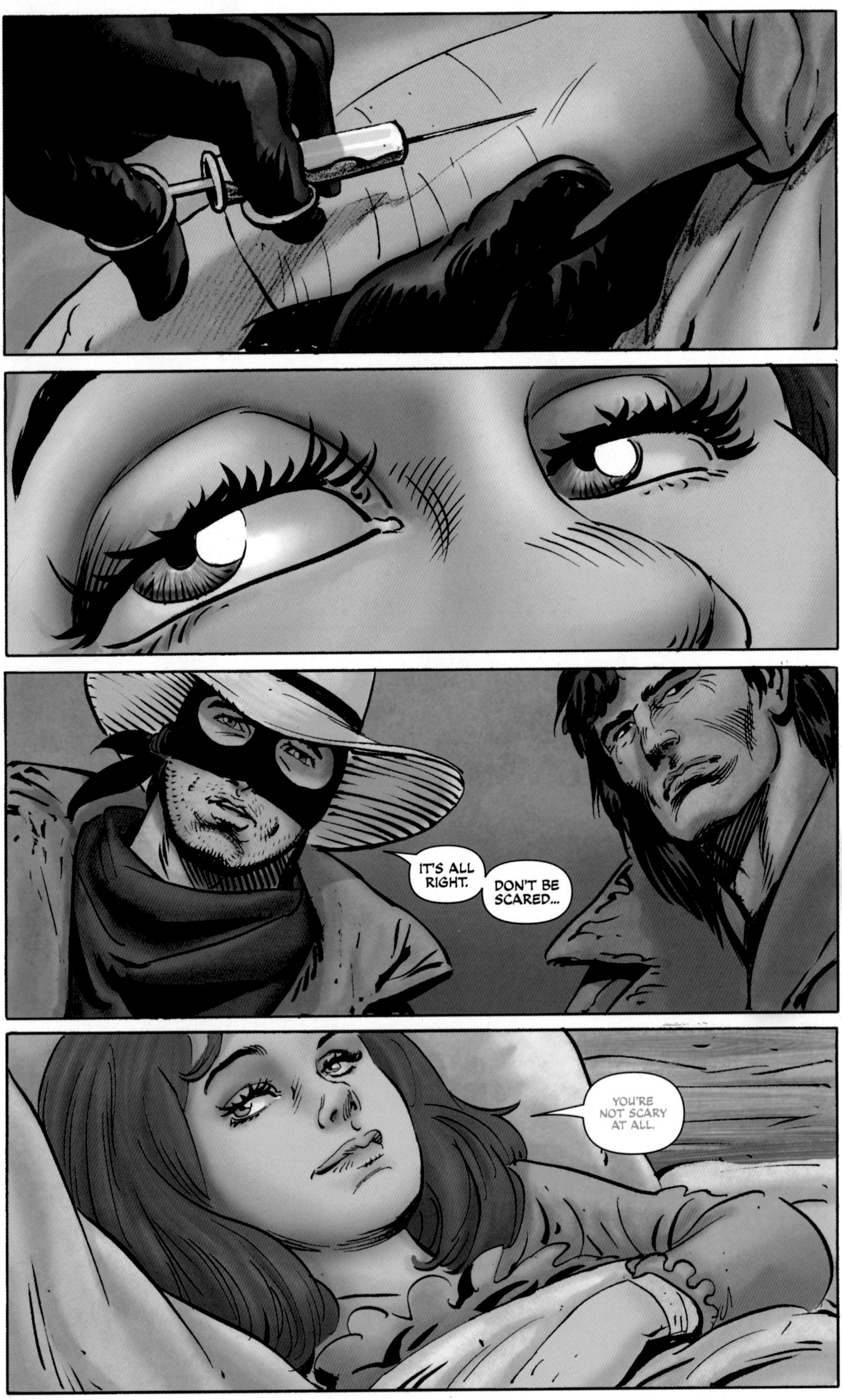

IT'S ALL RIGHT.
DON'T BE SCARED...
YOU'RE NOT SCARY AT ALL.

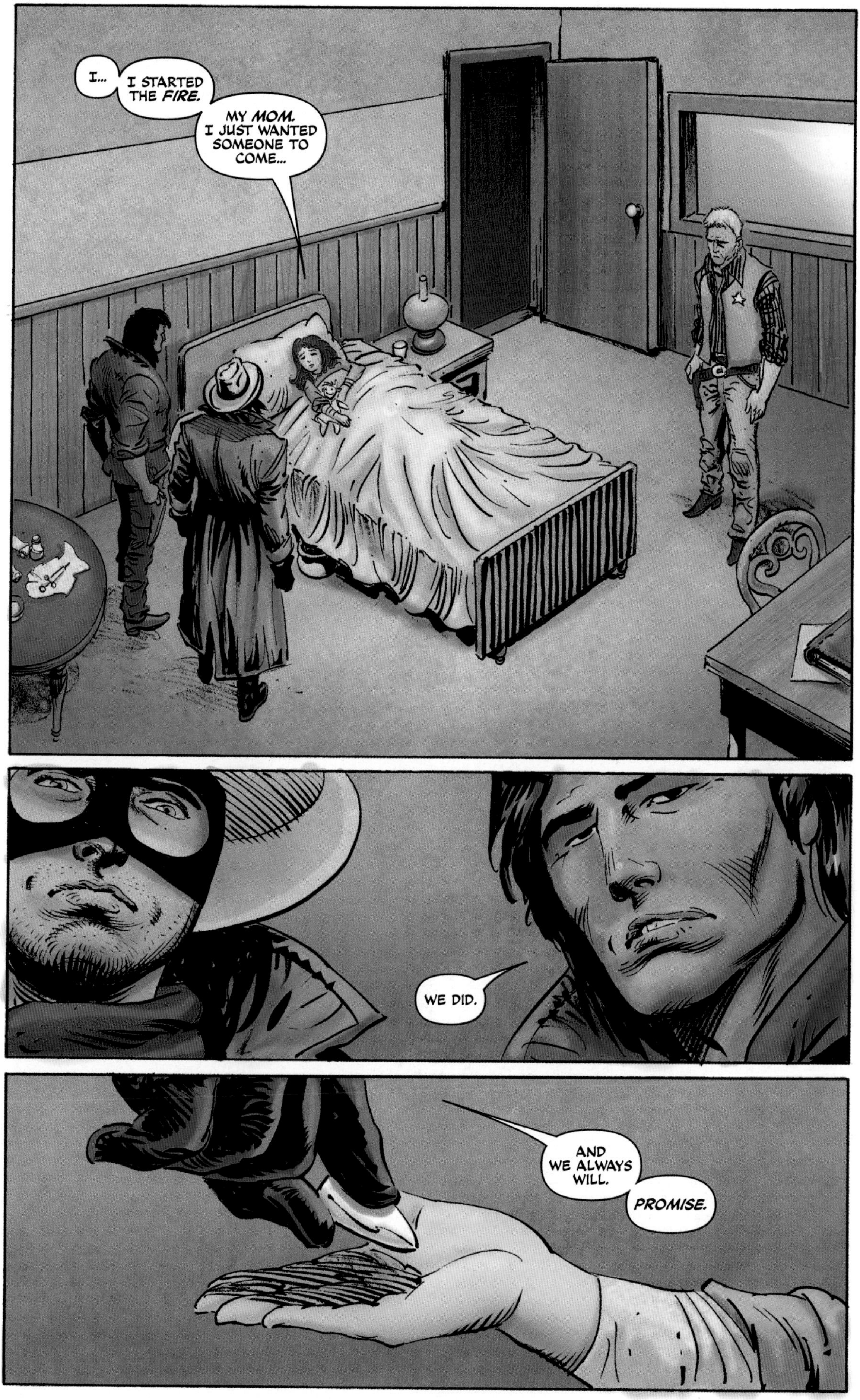
I...
I STARTED THE *FIRE.*
MY *MOM.* I JUST WANTED SOMEONE TO COME...
WE DID.
AND WE ALWAYS WILL.
PROMISE.

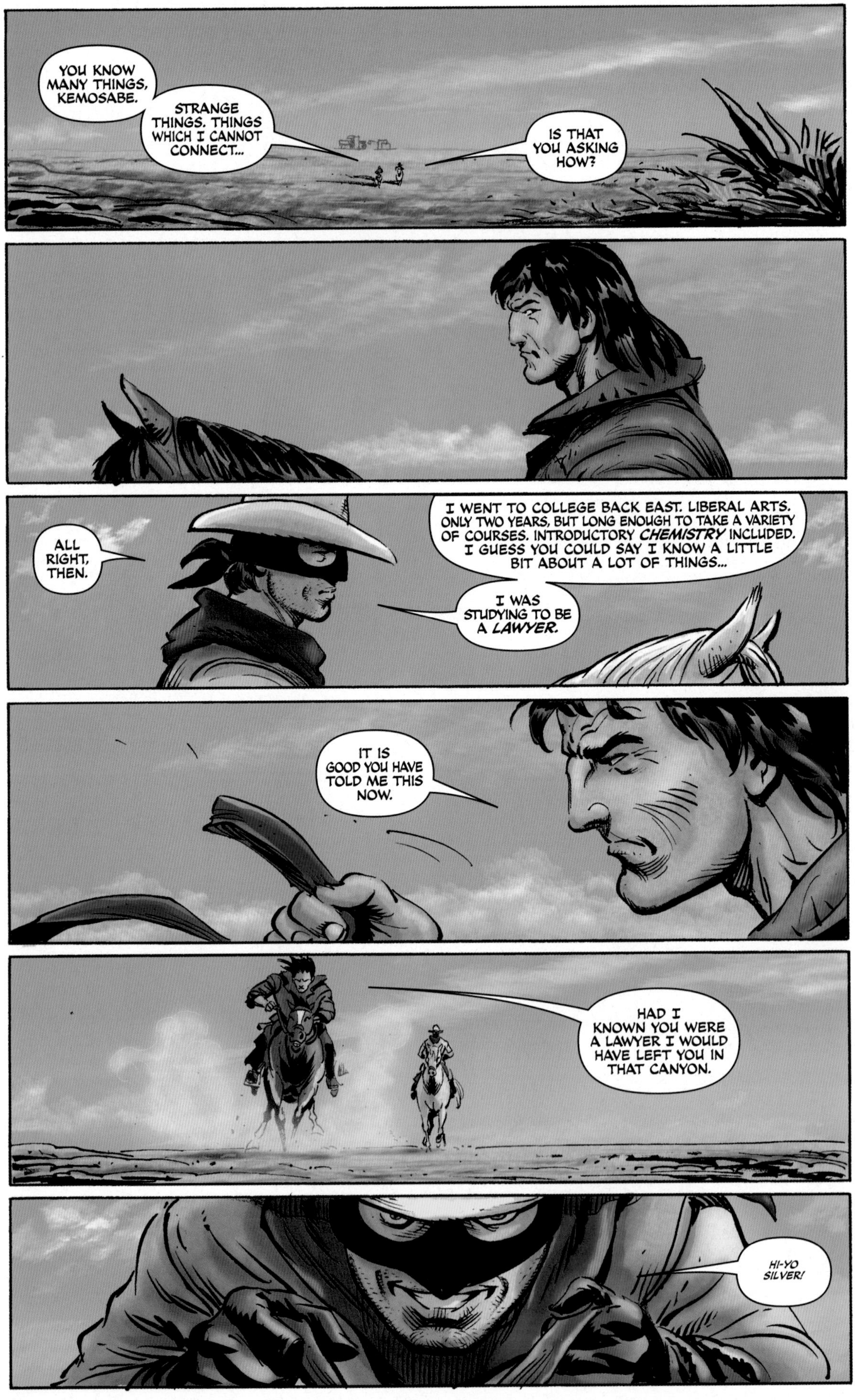
YOU KNOW MANY THINGS, KEMOSABE.
STRANGE THINGS. THINGS WHICH I CANNOT CONNECT...
IS THAT YOU ASKING HOW?
ALL RIGHT, THEN.
I WENT TO COLLEGE BACK EAST. LIBERAL ARTS. ONLY TWO YEARS, BUT LONG ENOUGH TO TAKE A VARIETY OF COURSES. INTRODUCTORY *CHEMISTRY* INCLUDED. I GUESS YOU COULD SAY I KNOW A LITTLE BIT ABOUT A LOT OF THINGS...
I WAS STUDYING TO BE A *LAWYER.*
IT IS GOOD YOU HAVE TOLD ME THIS NOW.
HAD I KNOWN YOU WERE A LAWYER I WOULD HAVE LEFT YOU IN THAT CANYON.
HI-YO SILVER!

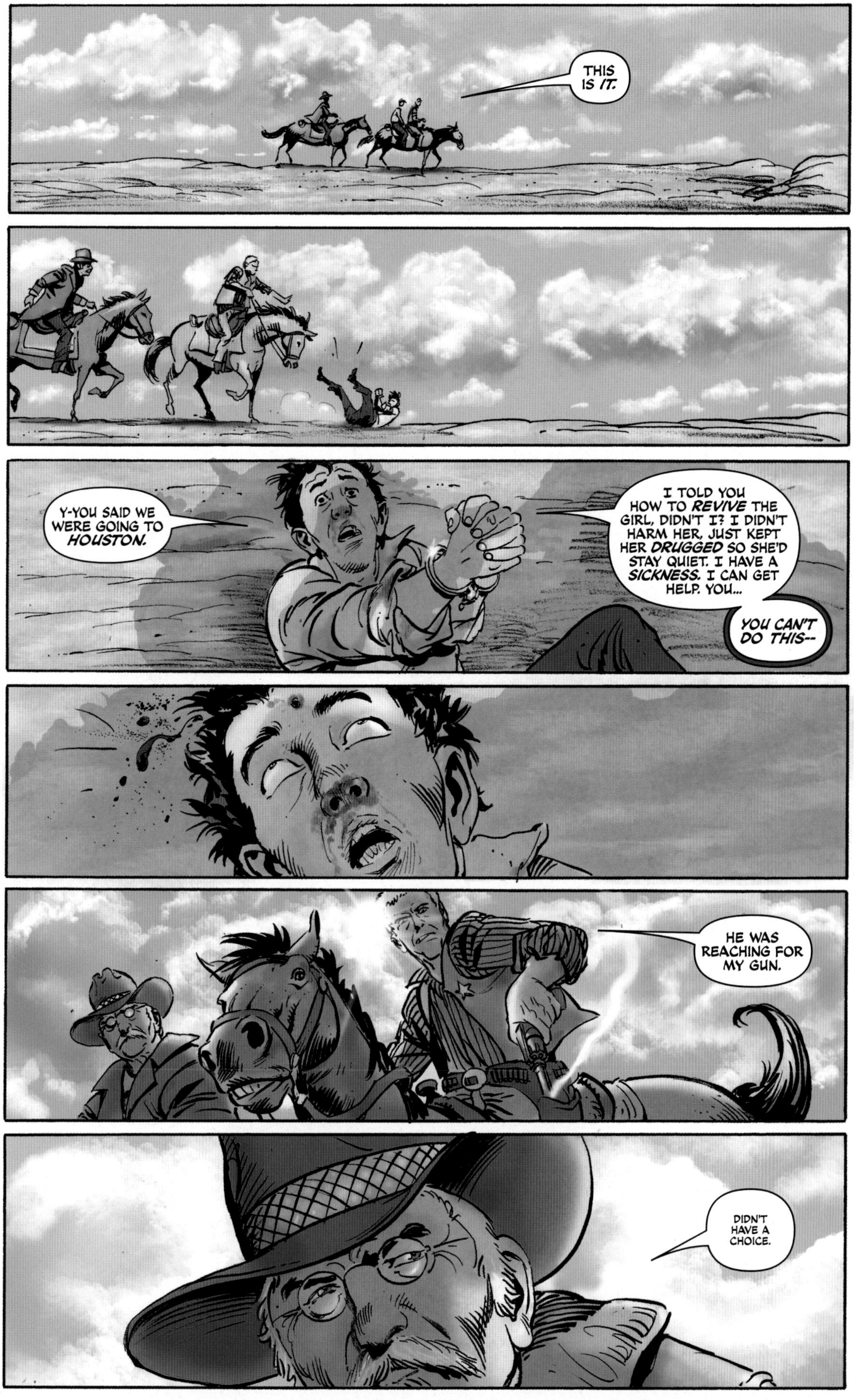
THIS IS IT.
Y-YOU SAID WE WERE GOING TO HOUSTON.
I TOLD YOU HOW TO REVIVE THE GIRL, DIDN'T I? I DIDN'T HARM HER, JUST KEPT HER DRUGGED SO SHE'D STAY QUIET. I HAVE A SICKNESS. I CAN GET HELP. YOU...
YOU CAN'T DO THIS--
HE WAS REACHING FOR MY GUN.
DIDN'T HAVE A CHOICE.

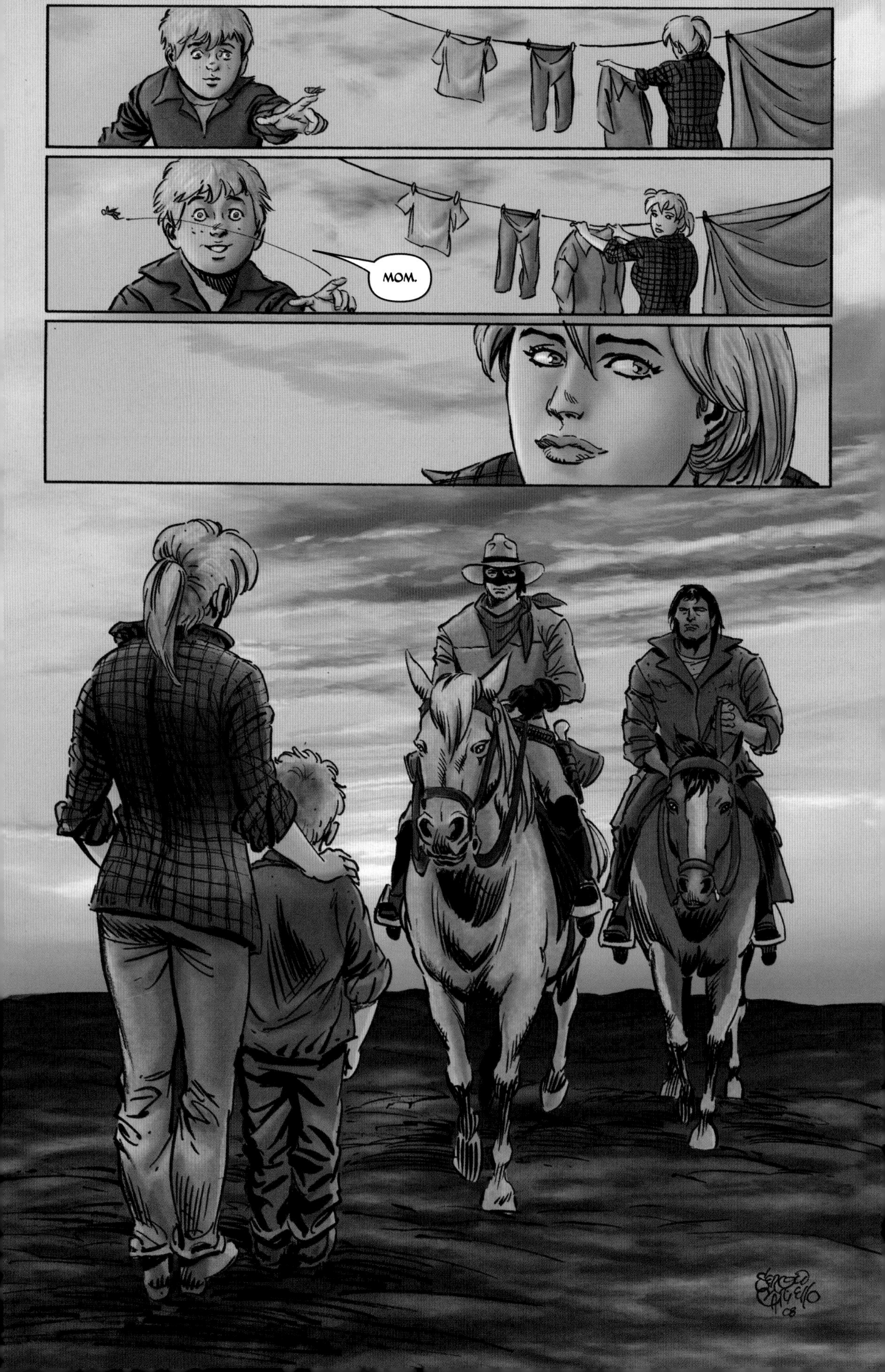
MOM.

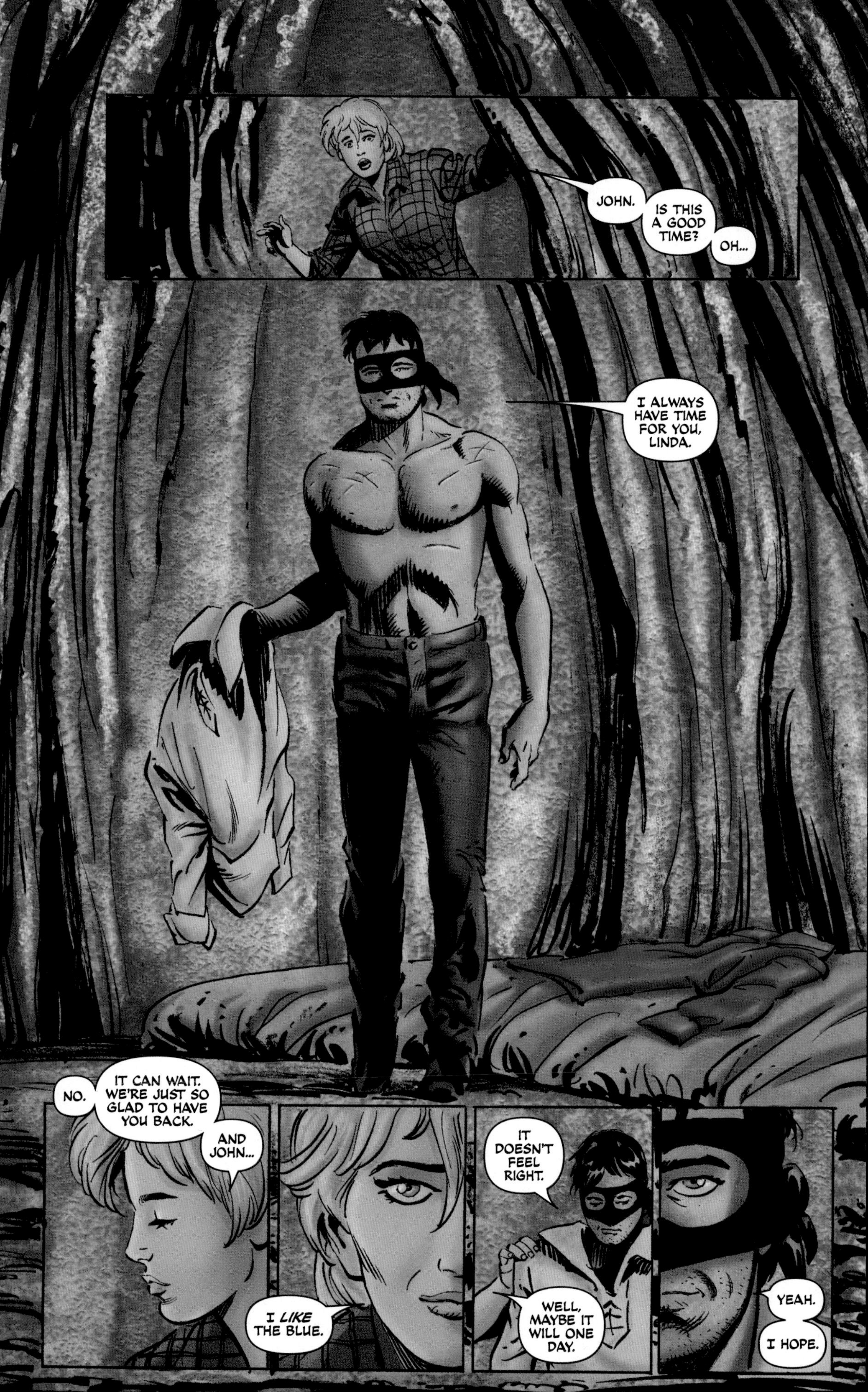
JOHN.
IS THIS A GOOD TIME?
OH...
I ALWAYS HAVE TIME FOR YOU, LINDA.
NO.
IT CAN WAIT. WE'RE JUST SO GLAD TO HAVE YOU BACK.
AND JOHN...
I *LIKE* THE BLUE.
IT DOESN'T FEEL RIGHT.
WELL, MAYBE IT WILL ONE DAY.
YEAH.
I HOPE.

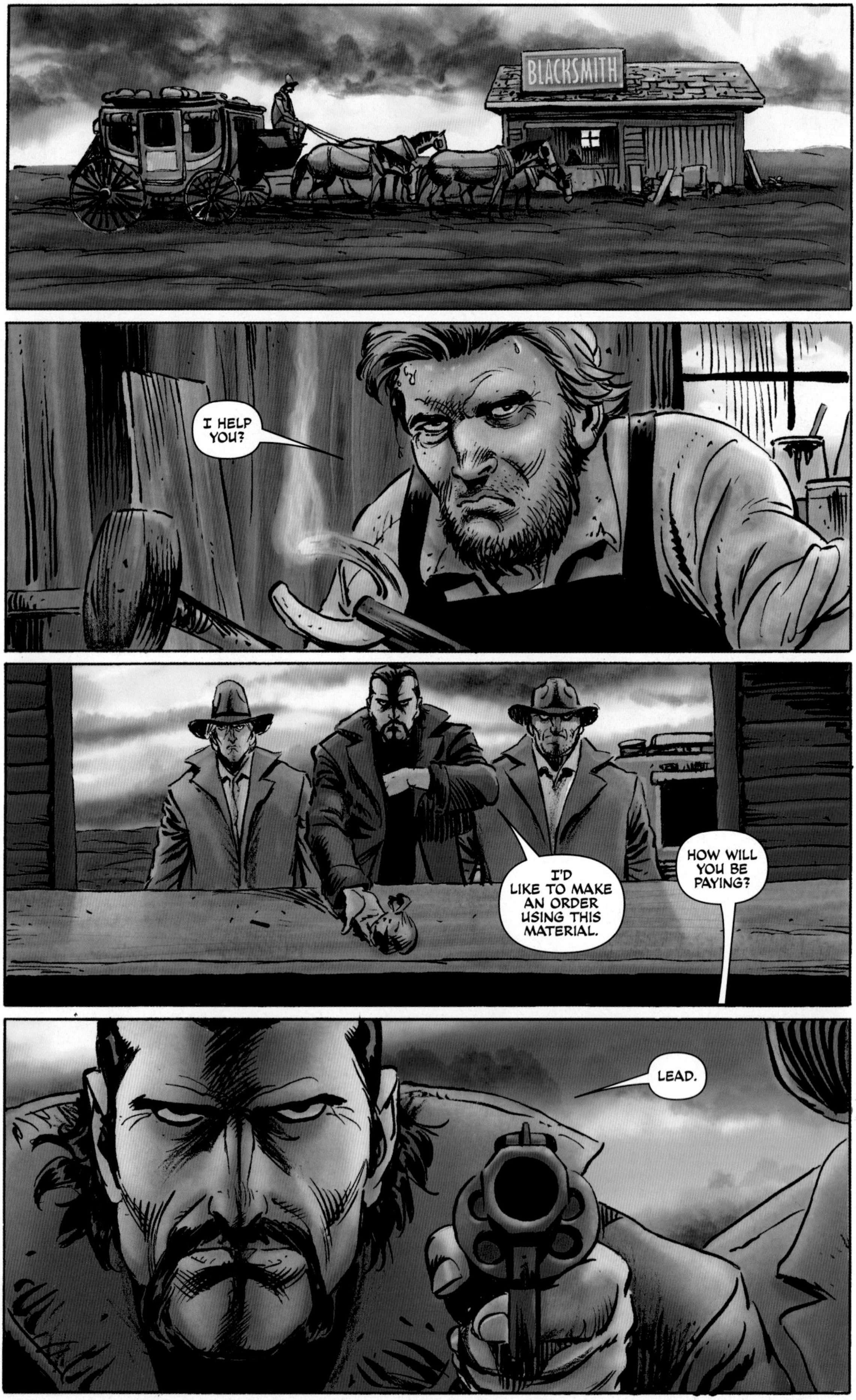
BLACKSMITH
I HELP YOU?
I'D LIKE TO MAKE AN ORDER USING THIS MATERIAL.
HOW WILL YOU BE PAYING?
LEAD.

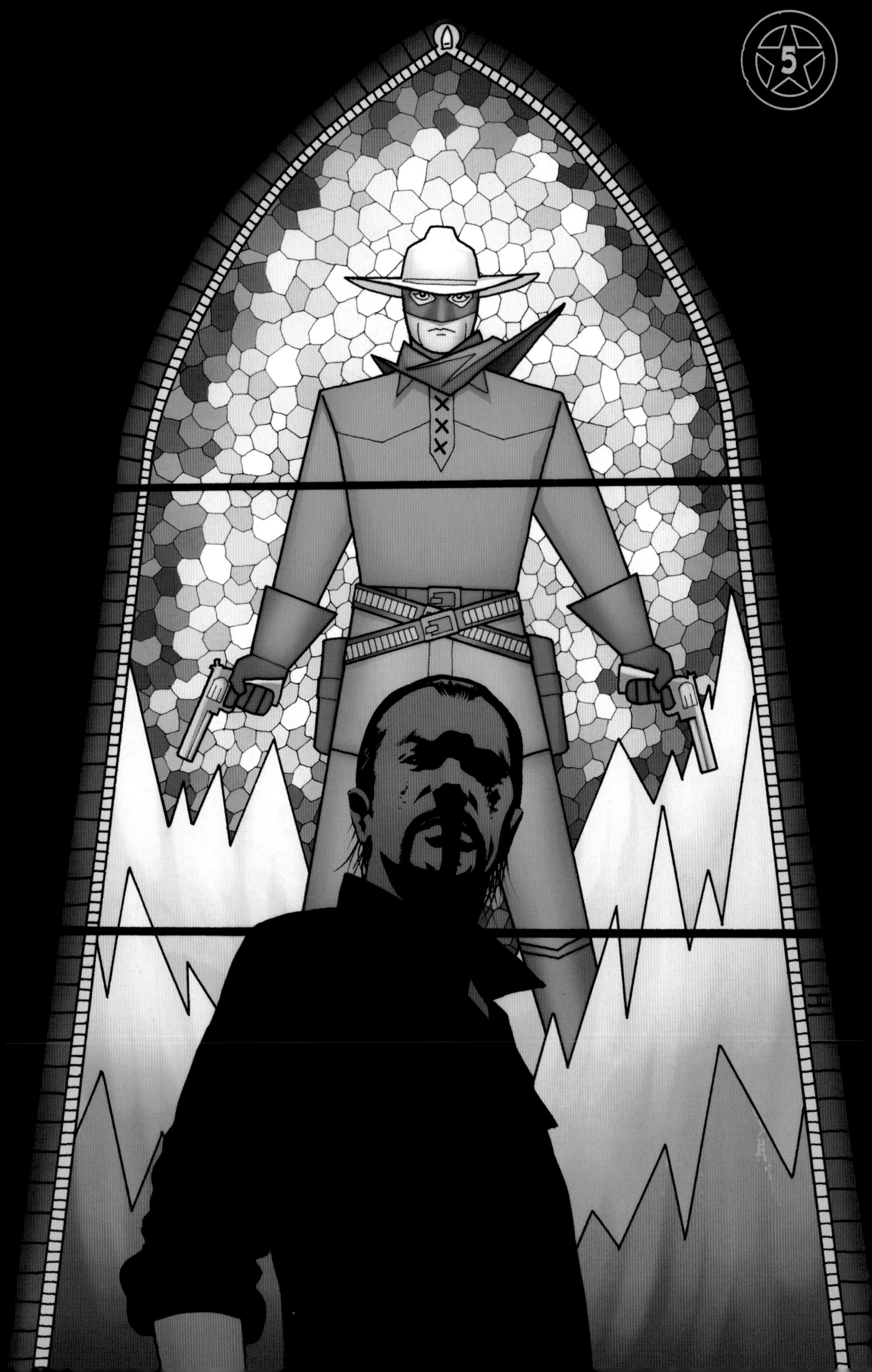
5

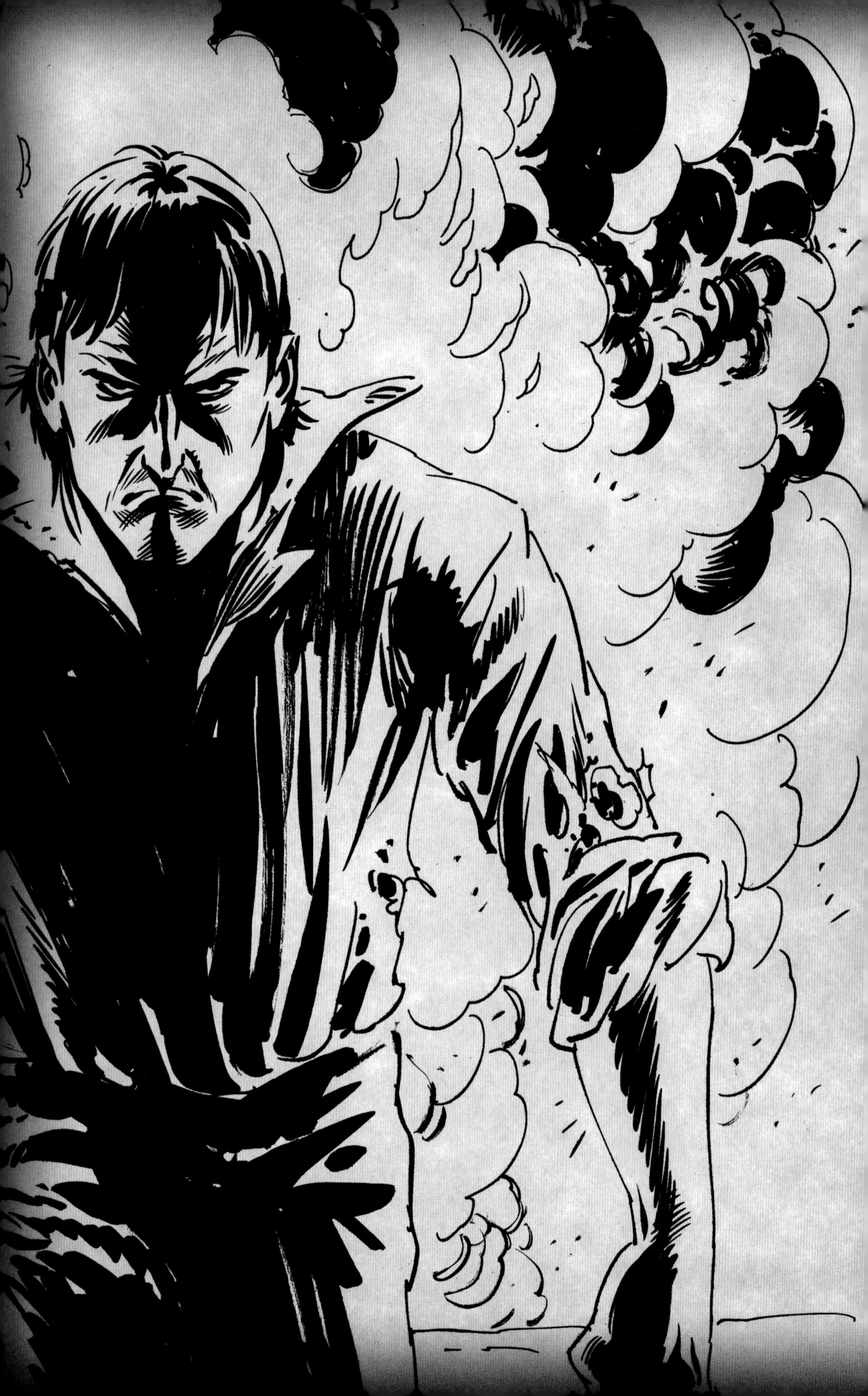

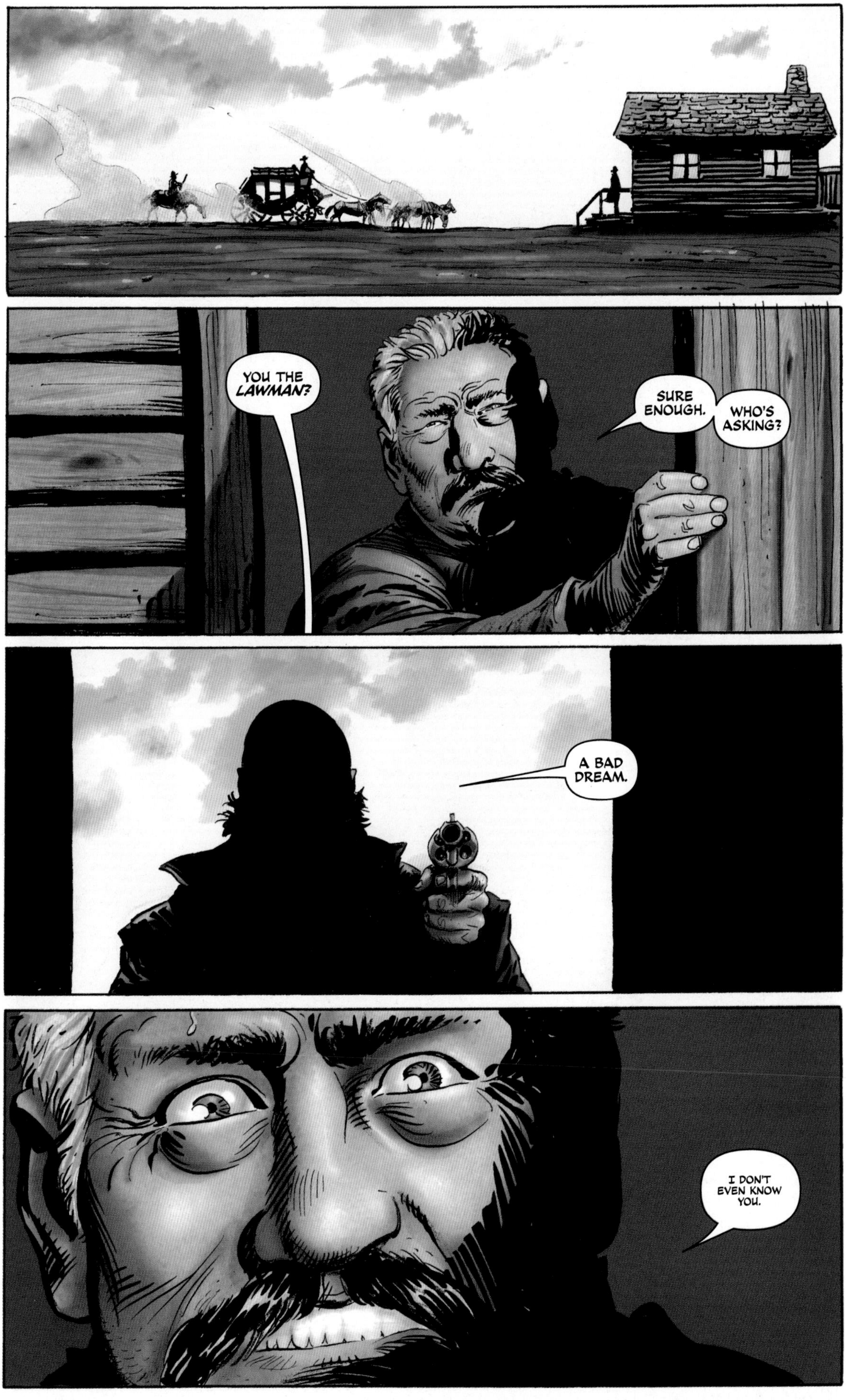
YOU THE LAWMAN?
SURE ENOUGH.
WHO'S ASKING?
A BAD DREAM.
I DON'T EVEN KNOW YOU.

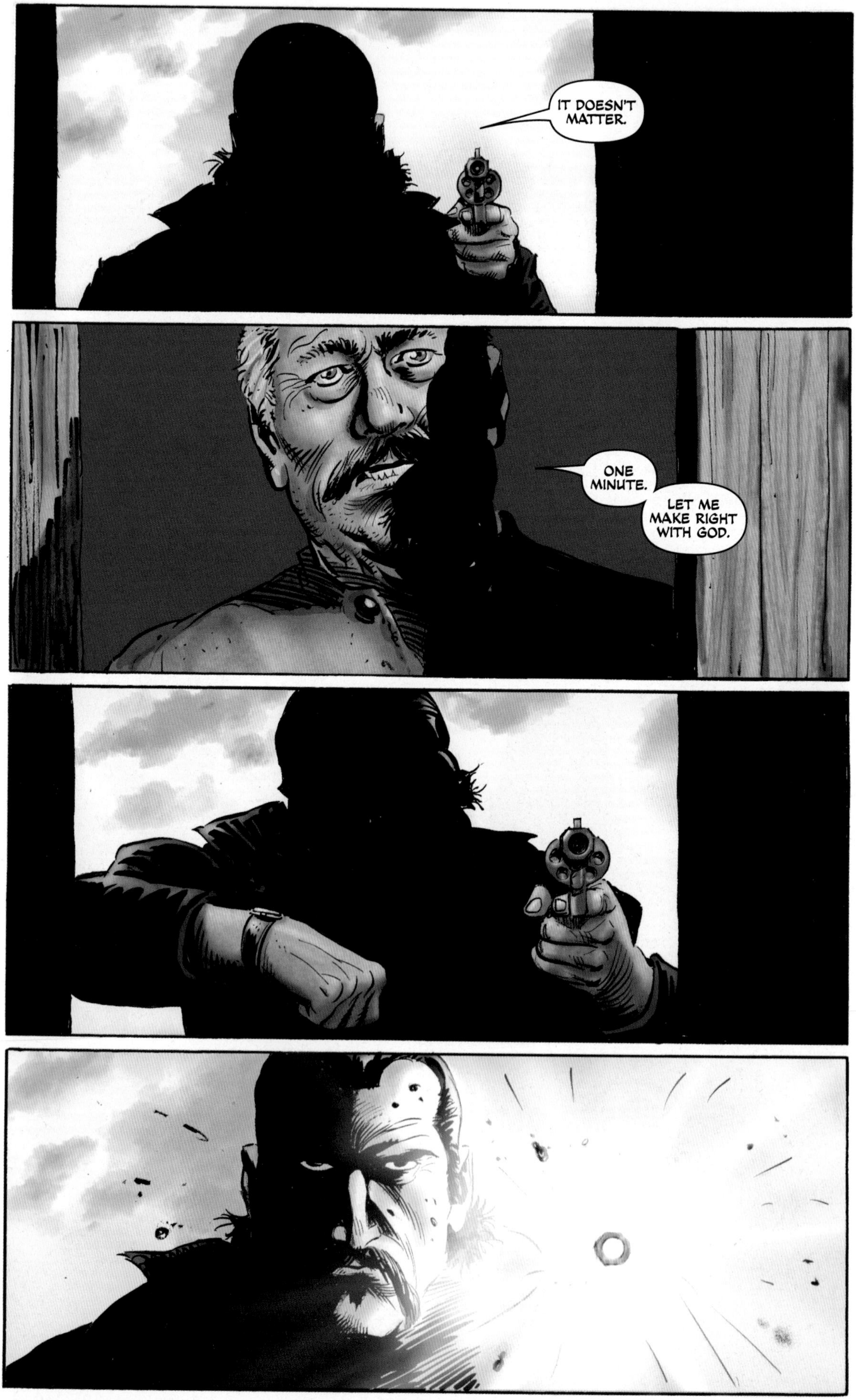
IT DOESN'T MATTER.
ONE MINUTE.
LET ME MAKE RIGHT WITH GOD.

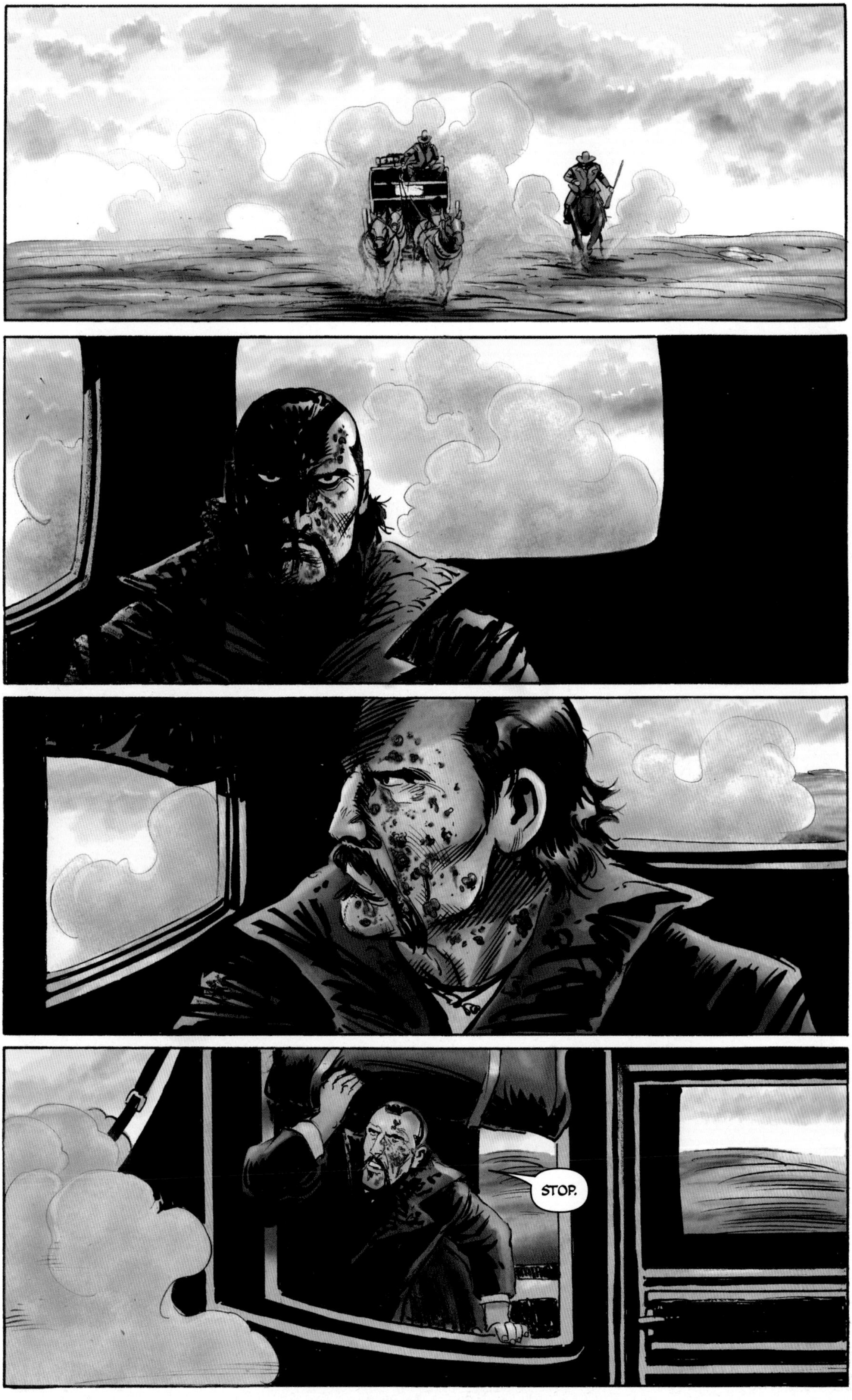
STOP.

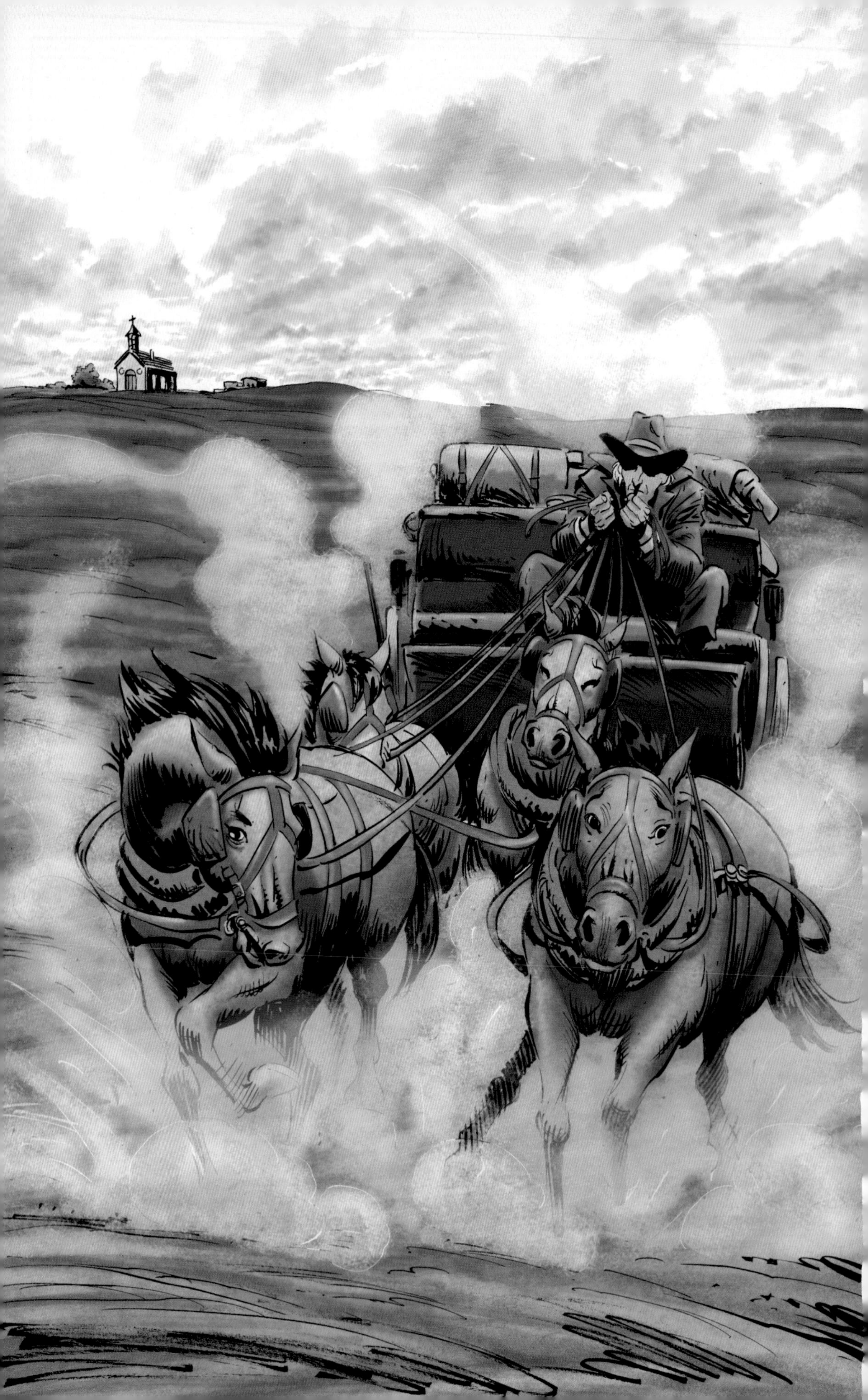

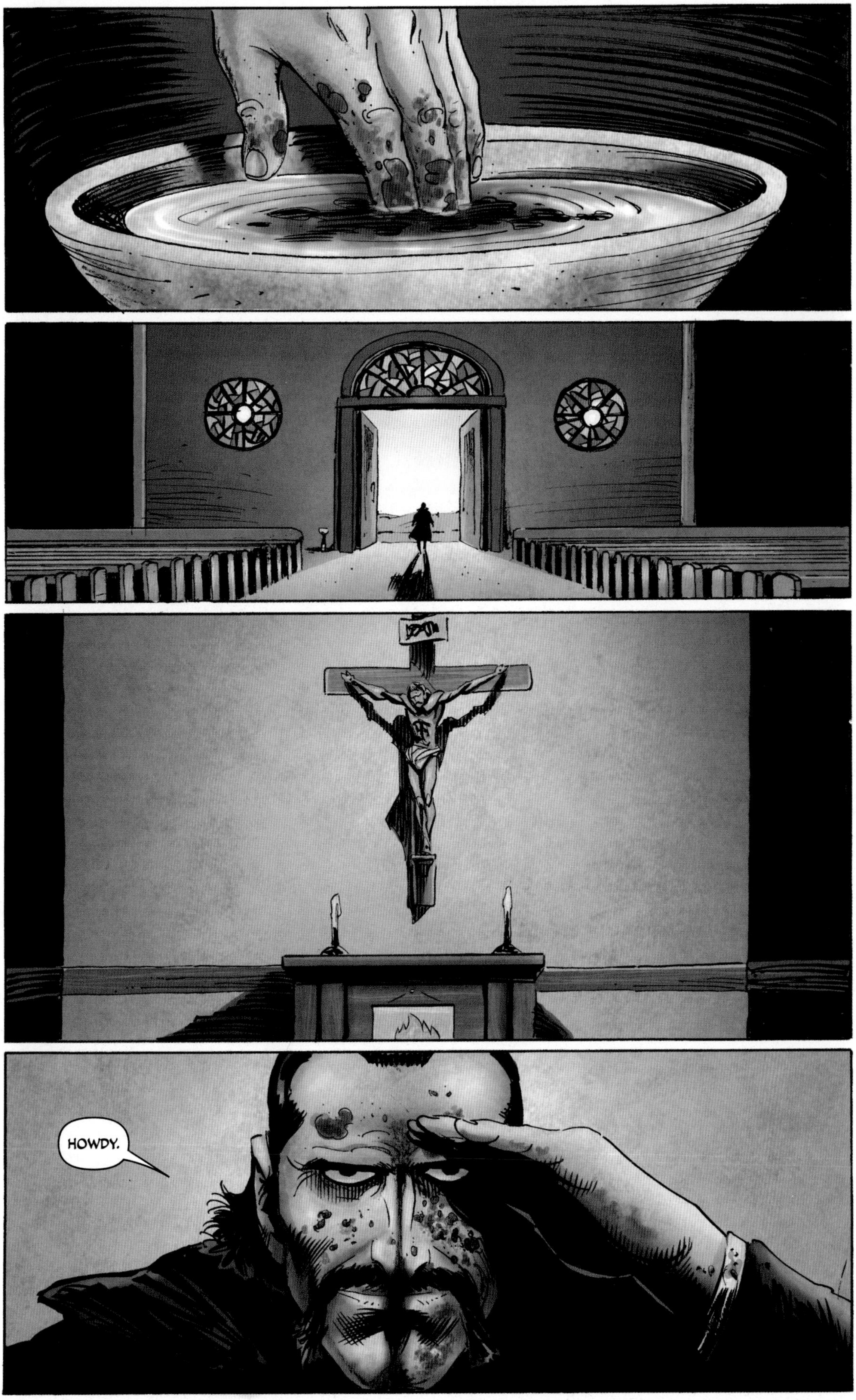
HOWDY.

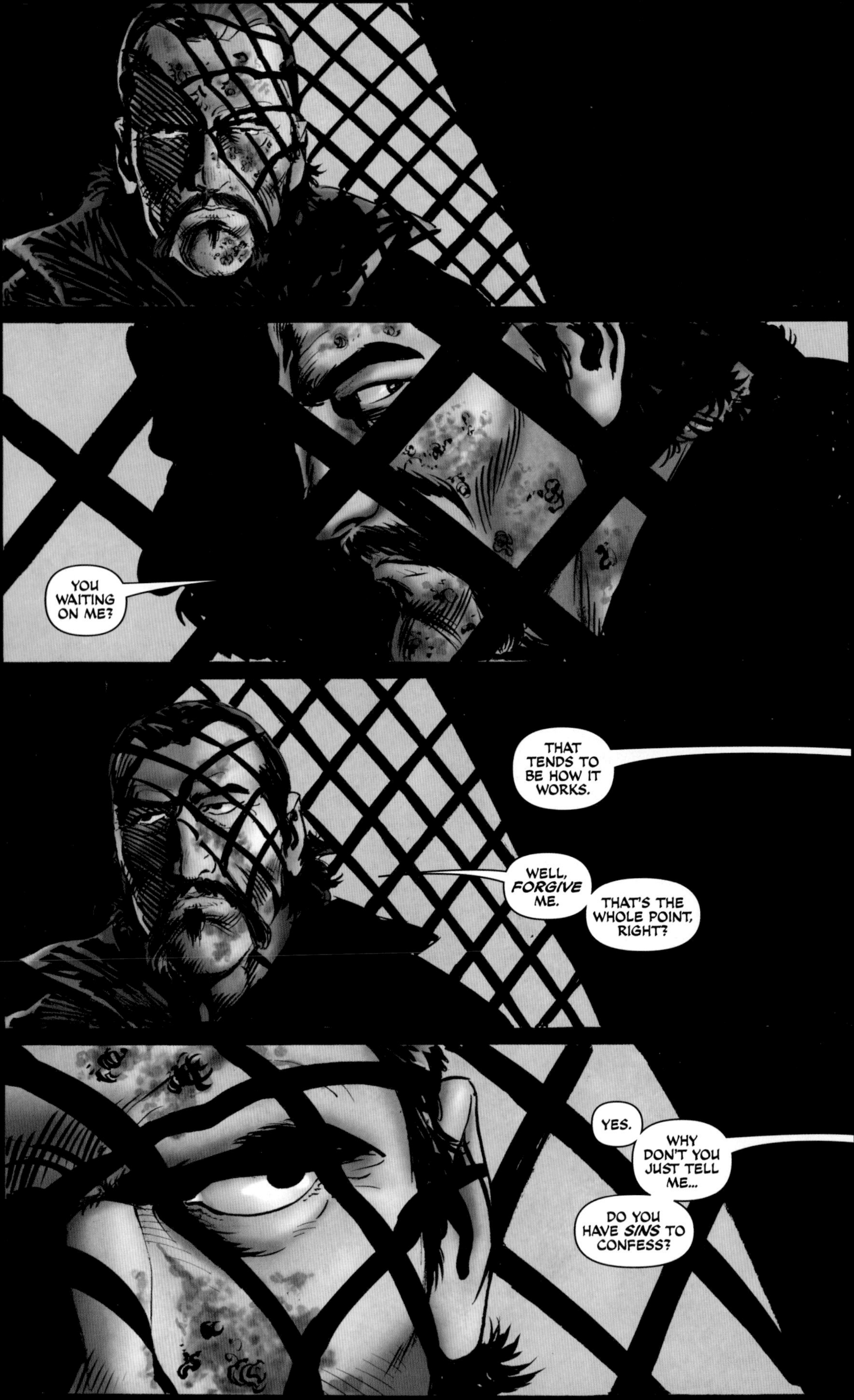
YOU WAITING ON ME?
THAT TENDS TO BE HOW IT WORKS.
WELL, FORGIVE ME.
THAT'S THE WHOLE POINT, RIGHT?
YES.
WHY DON'T YOU JUST TELL ME...
DO YOU HAVE SINS TO CONFESS?

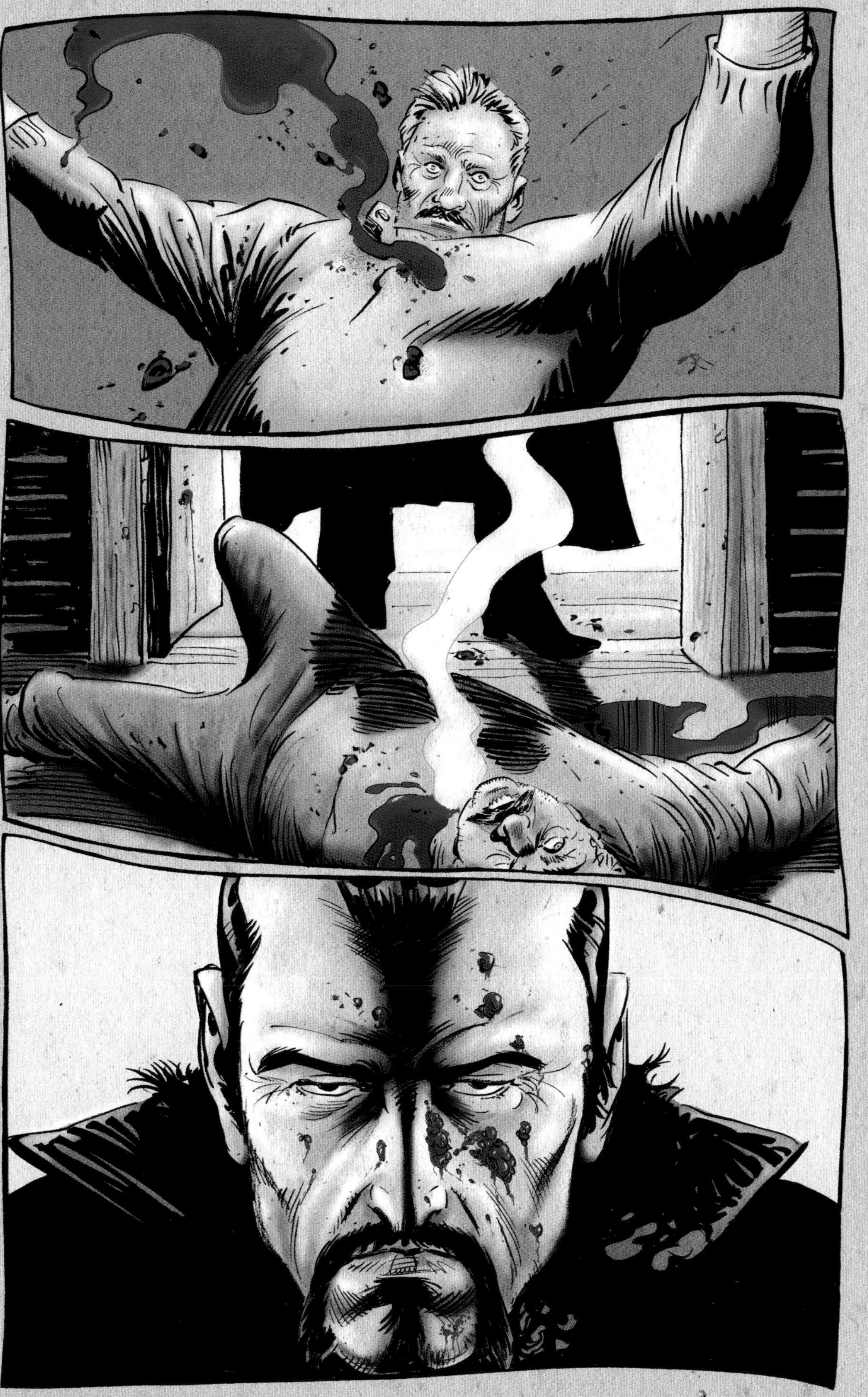

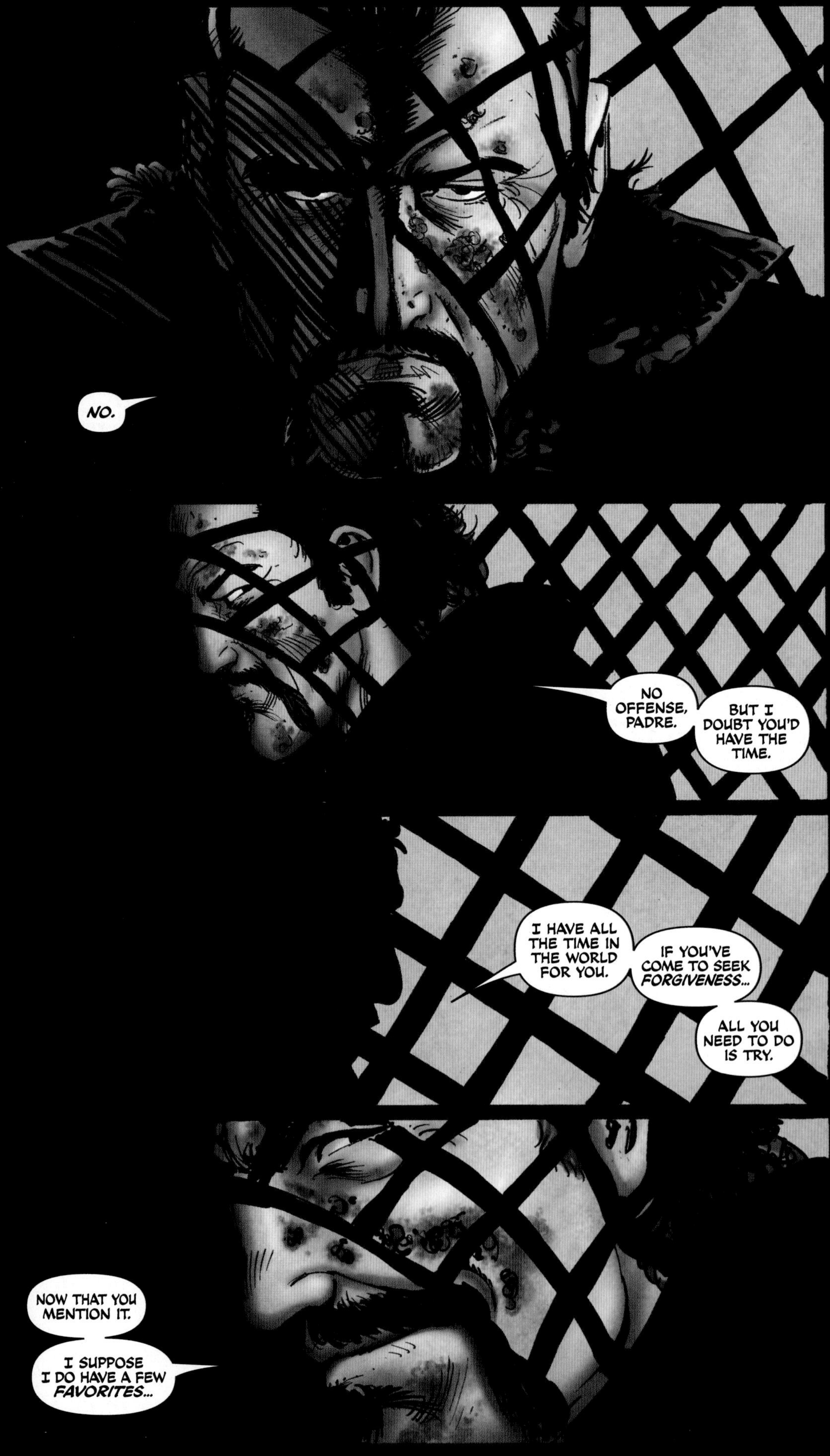
NO.
NO OFFENSE, PADRE.
BUT I DOUBT YOU'D HAVE THE TIME.
I HAVE ALL THE TIME IN THE WORLD FOR YOU.
IF YOU'VE COME TO SEEK *FORGIVENESS*...
ALL YOU NEED TO DO IS TRY.
NOW THAT YOU MENTION IT.
I SUPPOSE I DO HAVE A FEW *FAVORITES*...

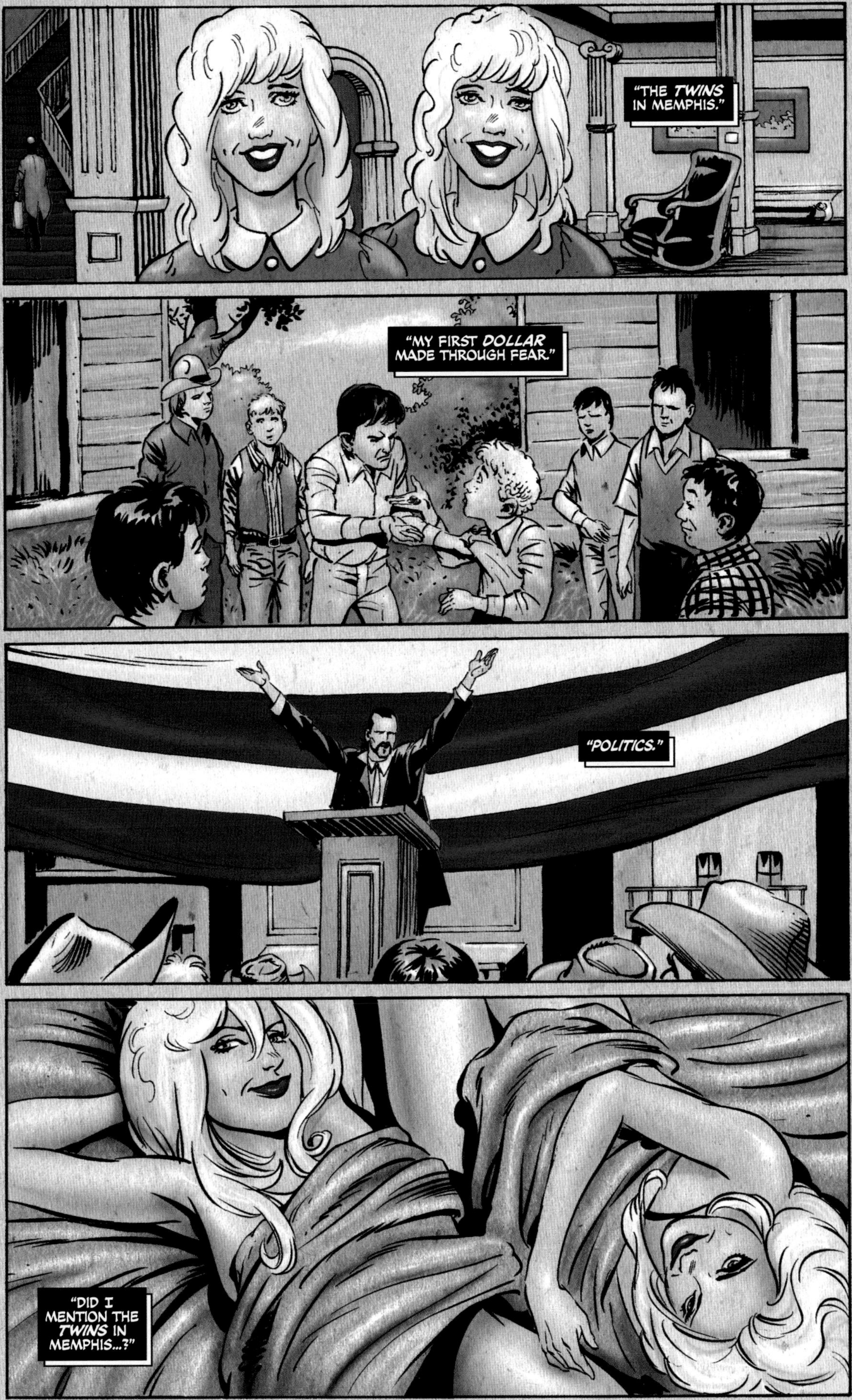
"THE TWINS IN MEMPHIS."
"MY FIRST DOLLAR MADE THROUGH FEAR."
"POLITICS."
"DID I MENTION THE TWINS IN MEMPHIS...?"

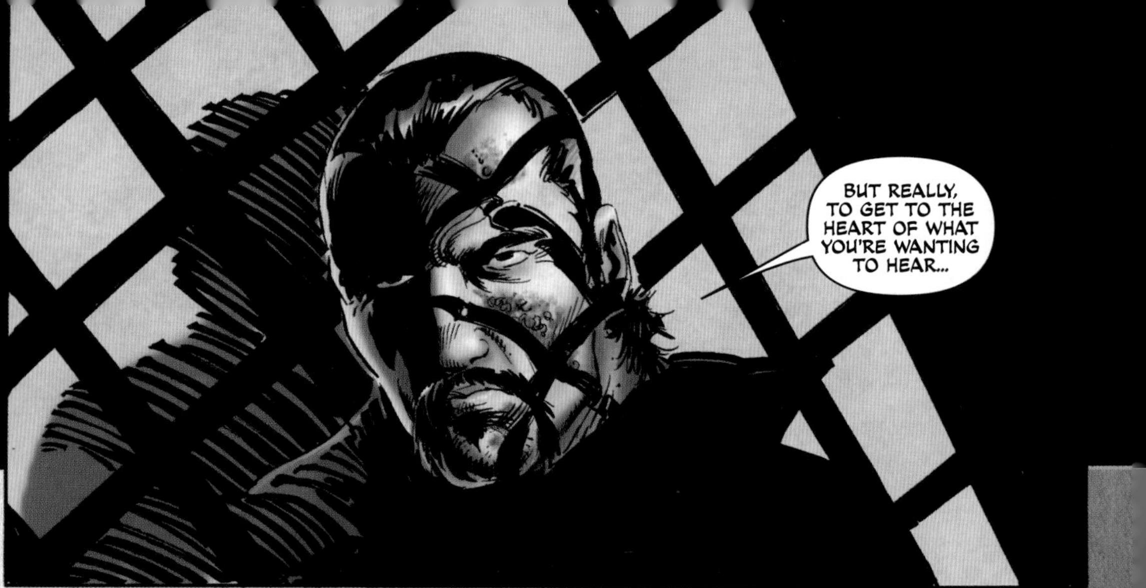
BUT REALLY, TO GET TO THE HEART OF WHAT YOU'RE WANTING TO HEAR...

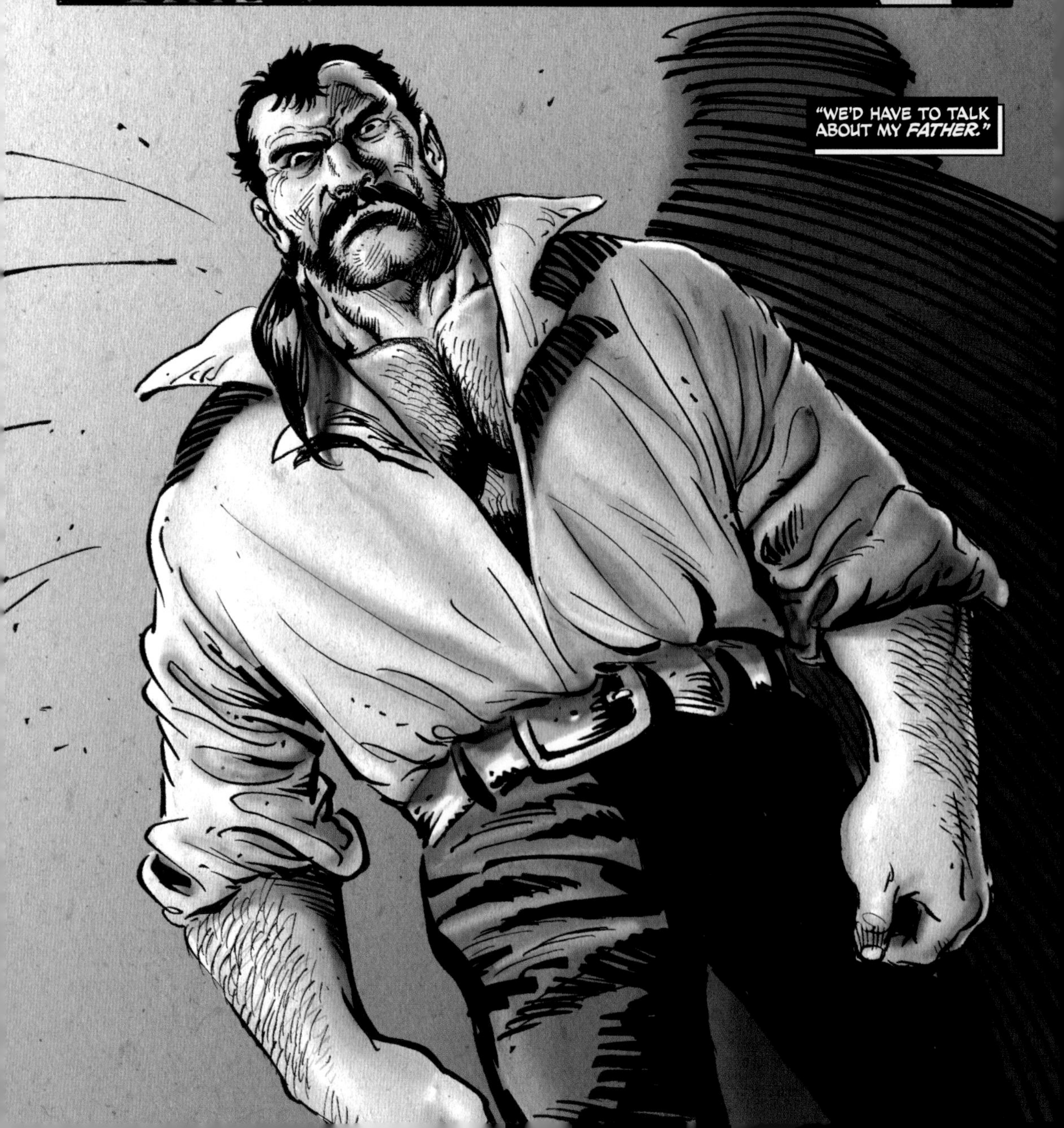
"WE'D HAVE TO TALK ABOUT MY *FATHER.*"

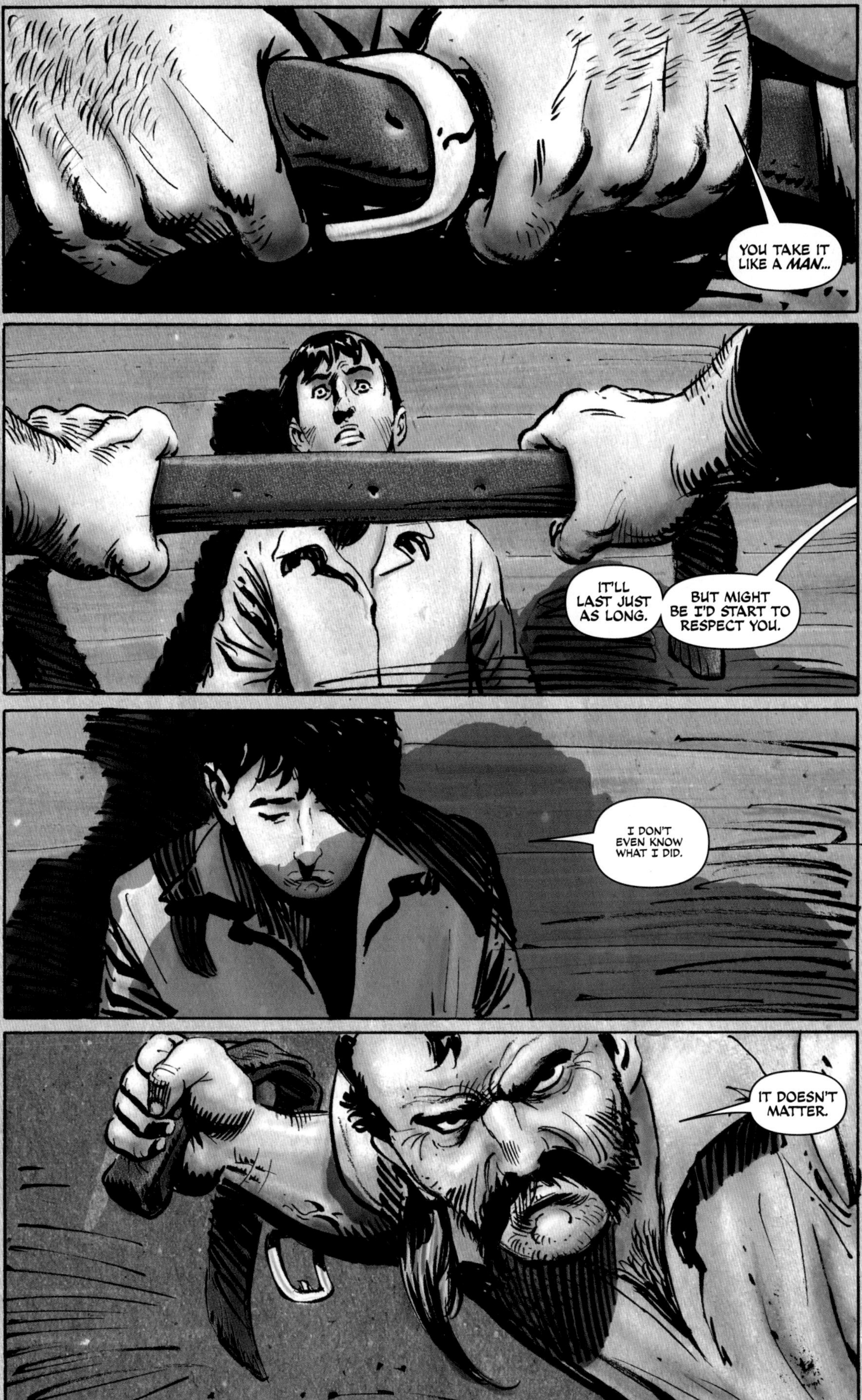
YOU TAKE IT LIKE A *MAN*...
IT'LL LAST JUST AS LONG.
BUT MIGHT BE I'D START TO RESPECT YOU.
I DON'T EVEN KNOW WHAT I DID.
IT DOESN'T MATTER.

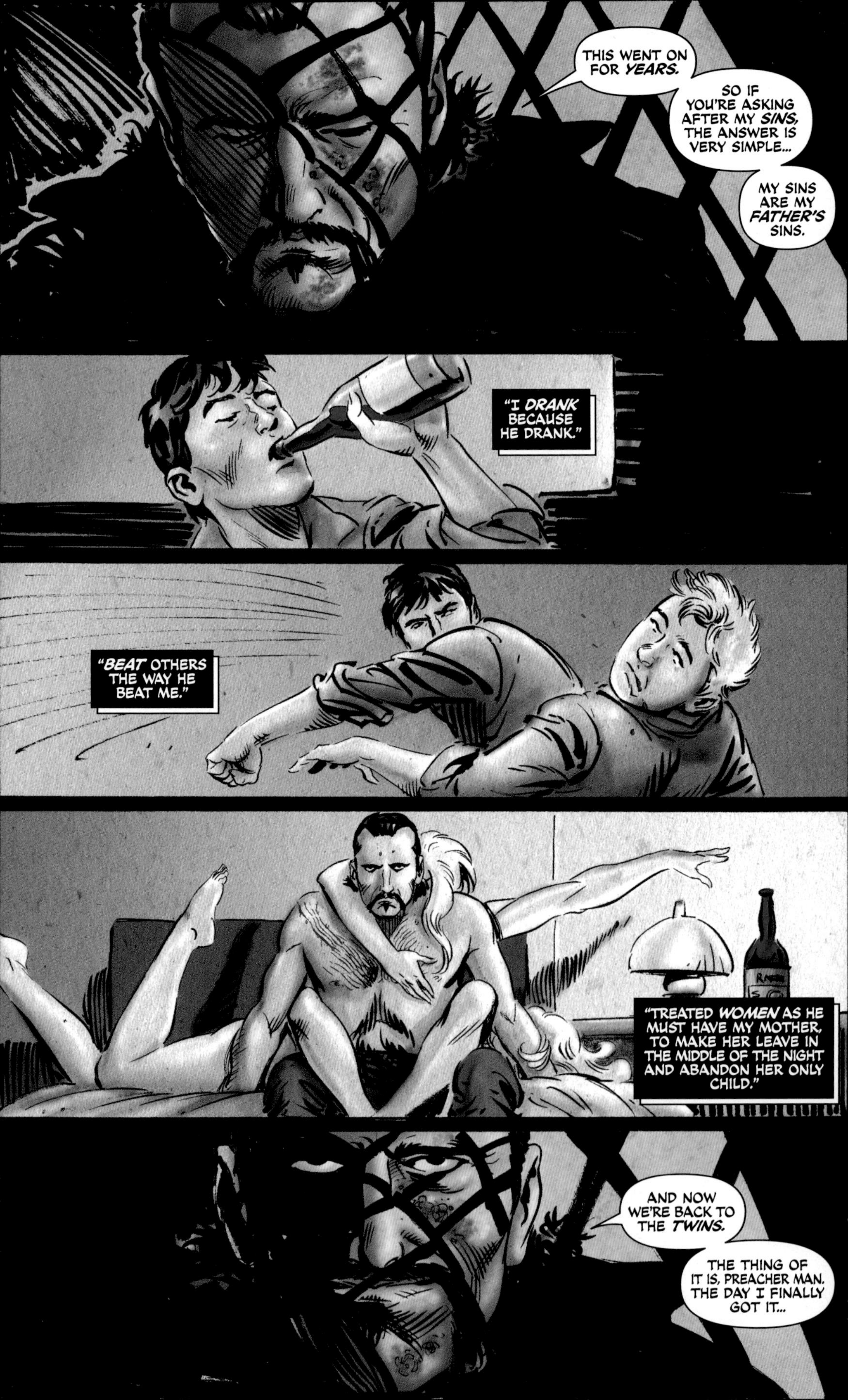
THIS WENT ON FOR YEARS.
SO IF YOU'RE ASKING AFTER MY SINS, THE ANSWER IS VERY SIMPLE...
MY SINS ARE MY FATHER'S SINS.
"I DRANK BECAUSE HE DRANK."
"BEAT OTHERS THE WAY HE BEAT ME."
"TREATED WOMEN AS HE MUST HAVE MY MOTHER, TO MAKE HER LEAVE IN THE MIDDLE OF THE NIGHT AND ABANDON HER ONLY CHILD."
AND NOW WE'RE BACK TO THE TWINS.
THE THING OF IT IS, PREACHER MAN. THE DAY I FINALLY GOT IT...

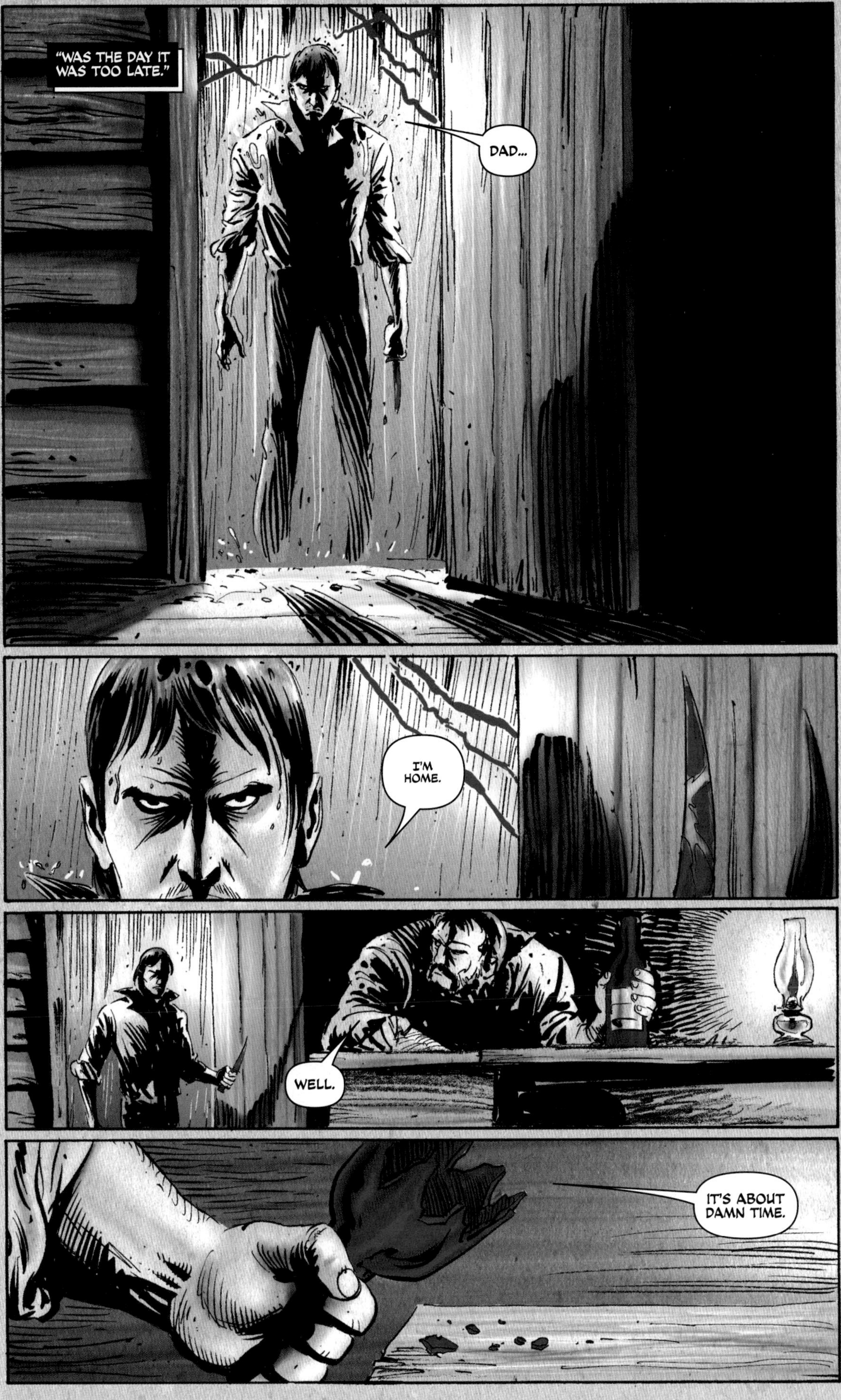
"WAS THE DAY IT WAS TOO LATE."
DAD...
I'M HOME.
WELL.
IT'S ABOUT DAMN TIME.

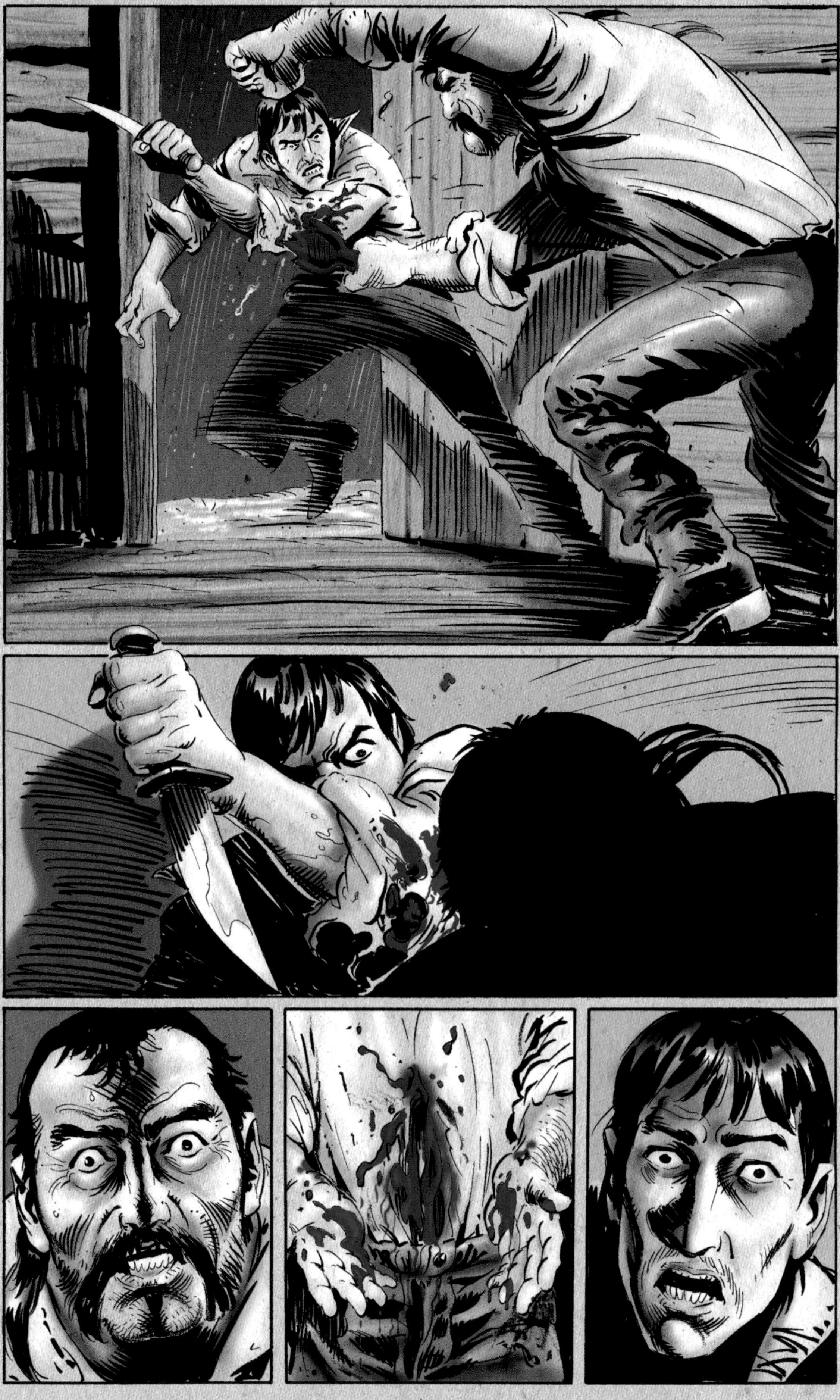

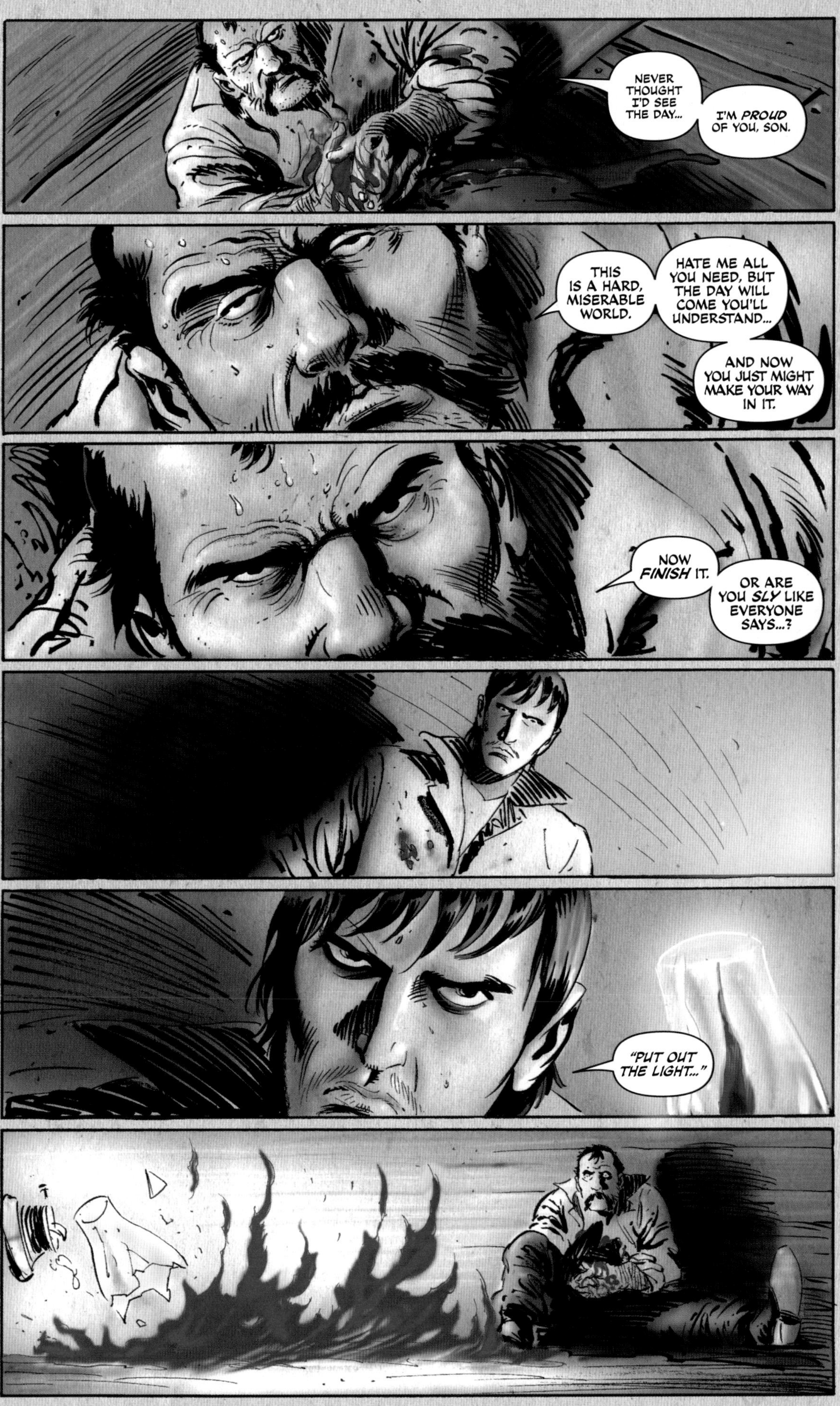
NEVER THOUGHT I'D SEE THE DAY...
I'M *PROUD* OF YOU, SON.
THIS IS A HARD, MISERABLE WORLD.
HATE ME ALL YOU NEED, BUT THE DAY WILL COME YOU'LL UNDERSTAND...
AND NOW YOU JUST MIGHT MAKE YOUR WAY IN IT.
NOW *FINISH* IT.
OR ARE YOU *SLY* LIKE EVERYONE SAYS...?
"PUT OUT THE LIGHT..."

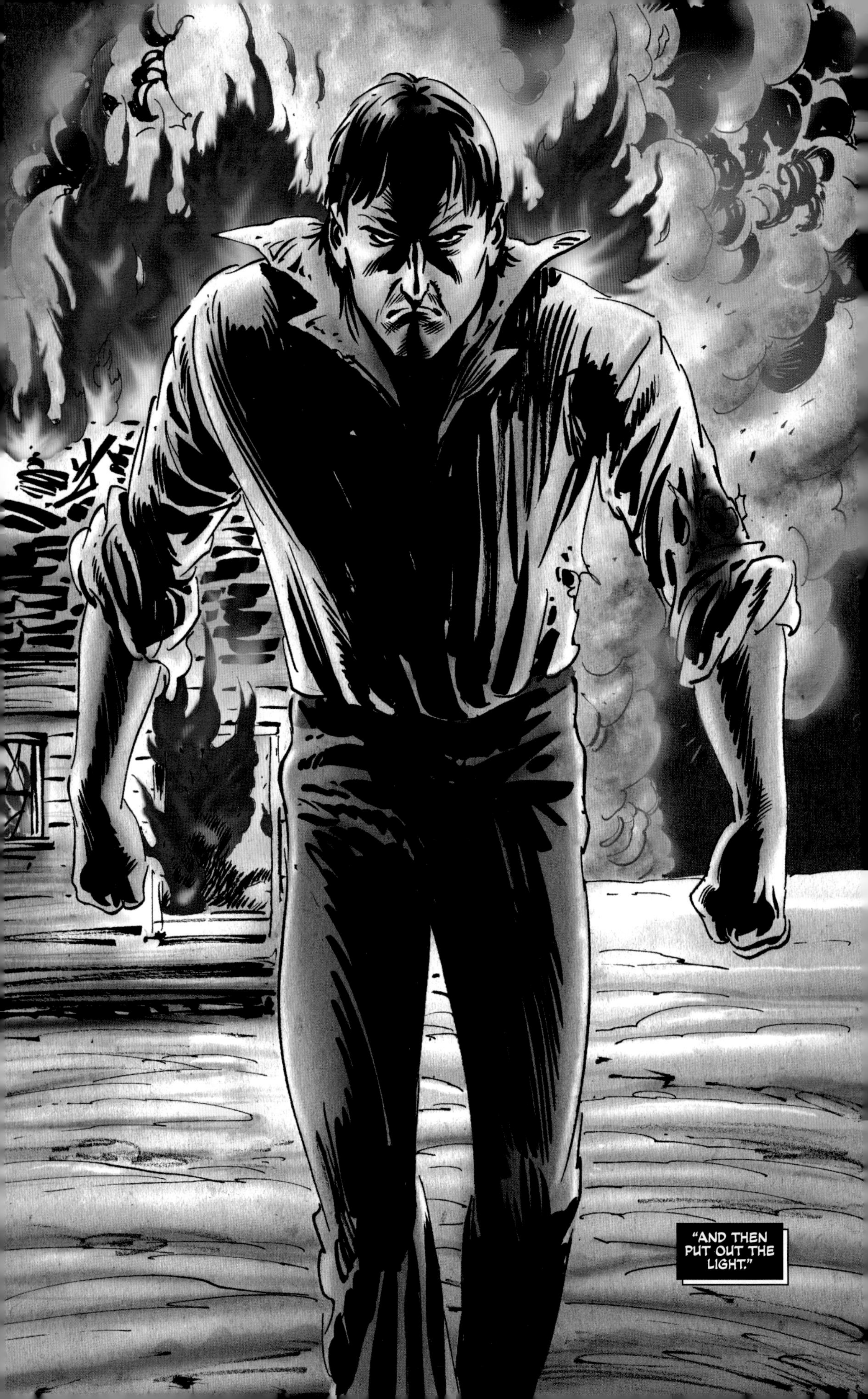
"AND THEN PUT OUT THE LIGHT."

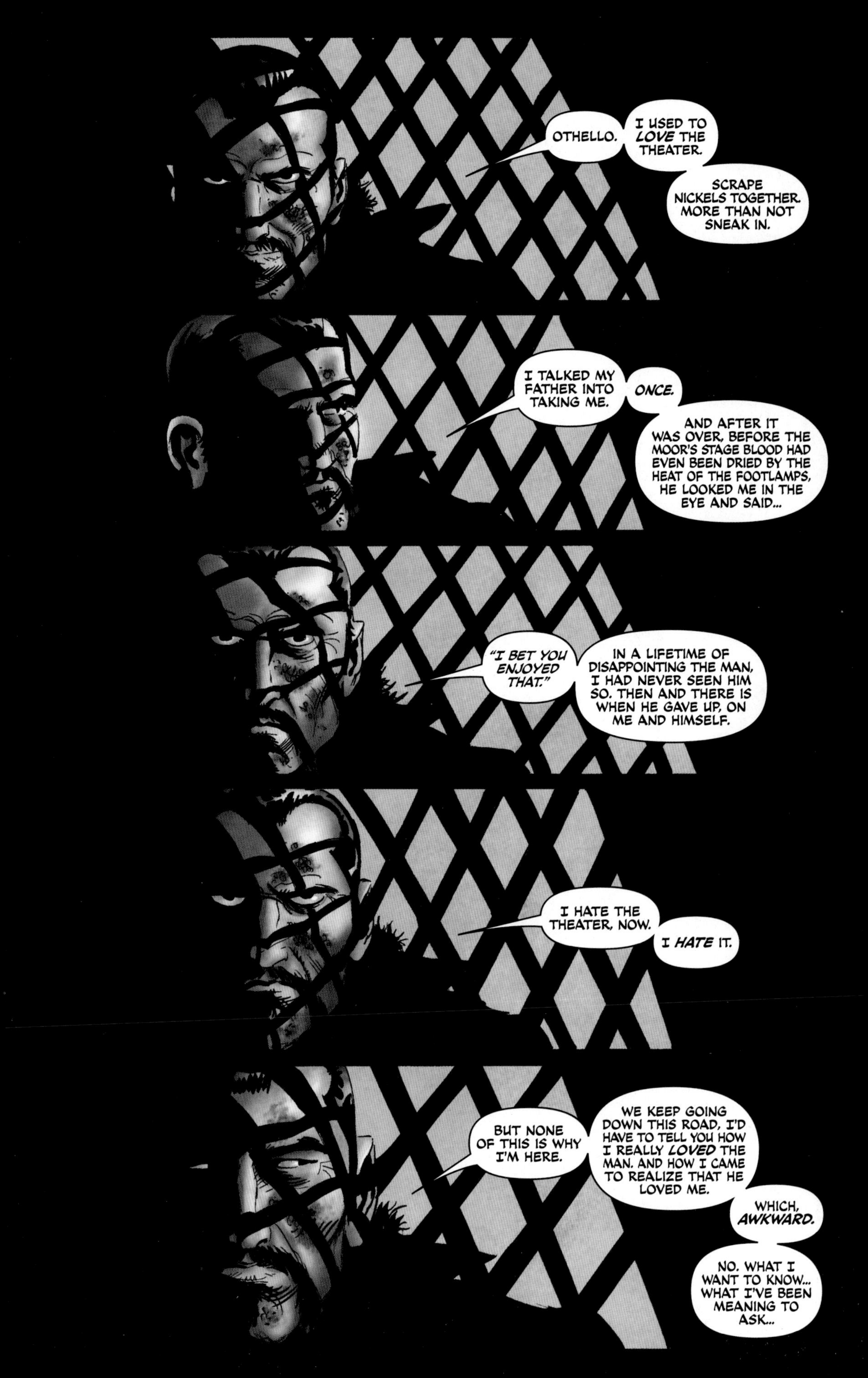

OTHELLO.
I USED TO *LOVE* THE THEATER.
SCRAPE NICKELS TOGETHER. MORE THAN NOT SNEAK IN.
I TALKED MY FATHER INTO TAKING ME.
ONCE.
AND AFTER IT WAS OVER, BEFORE THE MOOR'S STAGE BLOOD HAD EVEN BEEN DRIED BY THE HEAT OF THE FOOTLAMPS, HE LOOKED ME IN THE EYE AND SAID...
"I BET YOU ENJOYED THAT."
IN A LIFETIME OF DISAPPOINTING THE MAN, I HAD NEVER SEEN HIM SO. THEN AND THERE IS WHEN HE GAVE UP, ON ME AND HIMSELF.
I HATE THE THEATER, NOW.
I *HATE* IT.
BUT NONE OF THIS IS WHY I'M HERE.
WE KEEP GOING DOWN THIS ROAD, I'D HAVE TO TELL YOU HOW I REALLY *LOVED* THE MAN. AND HOW I CAME TO REALIZE THAT HE LOVED ME.
WHICH, ***AWKWARD.***
NO. WHAT I WANT TO KNOW... WHAT I'VE BEEN MEANING TO ASK...

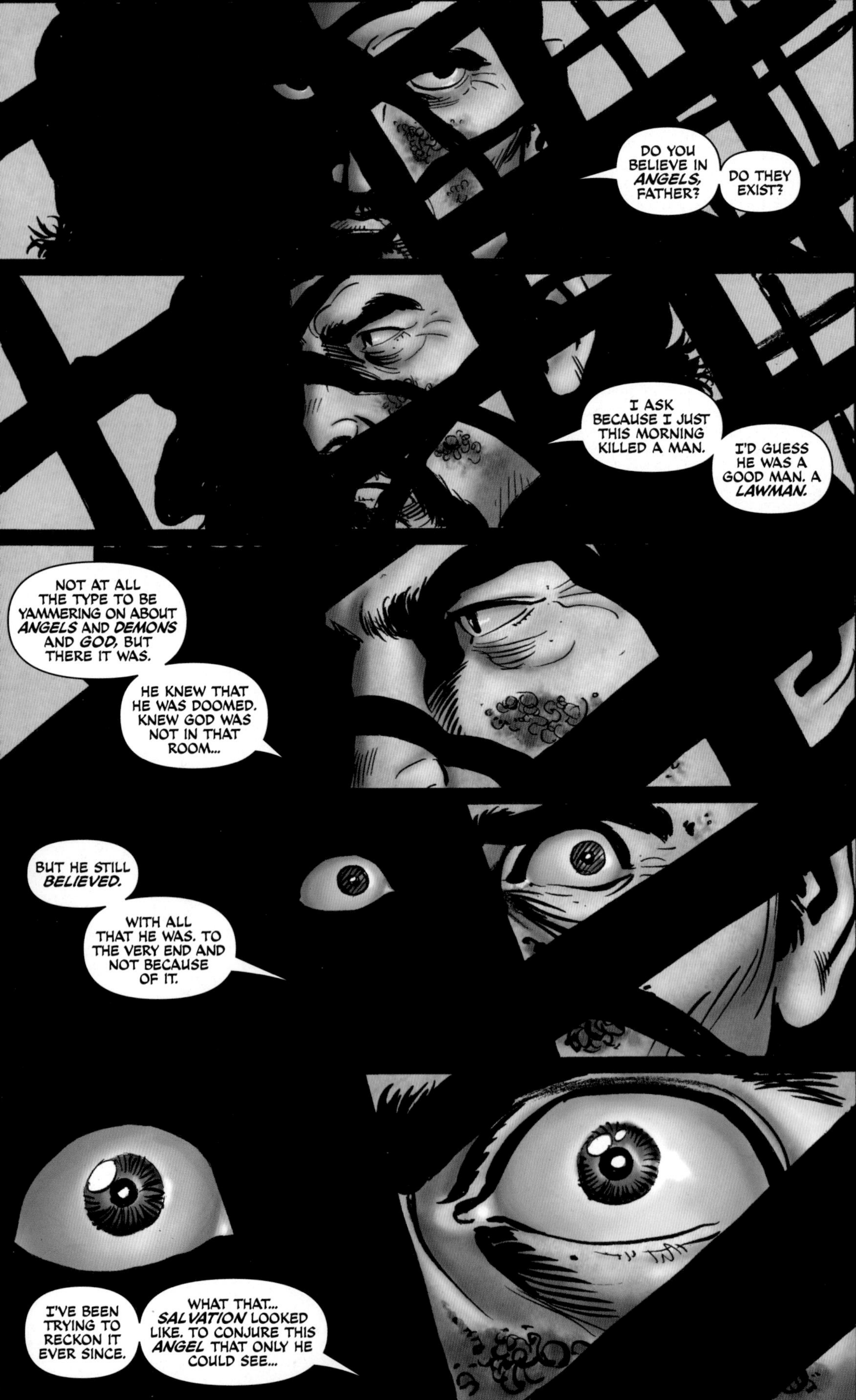
DO YOU BELIEVE IN *ANGELS,* FATHER?
DO THEY EXIST?
I ASK BECAUSE I JUST THIS MORNING KILLED A MAN.
I'D GUESS HE WAS A GOOD MAN. A *LAWMAN.*
NOT AT ALL THE TYPE TO BE YAMMERING ON ABOUT *ANGELS* AND *DEMONS* AND *GOD,* BUT THERE IT WAS.
HE KNEW THAT HE WAS DOOMED. KNEW GOD WAS NOT IN THAT ROOM...
BUT HE STILL *BELIEVED.*
WITH ALL THAT HE WAS. TO THE VERY END AND NOT BECAUSE OF IT.
I'VE BEEN TRYING TO RECKON IT EVER SINCE.
WHAT THAT... *SALVATION* LOOKED LIKE. TO CONJURE THIS *ANGEL* THAT ONLY HE COULD SEE...

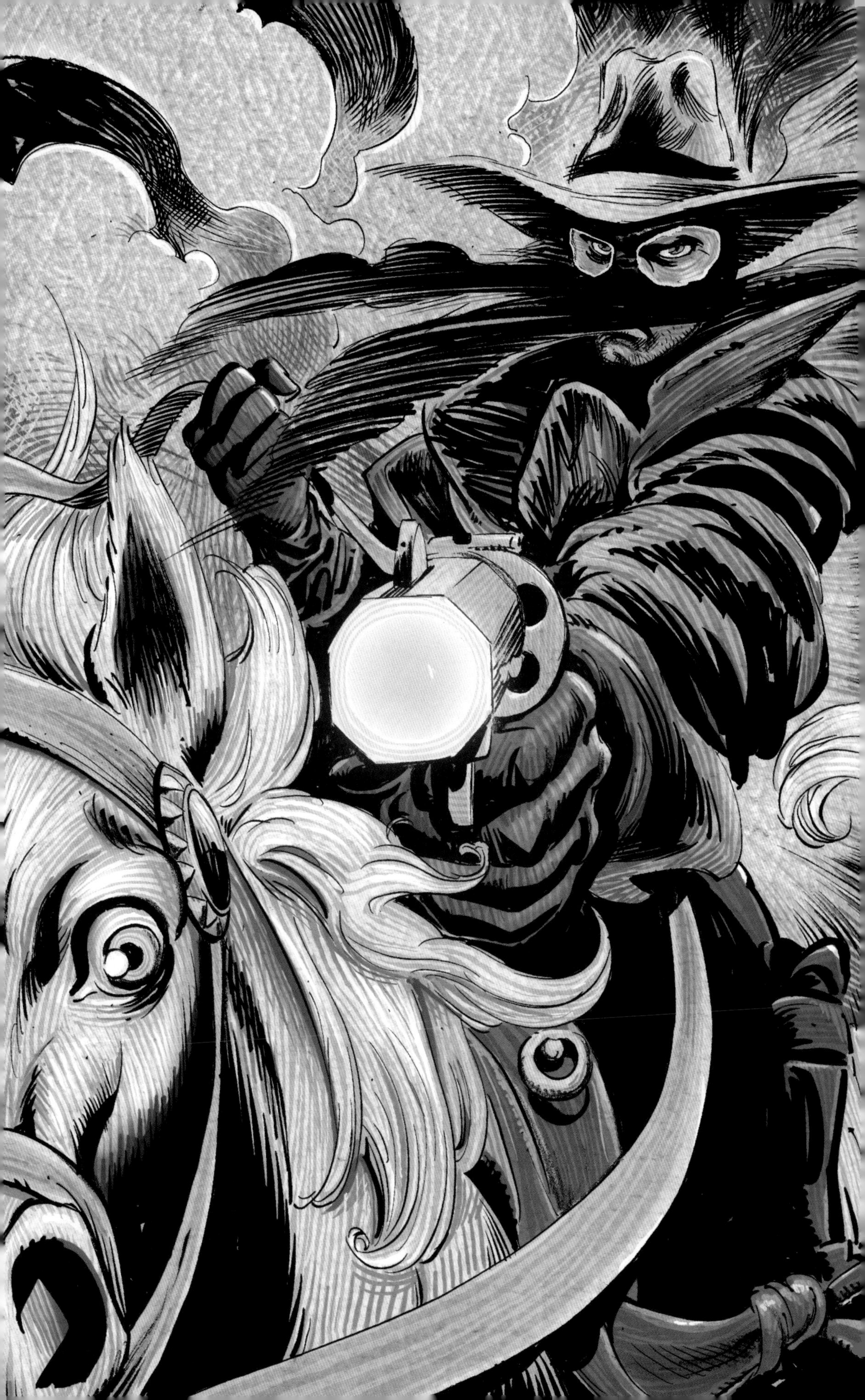

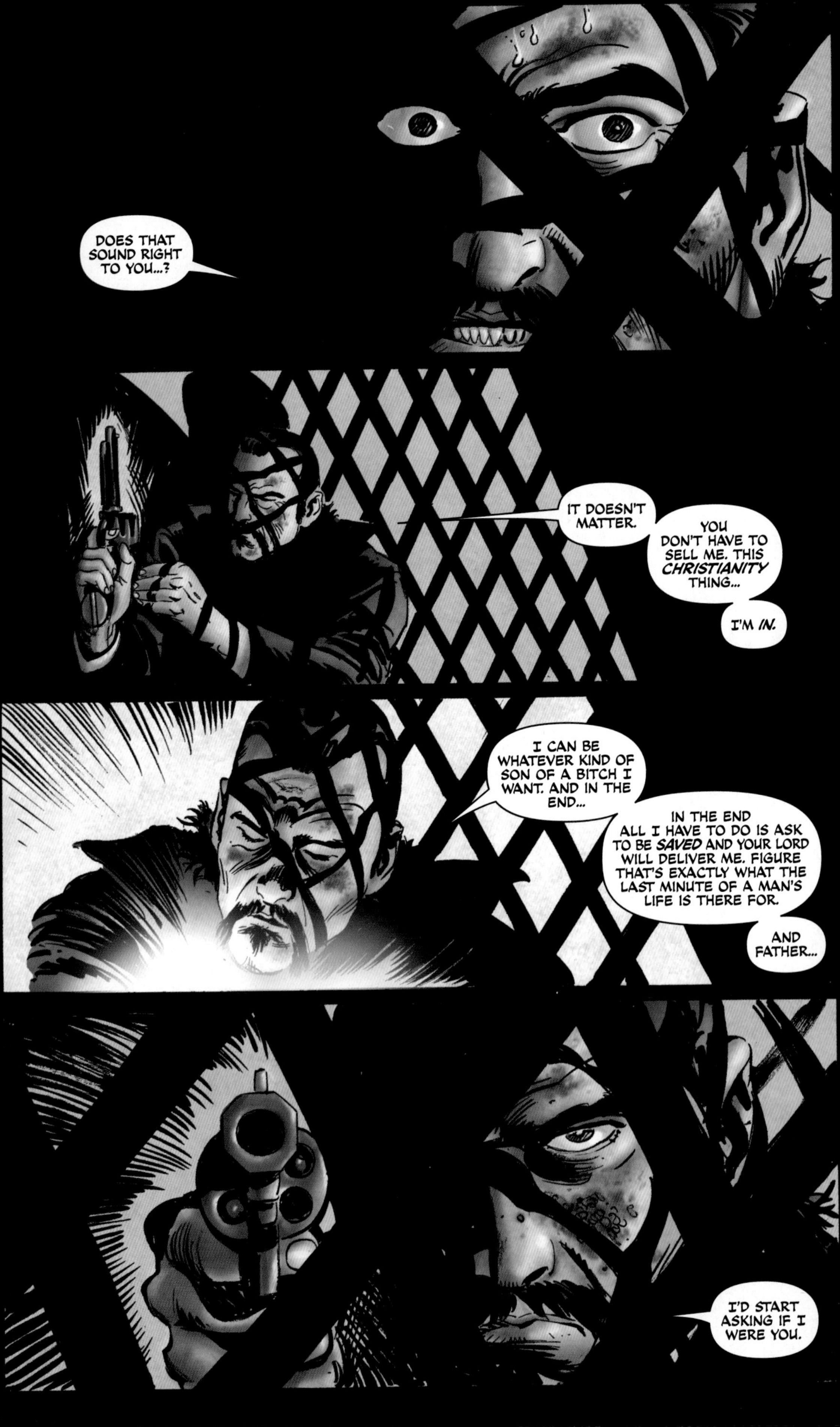
DOES THAT SOUND RIGHT TO YOU...?
IT DOESN'T MATTER.
YOU DON'T HAVE TO SELL ME. THIS *CHRISTIANITY* THING...
I'M *IN.*
I CAN BE WHATEVER KIND OF SON OF A BITCH I WANT. AND IN THE END...
IN THE END ALL I HAVE TO DO IS ASK TO BE *SAVED* AND YOUR LORD WILL DELIVER ME. FIGURE THAT'S EXACTLY WHAT THE LAST MINUTE OF A MAN'S LIFE IS THERE FOR.
AND FATHER...
I'D START ASKING IF I WERE YOU.

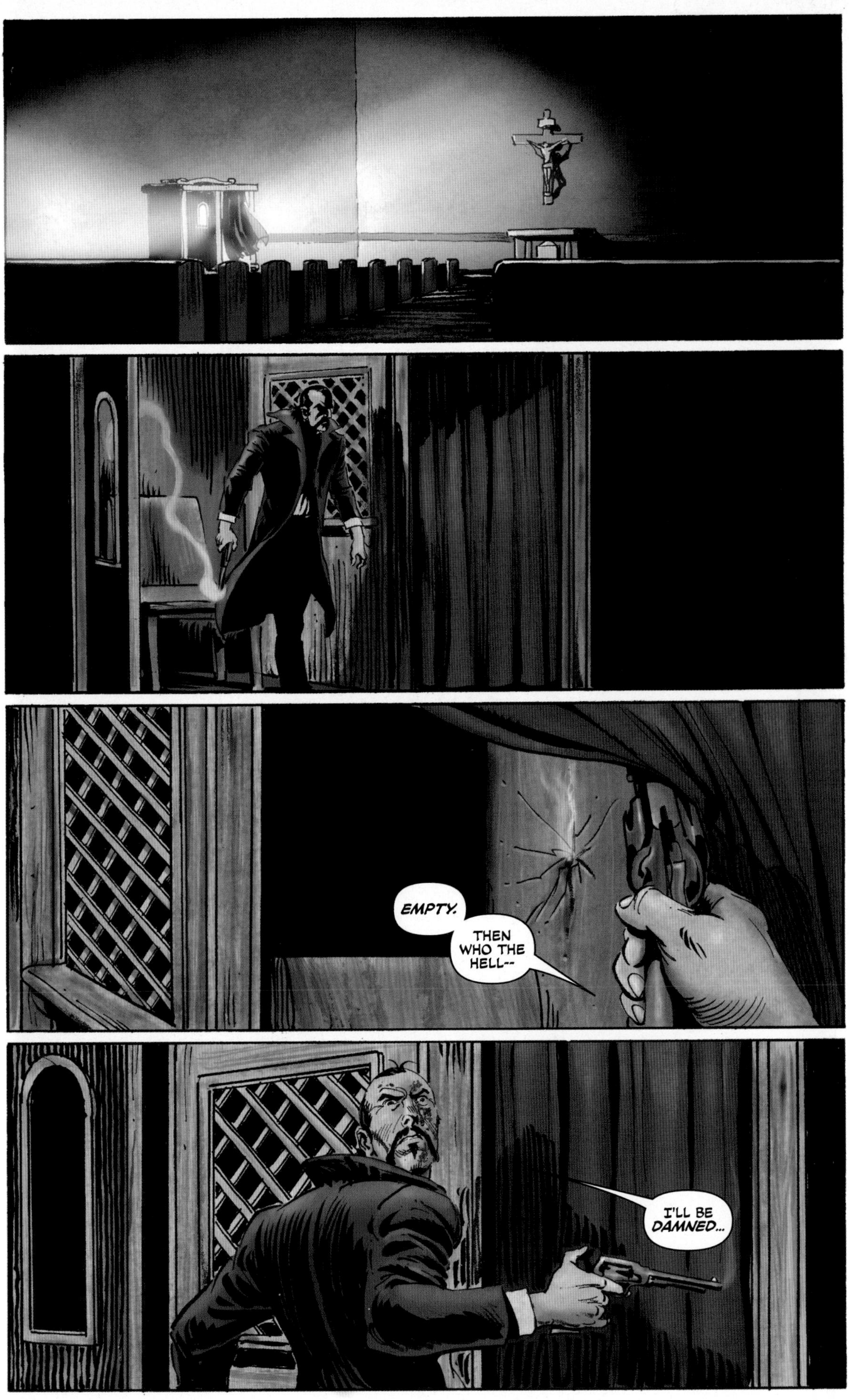
EMPTY.
THEN WHO THE HELL--
I'LL BE DAMNED...

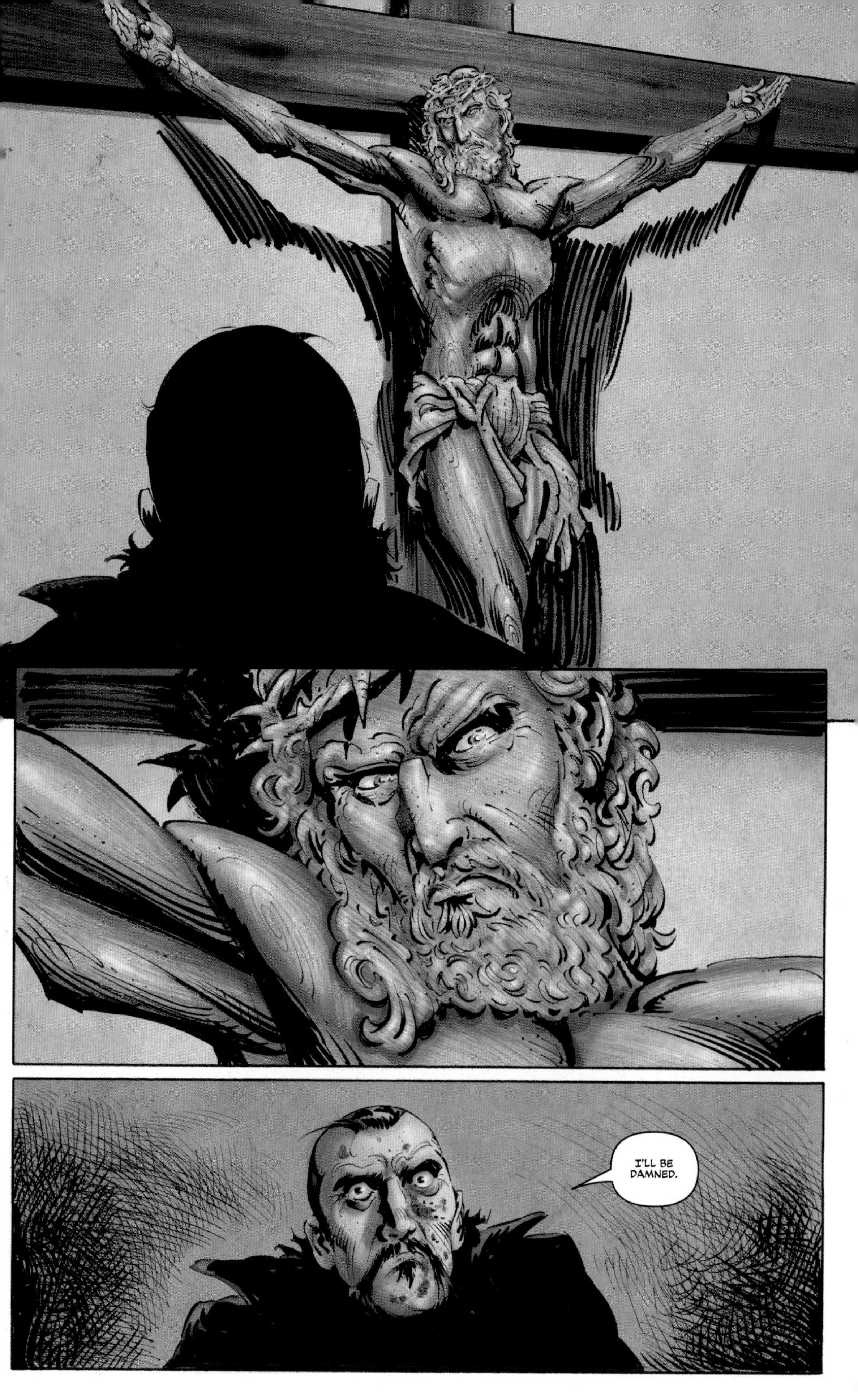
I'LL BE DAMNED.

THE LONE RANGER

SKETCHES & PENCILS BY SERGIO CARIELLO

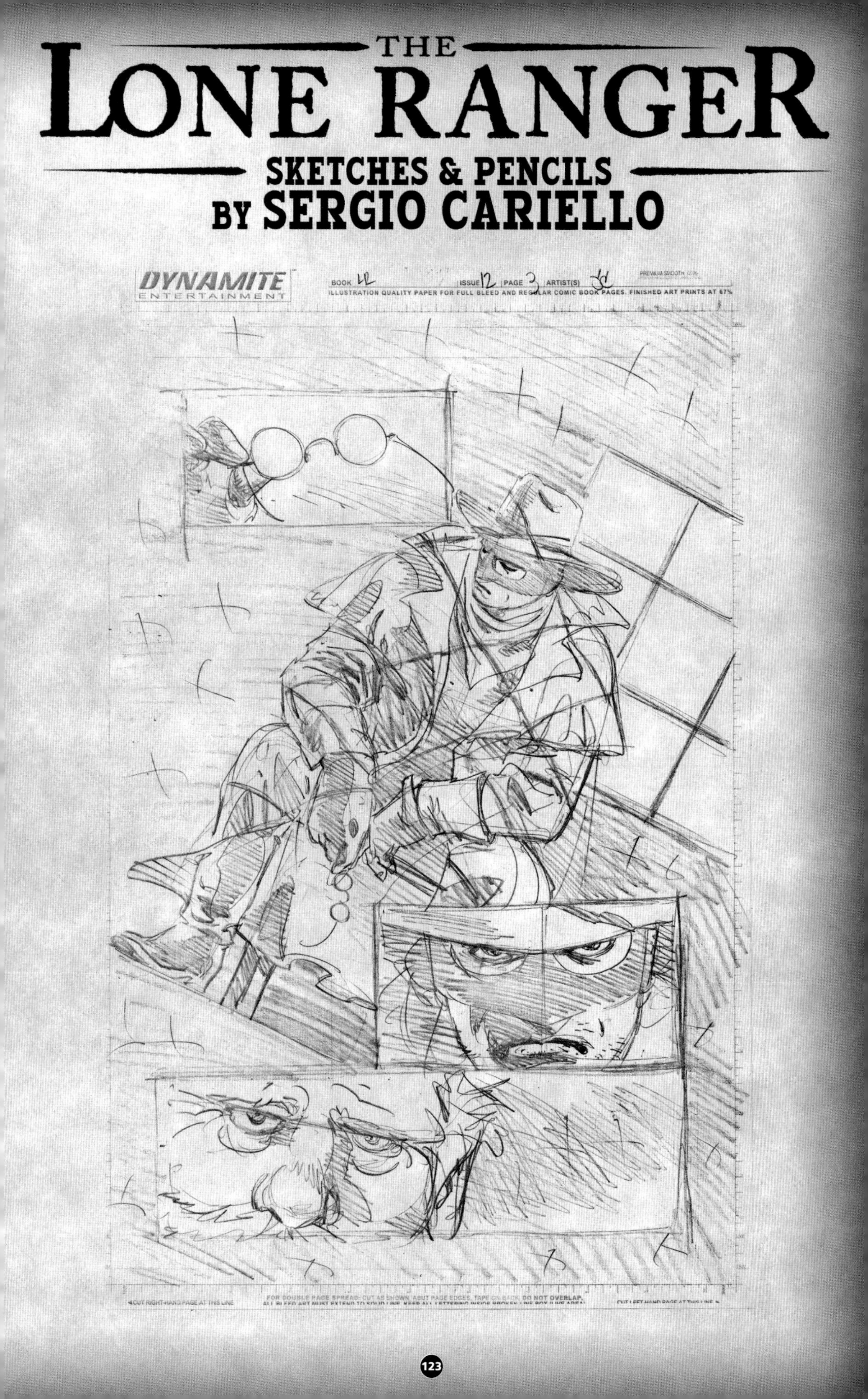
DYNAMITE ENTERTAINMENT
BOOK LR ISSUE 12 PAGE 3 ARTIST(S) SC
ILLUSTRATION QUALITY PAPER FOR FULL BLEED AND REGULAR COMIC BOOK PAGES. FINISHED ART PRINTS AT 67%

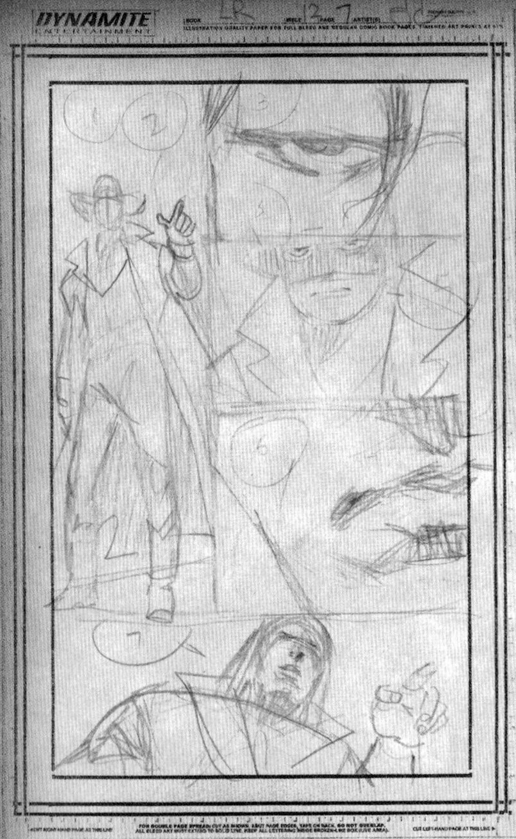

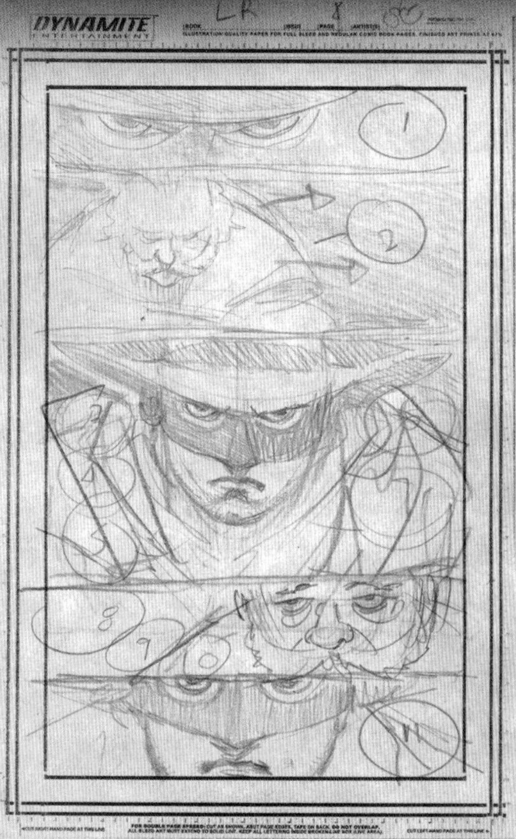

"I do my thumbs on 8 1/2x11 copy paper. I build myself a little booklet of all 22 pgs with the script on the right side and a 4x6 miniature template that contains the same crop marks, live art and bleed lines from the 11x17 boards on the left side. (I'm left handed). I like to keep the script and art together into one paper. Easier to keep the art according to script."

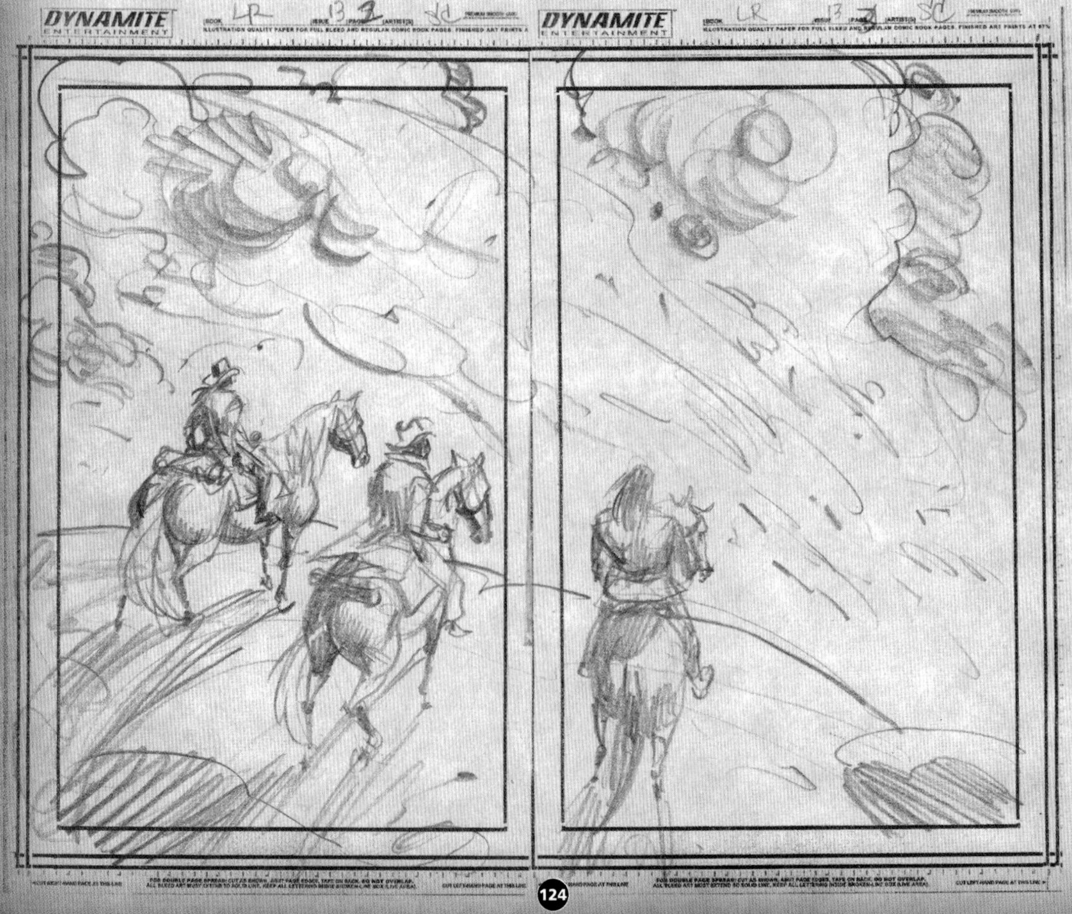

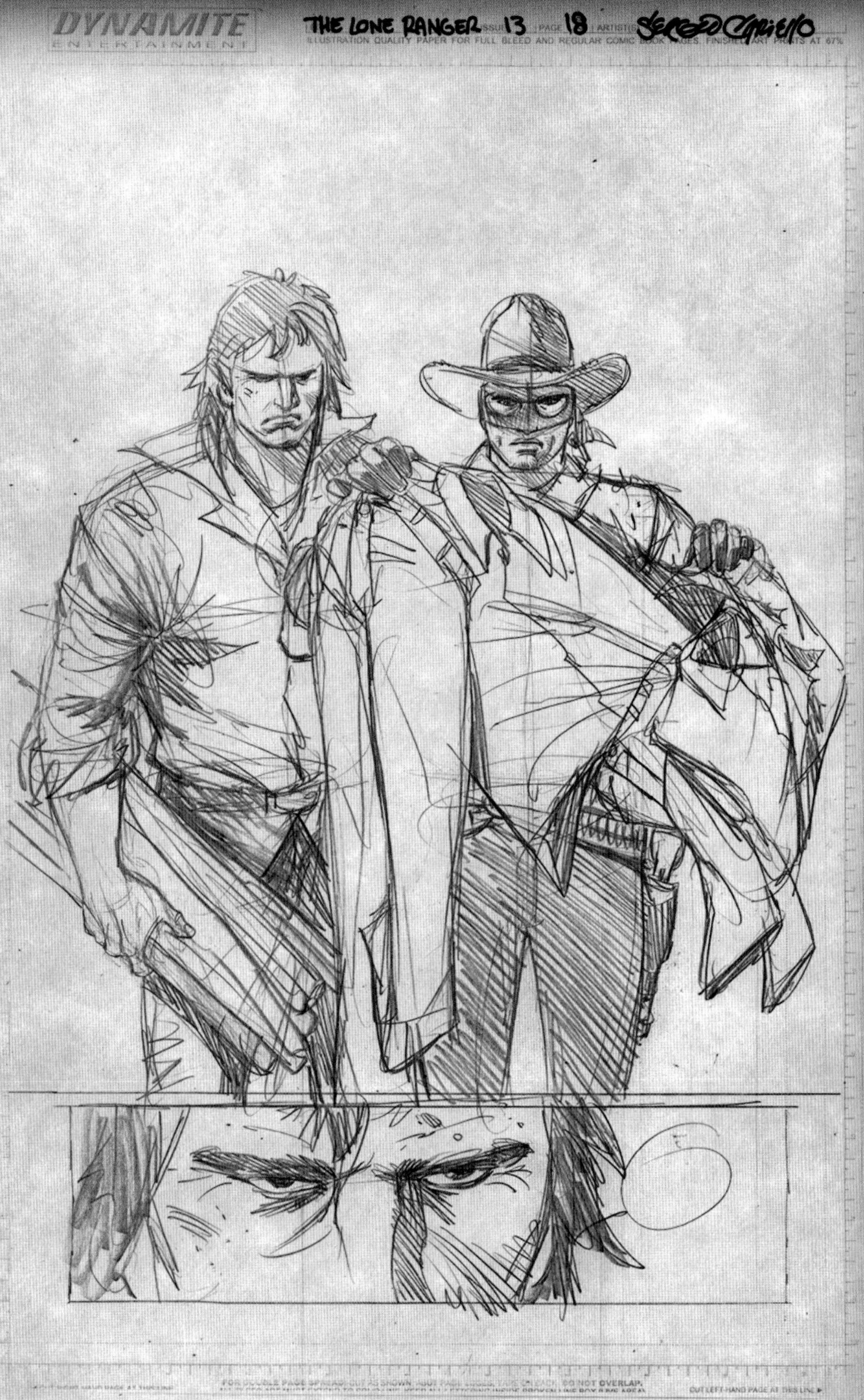
DYNAMITE
ENTERTAINMENT
THE LONE RANGER 13 18
ILLUSTRATION QUALITY PAPER FOR FULL BLEED AND REGULAR COMIC BOOK PAGES.

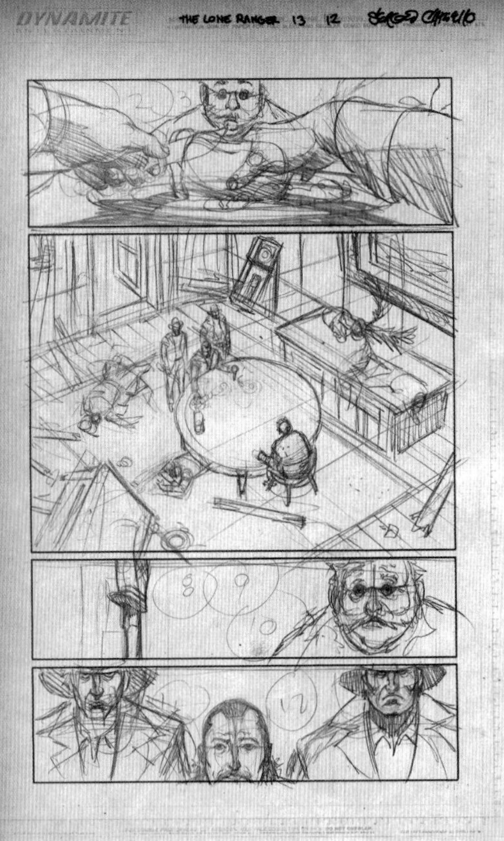
DYNAMITE
THE LONE RANGER 13 12

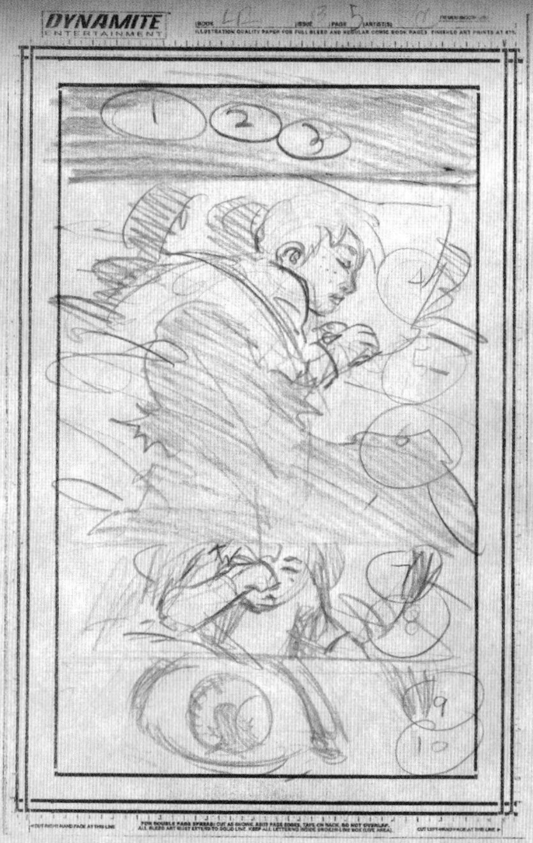
DYNAMITE
ENTERTAINMENT

I try to include as much information as possible in the thumbs, solving my light and shadow issues, proportions, expressions, background details pertaining to the storytelling, dynamics and design. Everything important to make it easier for me during transferring the thumbs to the actual boards. I can either light box the enlarged thumbs or use an artograph that projects the image onto my drawing board. The initial detailed thumbs also help Brett to see that all is in there and I didn't miss anything. I usually do all my adjusting and revisions in Photoshop.

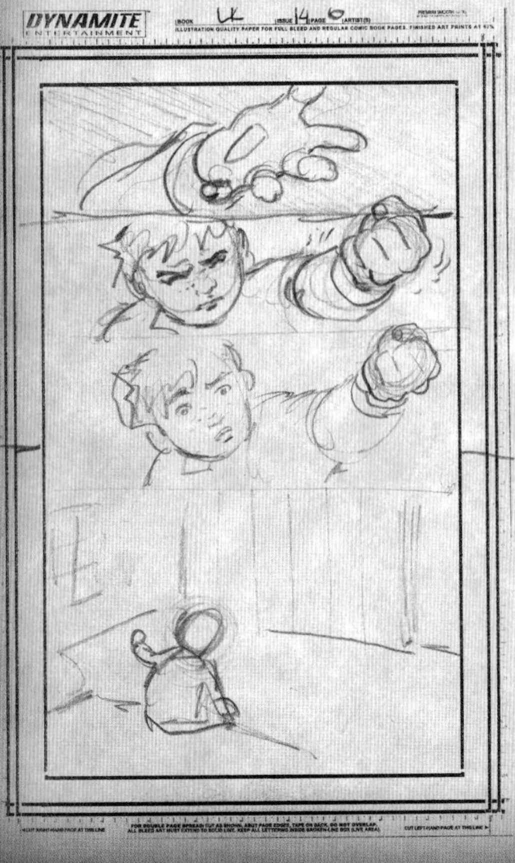
DYNAMITE
ENTERTAINMENT

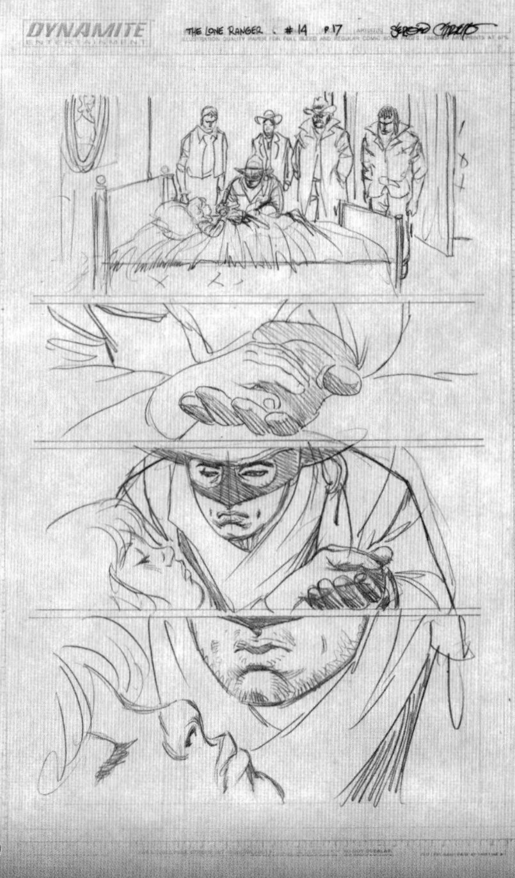
DYNAMITE
THE LONE RANGER # 14 # 17

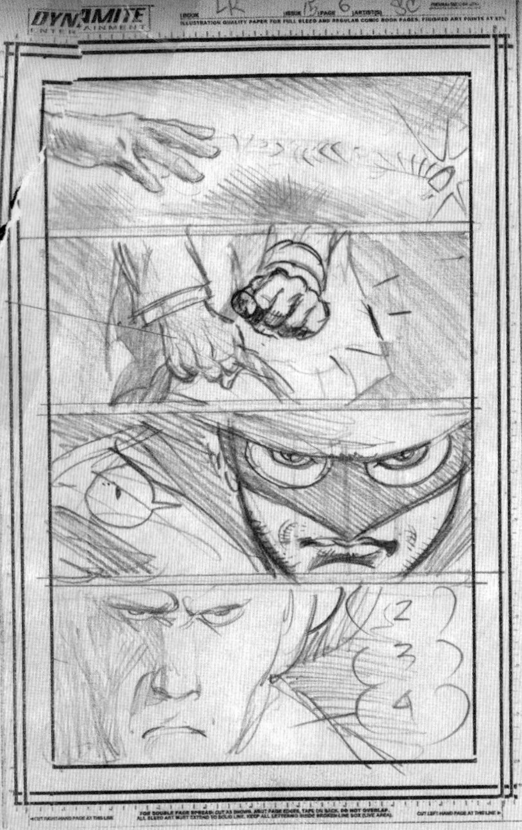
DYNAMITE
ENTERTAINMENT

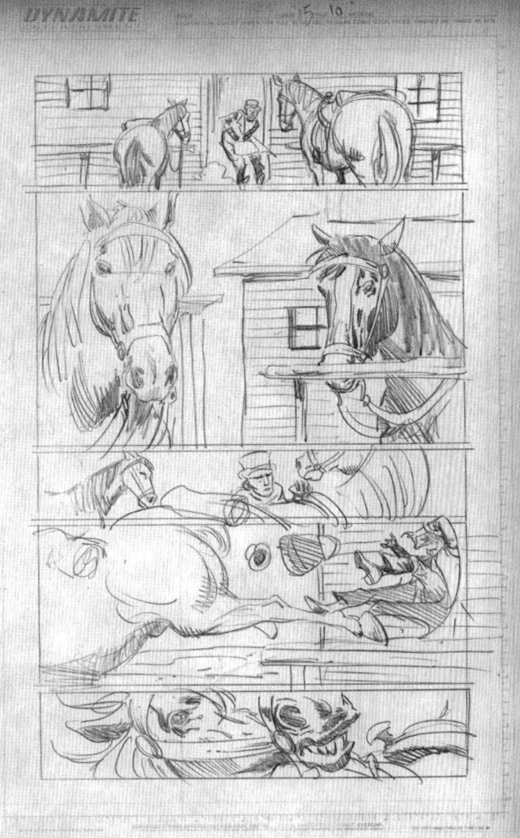
DYNAMITE

If my thumbs were done in detail then the inking will be much easier. Often my pencils are not as detailed as my thumbs (the important thing is to have enough info once, either in thumb or pencil stage for me to know how to ink it). If the thumbs are tight I only need a light indication on the pencils and I'll know what to do in the inks. The opposite also occurs. I do loose thumbs to tighten in the pencils. I use the blue pencil and/or 2B pencil lead (or a variation of leads depending on paper surface) for thumbs and pencil stage, whatever feels right at the moment.

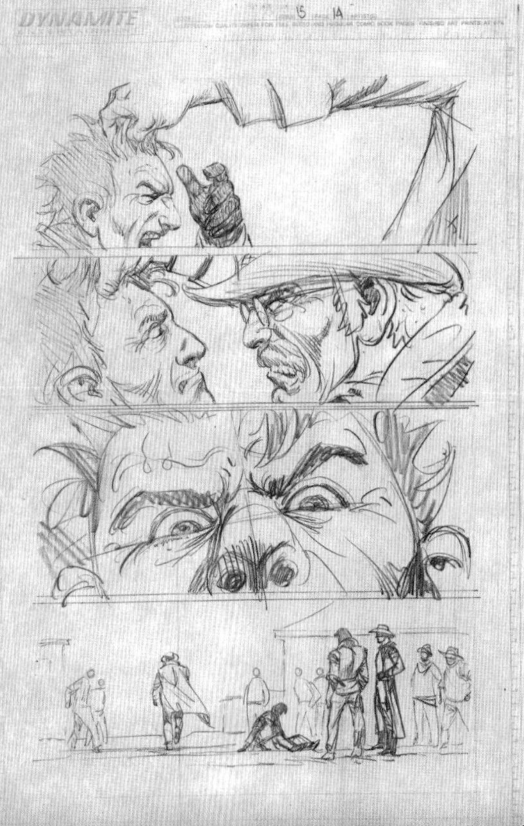
DYNAMITE

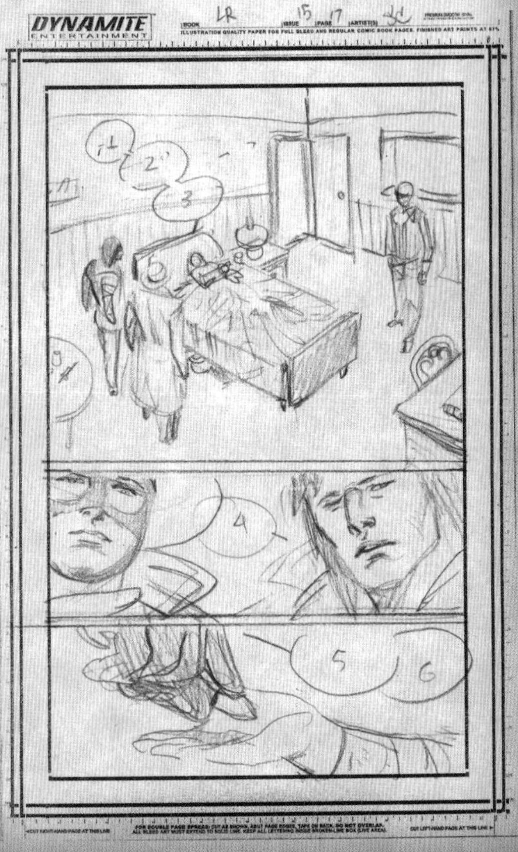
DYNAMITE
ENTERTAINMENT

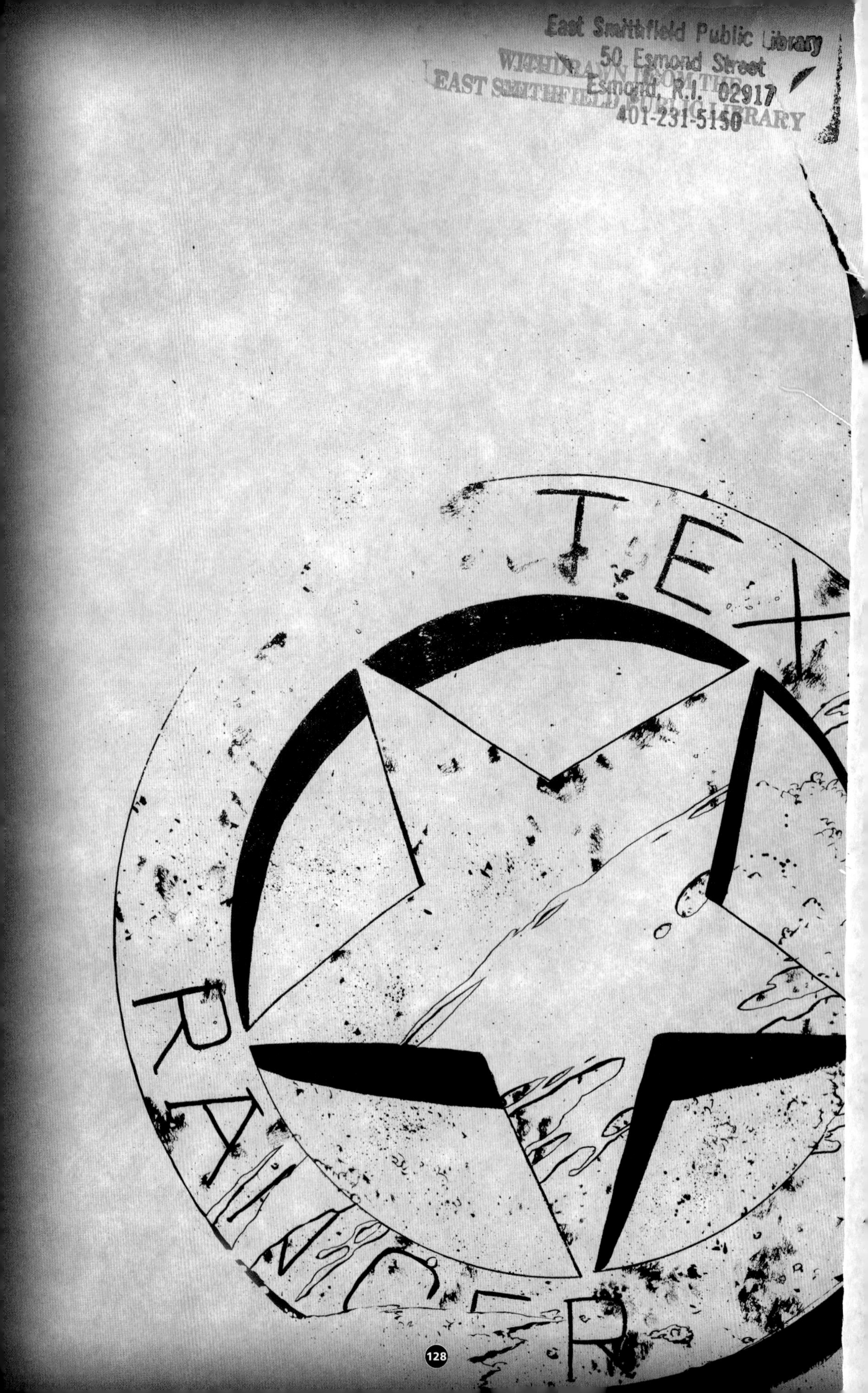
TEX
RANGER